METAPHYSICAL DISPUTATION II

EARLY MODERN CATHOLIC SOURCES

Volume 5

FRANCISCO SUÁREZ

METAPHYSICAL DISPUTATION II

ON THE ESSENTIAL CONCEPT OR CONCEPT OF BEING

Translated and annotated,
with corrected Latin text,
by SHANE DUARTE

THE CATHOLIC UNIVERSITY
OF AMERICA PRESS
Washington, D.C.

The paper used in this publication meets the minimum requirements of American National Standards for Information Science—Permanence of Paper for Printed Library Materials, ANSI Z39.48—1984.
∞

Cataloging-in-Publication Data available from the Library of Congress
Hardcover ISBN: 9780813236049
eBook ISBN: 9780813236056

For Michelle

CONTENTS

LATIN TEXT AND ENGLISH TRANSLATION

Contents

ACKNOWLEDGMENTS

I would like to thank a number of people for their help in the preparation of this volume. First, I should like to thank Christopher Shields and Andreas Waldstein for their careful reading of, and feedback on, my introduction to *DM* 2. I should also like to thank Christopher Shields for his sage advice and kind encouragement. For help in making sense of Suárez's references to Scotus, I offer my sincere thanks to Richard Cross and Stephen Dumont. I also wish to thank Lukáš Novák for reading and commenting on an earlier draft of my translation of *DM* 2. For their advice on several points, I would also like to thank the audience at the conference "Being Univocal, Being Equivocal: Scotus and Suárez" in London (July 12–13, 2018), organized by Christopher Shields and Richard Cross at the University of Notre Dame's Center for the Aristotelian Tradition. Finally, my deepest gratitude again goes to my wife, the incomparable Michelle Karnes.

INTRODUCTION

The first of Francisco Suárez's metaphysical disputations is introductory and devoted to the nature of metaphysics itself. Suárez begins the First Disputation (*DM* 1) by specifying this science's object and nature (sections 1 and 2), and then proceeds to discuss this science's unity (section 3), its end, utility, and functions (section 4), its status as both the most perfect natural science and true wisdom (section 5), and finally the thesis that it is the science most of all desired by means of a natural appetite (section 6).[1] The Second Disputation, in which the business of actual metaphysical inquiry begins in earnest, is therefore something of a fresh start. Indeed, in the introduction to it Suárez again outlines the structure of the entire *Metaphysical Disputations* and mentions his decision to abstain from lengthy explanations (*prolixa explicatio*) of the text of Aristotle's *Metaphysics*, focusing instead on an examination of things themselves (*rerum ipsarum examinatio*).

At the close of his introduction to *DM* 2, Suárez states that the topic of the disputation is the nature of first philosophy's adequate object, real being. His aim, he explains, is to settle the question, "What is being as being [*ens in quantum ens*]?" For *that* being is, he says, is so known *per se* as to require no explanation, and after the question of *whether* a thing is has been settled, the next in order is *what* it is. Moreover, Suárez observes, metaphysics cannot, like other sciences, take its subject as proved or explained by a higher science; it is therefore "necessary to hand it down [*tradere*] and explain it immediately at the beginning."

1. For an English translation of the First Disputation and a discussion of its contents, see Francisco Suárez, *Metaphysical Disputation I: On the Nature of First Philosophy or Metaphysics*, trans. Shane Duarte (Washington, D.C.: The Catholic University of America Press, 2021).

DM 2.1–3: The unity and precision of the formal and objective concepts of being

Suárez begins section 1 of *DM* 2 by introducing a distinction that he characterizes as commonplace (*vulgaris*), that between a formal concept and an objective concept (*conceptus formalis et conceptus obiectivus*). A formal concept—which is sometimes also called a mental concept (*conceptus mentalis*) or concept of the mind (*conceptus mentis*)—is described as the act by which the intellect conceives some thing or *ratio*. Suárez also refers to it here as a word (*verbum*)—namely, a mental or internal word—and a little later as an image (*imago*) (*DM* 2.1.11).[2] An objective concept, on the other hand, is said to be the thing or *ratio* that is properly and immediately cognized by means of a formal concept.[3] Accordingly, when I conceive human nature, the act or form that I produce in my mind in order to conceive that nature is a formal concept, while the nature cognized or represented by that act is an objective concept.

Suárez also takes note of a couple of important differences between formal and objective concepts. First, a formal concept is always a true and positive thing and, at least in the case of creatures, a quality inhering in the mind. An objective concept, on the other hand, need not be a true and positive thing, "for we sometimes conceive privations and other things that are called beings of reason because they only have *esse* objectively in the intellect" (*DM* 2.1.1).[4] Second, a formal concept is

2. On Suárez's identification of the act of conception with the mental word, or *verbum*, see Franco Riva, "La dottrina suareziana del concetto e le sue fonti storiche," *Rivista di Filosofia Neo-Scolastica* 71, no. 4 (1979): 686–99. On the Augustinian notion of a mental word, Aquinas's integration of it into Aristotelian psychology, and the subsequent development of the notion of a mental language, see Claude Panaccio, "From Mental Word to Mental Language," *Philosophical Topics* 20, no. 2 (1992): 125–47, and Claude Panaccio, *Mental Language: From Plato to William of Ockham*, trans. Joshua Hochschild and Meredith Ziebart (New York: Fordham University Press, 2017).

3. By a "*ratio*," in the sense relevant here, Suárez means an essence, nature, or quiddity. See "Remarks on the Latin Text and English Translation" for a list of possible renderings of this word.

4. Some scholars have interpreted Suárez as holding that an objective concept, even in cases where it is the objective concept of "a true and positive thing," has a special kind of being—that is, "objective being" (*esse obiectivum*)—in the mind, and that it is not to be identified with the true and positive thing outside the soul that is in such a case said to be cognized. For this view, see Eleuterio Elorduy, "El concepto objetivo en Suárez," *Pensamiento* 4

always a singular and individual thing, since it is something produced by the intellect and inhering in it. An objective concept, on the other hand, need not be singular and individual, since what we conceive is sometimes "universal, or confused and common, as are human being, substance, and the like" (*DM* 2.1.1).

Having introduced the distinction between formal and objective concepts, Suárez says that his principal aim in the Second Disputation is to explain the objective concept of being in its entire abstraction, according to which it is the object of metaphysics. Before doing this, however, he will focus, in section 1, on the corresponding formal concept, since he thinks that it can be better known.[5] Suárez's principal question in this section is whether there is a formal concept of being that is really and rationally one and also really and rationally prescinded (*praecisus*) from the formal concepts of being's inferiors (i.e., from the formal concepts of God, substance, quality, quantity, etc.). Sections 2 and 3 focus on the objective concept of being, and Suárez's principal question in these sections is whether there is an objective concept of being that is rationally one and somehow prescinded from the objective concepts of all other things.

(1948): 335–423, and Timothy J. Cronin, *Objective Being in Descartes and in Suárez* (Rome: Gregorian University Press, 1966), 78–89. It is worth noting, however, that Suárez explicitly states that the objective concept of the human being—which, he thinks, can have only a formal or fundamental unity, and not a real or numerical one (see *DM* 2.2.8 and 2.2.14)—is only "rationally prescinded from Peter, Paul and other singulars" and does not differ in reality from them (*DM* 2.2.16; cf. *DM* 2.2.21). This seems clearly to imply that the objective concept of the human being is just the human nature found in individual human beings, insofar as it serves as the object of the corresponding formal concept. For more on this and other matters related to formal and objective concepts in Suárez, see James C. Doig, "Suárez, Descartes, and the Objective Reality of Ideas," *The New Scholasticism* 51, no. 3 (1977): 350–71; Jorge J. E. Gracia, "Suárez's Conception of Metaphysics: A Step in the Direction of Mentalism?" *American Catholic Philosophical Quarterly* 65, no. 3 (1991): 287–309; Norman J. Wells, "*Esse Cognitum* and Suárez Revisited," *American Catholic Philosophical Quarterly* 67, no. 3 (1993): 339–48; Jorge J. E. Gracia, "Suárez and Metaphysical Mentalism: The Last Visit," *American Catholic Philosophical Quarterly* 67, no. 3 (1993): 349–54; Marco Forlivesi, "La distinction entre concept formel et concept objectif: Suárez, Pasqualigo, Mastri," *Les Études philosophiques* 1 (2002): 3–30; and Michael Renemann, "Suárez's Doctrine of Concepts: How Divine and Human Intellection Are Intertwined," in *A Companion to Francisco Suárez*, ed. Victor M. Salas and Robert L. Fastiggi, 313–35 (especially 329–30) (Leiden & Boston: Brill, 2015).

5. That Suárez begins with the formal concept, rather than the objective concept, is sometimes thought to be a significant development in the history of metaphysics. See Victor Salas, "Francisco Suárez: End of the Scholastic ἐπιστήμη?" in *Francisco Suárez and His Legacy: The Impact of Suárezian Metaphysics and Epistemology on Modern Philosophy*, ed. Marco Sgarbi, 9–28 (Milano: Vita e Pensiero, 2010).

Informing Suárez's inquiry here, as well as the terms in which it is framed, is the centuries-long debate on the question of whether "being" is univocal or analogical. His own position in this debate, it should be noted, comes only partially into view in *DM* 2; for a complete statement of his position, the reader must wait until *DM* 28.3 (where he argues that being is said analogically of God and creatures) and *DM* 32.2 (where he argues that being is said analogically of substance and accidents). This fact notwithstanding, it remains the case that an adequate understanding of Suárez's discussion in *DM* 2, sections 1 through 3, requires some familiarity with the debate over the analogy of being. An introduction to this debate is accordingly in order.

Competing theories of analogy

At the beginning of the *Categories*, Aristotle explains that two or more things count as equivocals (ὁμώνυμα) when they have a name in common but the essential account corresponding to that name (ὁ κατὰ τοὔνομα λόγος τῆς οὐσίας) varies depending on which of the things is named (1a1–2). Aristotle's example here relies on a peculiarity of the Greek language in his day, the fact that the word "ζῷον"—which was invariably rendered into Latin as "*animal*"—could be used to mean either an animal or a picture, whether the picture was of an animal or something else (1a2–3). Thus, in Greek, both a horse and a landscape painting can be called a ζῷον. Of course, it is also the case that for a horse to be a ζῷον is for it to be a sensitive living substance, whereas for a painting to be a ζῷον is for it to be an artistic representation (1a4–6). Accordingly, a horse and a painting are equivocals, since they have the name "ζῷον" in common, but the essential account corresponding to this name varies as the name is applied first to a horse and then to a painting, or vice versa.

It is worth noting that the polysemous character of the Greek word "ζῷον" was not always recognized in the Latin West, and that the Latin word "*animal*" cannot be used to refer to pictures generally. Accordingly, it was often assumed that in giving this example Aristotle had in mind a picture of an animal, or a painted animal.[6] After all, a museum

6. See, for example, *DM* 28.3.20 and Cajetan, *Scripta Philosophica: De Nominum*

guide might sensibly point to a picture depicting several animals, as well as various other things, and say, "Look carefully at the animals." Even on this understanding of Aristotle's meaning, however, it remains the case that the essential account corresponding to the name will vary according to the name's use, since for a horse to be an animal is for it to be a sensitive living substance, whereas for a painted horse to be an animal is for it to be an artistic representation of such a substance.

In the first chapter of the *Categories*, Aristotle also explains that two or more things count as univocals (συνώνυμα) when they have a name in common and the essential account that corresponds to the name is the same regardless of which thing is named (1a6–7). Aristotle's example here again appeals to the word "ζῷον," but this time as said of a human being and an ox: not only is the name common to both, it is also the case that, for both a human being and an ox, to be an animal is to be a sensitive living substance (1a7–12).

Finally, in the remainder of chapter 1 of the *Categories*, Aristotle explains that things are called denominatives (παρώνυμα) when they get their name from something else, but with a change of ending, in the way the grammarian (γραμματικός), for example, gets his name from grammar (γραμματική), that is, from his knowledge of grammar (1a12–15).

Several features of the doctrine presented in *Categories*, ch. 1, are worth underlining. First, Aristotle does not classify *words* as equivocal or univocal, but *things*, even if this classification applies to things not as they are in themselves, but insofar as they are signified by words. Nevertheless, medieval and early modern scholastic philosophers commonly speak of univocal and equivocal names or terms, although they standardly specify the things in relation to which a given term is univocal or equivocal. They will, for example, say that the term "dog" (*canis*), as said of this barking animal, Rex, and that one, Rover, is univocal, while also affirming that the same term is equivocal when said of a barking animal and the star Sirius (i.e., the so-called Dog Star, which was also called *canis* in Latin). This distinction between equivocal words and things, moreover, was often marked by a terminologi-

Analogia, De Conceptu Entis, ed. N. Zammit, rev. ed. H. Hering (Romae: apud Institutum "Angelicum," 1952), p. 20, n. 19.

cal distinction: equivocal words were standardly called "equivocating equivocals" (sing.: *aequivocum aequivocans* / plur.: *aequivoca aequivocantia*), while equivocal things were called "equivocate equivocals" (sing.: *aequivocum aequivocatum* / plur.: *aequivoca aequivocata*), or just "equivocates." Similarly, univocal words were called "univocating univocals" (sing.: *univocum univocans* / plur.: *univoca univocantia*), while univocal things were called "univocate univocals" (sing.: *univocum univocatum* / plur.: *univoca univocata*), or just "univocates."[7] This terminology was also adapted to the case of analogy: both words and things are termed "analogicals" (sing.: *analogum* / plur.: *analoga*), but analogical words are more specifically called "*analoga analogantia*" (sing.: *analogum analogans*) and analogical things "*analoga analogata*" (sing.: *analogum analogatum*). (In what follows, I shall use the word "analogate" to refer to analogical things and "analogical" to characterize both words and things.)

Second, it is worth noting that it is possible for the same things to be both univocals and equivocals, that is, univocals with respect to one name and equivocals with respect to another. For example, a dog and the star Sirius are equivocals with respect to the Latin word "*canis*," but they are univocals in relation to the word "substance."

Third, the Greek words "ὁ κατὰ τοὔνομα λόγος τῆς οὐσίας," which I have rendered into English as "the essential account corresponding to the name," are rendered by Boethius (ca. 475/7–526?) and William of Moerbeke (ca. 1215–86) in their translations of the *Categories* as "*secundum nomen ratio substantiae*."[8] This *ratio substantiae*, moreover, was variously interpreted. Thomas Aquinas (1225–74), for example, seems to interpret it as "the intellect's conception of the thing signified by a name" (*ST* I, q. 13, art. 4),[9] whereas Hervaeus Natalis (ca. 1250/60–1323) takes it to be the very thing or nature understood by means of a mental concept, that is, what would come to be called the objective concept.[10]

7. See, for example, Francisco de Toledo, *Commentaria una cum quaestionibus in universam Aristotelis logicam* (Venetiis: apud Juntas, 1580), fol. 43ra.

8. Aristotle, *Aristoteles Latinus I.1–5, Categoriae vel Praedicamenta*, ed. L. Minio-Paluello (Bruges & Paris: Desclée de Brouwer, 1961), pp. 5 and 85.

9. Thomas Aquinas, *Sancti Thomae Aquinatis opera omnia*, t. 4 (Romae: Ex Typographia Polyglotta, Sacra Congregatio de Propaganda Fide, 1888), p. 144b: "Ratio enim quam significat nomen est conceptio intellectus de re significata per nomen."

10. Hervaeus Natalis, *Quolibeta* (Venetiis: Heredes Octaviani Scoti, 1513), fol. 43rb.

Pedro da Fonseca (1528–99), on the other hand, grants that "*ratio substantiae*" can be understood to refer either to a formal concept or to an objective concept, although, for reasons that need not detain us here, he thinks that it is best taken as referring to a formal definitive concept (*conceptus formalis definitivus*), which is the sort of concept by means of which the intellect conceives a thing's definition.[11] Suárez, for his part, understands the *ratio substantiae* to be an objective concept and what is immediately signified by a name, as does Antonio de Olivera (1583–1637) (aka Antonio de la Madre de Dios), the author of the *Collegium Complutense* textbook of Aristotelian logic.[12] Notwithstanding this difference of opinion, however, scholastic philosophers agree in holding that a univocal name (e.g., "animal") signifies the proper *rationes* of its univocates (e.g., the *rationes* of the human being, horse, and sparrow) only mediately, by virtue of immediately signifying a *ratio substantiae* common to them all (e.g., the *ratio* of animal), whereas an equivocal name (e.g., "*canis*") does not immediately signify a *ratio substantiae* common to its equivocates (e.g., the *rationes* of dog and a particular star), since there is no such *ratio*; an equivocal name instead immediately signifies the proper *rationes* of the equivocates themselves.[13, 14]

11. Pedro da Fonseca, *Commentariorum Petri Fonsecae Lusitani, Doctoris Theologi Societatis Iesu, In Libros Metaphysicorum Aristotelis Stagiritae Tomi Quatuor. Continet hic Tomus Primus quatuor priorum librorum explicationem* (Coloniae: Sumptibus Lazari Zetzneri Biblipolae, 1615) [hereinafter Pedro da Fonseca, *Commentaria in Libros Metaphysicorum Aristotelis Stagiritae*, vol. 1], cols. 720–21.

12. Collegium Complutense Sancti Cyrilli, *Artium Cursus sive Disputationes in Aristotelis Dialecticam, et Philosophiam naturalem* (Compluti: apud Ioannem de Orduña, 1624), p. 398a.

13. See Hervaeus Natalis, *Quolibeta*, fols. 44vb–45ra; cf. Cajetan, *In De Ente et Essentia D. Thomae Aquinatis Commentaria* (Taurini: Marietti, 1934), p. 24.

14. For the purposes of distinguishing univocal and equivocal terms, it doesn't much matter whether the *ratio substantiae* signified by a term is understood to be a formal concept or an objective concept, at least when a term has exactly as many formal concepts corresponding to it as it does objective concepts. In that case, if a term signifies more than one objective (or formal) concept, it is equivocal, and if it signifies only one objective (or formal) concept, it is univocal. The situation is more complicated if one holds—as some did hold—that a term can have exactly one formal concept but more than one objective concept. Suárez himself thinks that formal concepts are individuated by their objects and that a term therefore has the same number of formal and objective concepts (see *DM* 2.1.9 and *DM* 2.2.3). Cf. Antonio Rubio, *Logica Mexicana* (Lugduni: Sumptibus Antonii Pillehotte, 1620), p. 199, n. 28.

Fourth, Aristotelians standardly distinguish between three things in every case of denomination. First, there is the thing from which a denominative gets its name—for example, the whiteness from which a wall is denominated white. This is often understood to be a form of some sort,[15] and it is standardly referred to as the "denominating form" (*forma denominans*). Second, there is the thing denominated (*res denominata*), for example, the wall which is denominated white from the whiteness existing in it. Third, there is the denominative (*denominativum*) itself, for example, the concrete white thing (*album*). Scholastic philosophers also distinguish between two kinds of denomination, intrinsic and extrinsic. A denomination is intrinsic when the denominating form exists in the thing denominated, while a denomination is extrinsic when the denominating form exists in some other subject. For example, when a wall is denominated white from the whiteness existing in it, the denomination is intrinsic, but when it is denominated seen from an act of vision, which is conceived to be a form existing in the seer, the denomination is extrinsic.

Although they are not explicitly mentioned in the *Categories*, two further ways of classifying things in relation to names are found in Aristotle's works.[16] Both are commonly classed by scholastic philosophers under the general heading of analogy, although Aristotle himself only ever uses the term "analogy" (or "ἀναλογία") in connection with one of them, namely, the so-called "analogy of proportionality" (*analogia proportionalitatis*). In this kind of analogy, a comparison of two relations involving four terms is at work, as when "to see" is used of both an act of understanding and an act of seeing because the former is related to the intelligible as the latter is related to the visible (act of seeing : visible :: act of understanding : intelligible). Another common example of this sort of analogy involves the word "smiling" or "laughing" (*ridere*) as said of both a human being and a meadow (*pratum*). The thought

15. Though not invariably, since things can be denominated from privations, too—e.g., "*caecus*" ("blind").

16. For useful discussions of issues touched on here, see the following papers: E. J. Ashworth, "Signification and Modes of Signifying in Thirteenth-Century Logic: A Preface to Aquinas on Analogy," *Medieval Philosophy and Theology* 1 (1991): 39–67; E. J. Ashworth, "Analogy and Equivocation in Thirteenth-Century Logic: Aquinas in Context," *Mediaeval Studies* 54 (1992): 94–135; E. J. Ashworth, "Analogical Concepts: The Fourteenth-Century Background to Cajetan," *Dialogue* 31, no. 3 (1992): 399–413.

is that smiling is related to the human being as verdancy (*viriditas*) or loveliness (*amoenitas*) is related to the meadow.

The other principal species of analogy discussed by scholastic philosophers, the so-called analogy of attribution (*analogia attributionis*), corresponds to what is now referred to as Aristotle's notion of *pros hen* (πρὸς ἕν) equivocation.[17] Perhaps the most common example of this is "healthy" (*sanum*) as said of an animal, food, and urine. The idea here is that an animal is called healthy by virtue of its possessing, or being the subject of, health, which is a particular state of a living body. Food, on the other hand, is called healthy not because it possesses health, but because it is conducive to health in an animal. Similarly, urine is called healthy not because it possesses health, but because it is a sign or indication of health in the animal. Otherwise put, an animal is denominated healthy intrinsically from the health present in it, while food and urine are denominated healthy extrinsically from the animal's health.

Since neither of these ways of classifying things in relation to names is discussed in the *Categories*, Aristotle's interpreters were left with the task of determining how analogy is related to equivocation and univocation. To be sure, analogy was commonly understood to be intermediate between equivocation and univocation, but it is not at first sight clear how this can be the case, since it would seem that every name or significant utterance (*vox significativa*) must be either univocal or equivocal, given that it must immediately signify either exactly one *ratio*, in which case it is univocal, or more than one *ratio*, in which case it is equivocal.[18]

The most common response was to distinguish between two species of equivocation, identify analogy with one of these, and assert that analogy is intermediate between univocation and the other species of equivocation. In his commentary on the *Categories*, Boethius, following Porphyry (234?–305? CE), had distinguished between so-called chance

17. As Suárez notes at *DM* 28.3.4, the expression "analogy of proportion" is sometimes treated as a terminological variant equivalent to "analogy of attribution" and sometimes as a terminological variant of "analogy of proportionality." In other words, where the analogy of proportion is opposed to, and distinguished from, the analogy of proportionality, it is equivalent to the analogy of attribution, but where it is opposed to, and distinguished from, the analogy of attribution, it is equivalent to the analogy of proportionality. In what follows I avoid using the expression "analogy of proportion."

18. Cf. Hervaeus Natalis, *Quolibeta*, fol. 44ra.

equivocals (*aequivoca a casu*) and deliberate equivocals (*aequivoca a consilio*).[19] Equivocals of the former sort—for example, the financial institution and the strip of land adjacent to a river, both called "bank"—are such that their having the same name is thought to be a product of coincidence and unmotivated by the recognition of some relation obtaining between them. The equivocation at work in their case was often termed "pure equivocation" (*mera* or *pura aequivocatio*). Deliberate equivocals, commonly identified with analogicals and conceived to be intermediate between univocals and chance equivocals, are such that their sharing a name is thought to be the product of some recognized relation obtaining between them.

Of course, on this conception, according to which analogy is identified with deliberate equivocation, there is no single *ratio* or nature that is immediately signified by an analogical term and common to the analogates. The word "healthy," for example, does not signify some single *ratio*, form, or nature common to a healthy animal, healthy food, and healthy urine (even if a relation to health is something found in all three). For an animal to be healthy is for it to possess health, for food to be healthy is for it to be such as to cause or preserve health in the animal that eats it, and for urine to be healthy is for it to be the sort that a healthy animal produces. Here we have three different *rationes* or natures. Likewise, the word "smiling" does not signify some one *ratio* common to a smiling human being and a meadow in bloom. For a human being to smile is one thing; for a meadow to smile is another.

Following what they took to be Aristotle's teaching, scholastic philosophers frequently (though not invariably) held that "being" is said analogically of both substance and accidents.[20] According to those who identified analogy with deliberate equivocation, then, "being" does not

19. Boethius, *In Categorias Aristotelis libri quatuor*, Patrologiae Cursus Completus: Series Latina 64, ed. J.-P. Migne (Paris: apud Garnier Fratres, 1891), col. 166B. Cf. Porphyry, *In Categorias*, vol. 4, part 1 of *Commentaria in Aristotelem graeca*, ed. Adolfus Busse (Berolini: Typis et Impensis Georgii Reimer, 1887), p. 65, ll. 18–19.

20. Two Aristotelian texts commonly cited by scholastics in their discussions of the analogy of being are *Metaph.* IV, ch. 2, 1003a33–b10, and *Metaph.* VII, ch. 1, 1028a10–31. Cf. Thomas Aquinas, *In duodecim libros metaphysicorum Aristotelis expositio* (Taurini & Romae: Marietti, 1950), pp. 151b–52b, ns. 535–43; and pp. 315a–17a, ns. 1245–56. Cf. Pierre Aubenque, "Sur la naissance de la doctrine pseudo-Aristotélicienne de l'analogie de l'être," *Les Études philosophiques* 3/4 (1989): 291–304.

immediately signify a single *ratio substantiae* common to the categories of being, but rather several related *rationes substantiae*, for example, the proper *rationes* of the categories or (alternatively) the proper *rationes* of substance and accident. They also frequently held that no term—whether "being" or "wise" or "just"—is said univocally of both God and any creature.[21] Thinkers who identified analogy with deliberate equivocation accordingly held that the term "wisdom" (say) does not immediately signify a *ratio substantiae* common to created and uncreated wisdom, but rather two different (albeit somehow related) *rationes*. As John Duns Scotus (1265/66–1308) pointed out, however, both of these opinions pose significant problems. For example, granted the widely held view that substance does not directly give rise in us to an intellection of itself, but is instead known by us only through the mediation of sensible accidents, it is not at all clear how we can acquire a quidditative concept of substance on the basis of our grasp of accidents if in fact there is no single concept of being, common to both substance and accidents, abstractable from the concept of accident.[22] A similar problem presents itself regarding our natural cognition of God. For God is supposed to admit of being cognized in some way through his creatures (see Romans 1:20, "The invisible things of God . . . are clearly seen, being understood through the things that are made"). However, the view that no term is predicated univocally of God and creatures makes it difficult to see how we can arrive at (say) a concept of God's wisdom on the basis of our concept of creaturely wisdom. For, it might be thought, such a concept of uncreated wisdom could only be arrived at by means of a concept common to both created and uncreated wisdom, abstracted by us from the concept of creaturely wisdom.[23]

Problems such as these may have served to make an alternative understanding of analogy attractive to at least some thinkers. As E. Jen-

21. See, for example, Thomas Aquinas, *ST* I, q. 13, art. 5, in *Opera omnia*, t. 4, pp. 146–47.

22. Scotus, *Ord.* I, d. 3, p. 1, q. 3, n. 139, in John Duns Scotus, *Opera omnia*, vol. 3 (Civitas Vaticana: Typis Polyglottis Vaticanis, 1954), pp. 86–87.

23. Scotus, *Ord.* I, d. 3, p. 1, q. 1–2, ns. 38–40, in John Duns Scotus, *Opera omnia*, vol. 3 (Vaticana), pp. 25–27. For a discussion of Thomist responses to the challenges posed by Scotus's arguments, see Joshua P. Hochschild, *The Semantics of Analogy: Rereading Cajetan's* De Nominum Analogia (Notre Dame, Ind.: University of Notre Dame Press, 2010), and Domenic D'Ettore, *Analogy after Aquinas: Logical Problems, Thomistic Answers* (Washington, D.C.: The Catholic University of America Press, 2019).

nifer Ashworth has shown, there existed a different way of classifying analogy in relation to univocation and equivocation, one that has roots which predate Scotus.[24] On this conception, a distinction is to be drawn between analogical terms that immediately signify multiple *rationes* and analogical terms that immediately signify a single *ratio* which is present in a prior way in one analogate and in a posterior way in other analogates. A term of the former sort is a deliberate equivocal, but a term of the latter type is conceived to be intermediate between a univocal and a deliberate equivocal, since, like a univocal term and unlike an equivocal term, it immediately signifies a single *ratio*, but unlike a univocal term, it immediately signifies a *ratio* that is not participated in equally or in the same way by all the things that participate in it.[25]

Suárez subscribes to a version of this second way of classifying analogical terms. In particular, he grants that terms analogical by the analogy of proportionality each immediately signify multiple *rationes*, but he draws a distinction in the case of terms analogical by the analogy of attribution. In some cases, he explains, the denominating form is found only in one of the analogates, and the other analogates are denominated extrinsically from it. Such is the case with "healthy" as said of an animal, food, and urine. Suárez calls this kind of analogy the analogy of extrinsic attribution, and he holds that a term which is in this way analogical immediately signifies multiple *rationes*. On the other hand, he says, sometimes the denominating form is present in all of the analogates, although it is present in the primary analogate absolutely and in the other analogates by virtue of some relation (*per habitudinem*) that they bear to the primary analogate (*DM* 28.3.14). Suárez calls this kind

24. E. J. Ashworth, "Suárez on the Analogy of Being: Some Historical Background," *Vivarium* 33, no. 1 (1995): 50–75.

25. It should be noted that talk of unequal participation in a single *ratio* is found also in thinkers who cannot be said to subscribe to this classification of analogy in relation to univocation and equivocation, and this because both the notion of a single *ratio* and the notion of unequal participation are susceptible to various interpretations. Dominic of Flanders, for example, invokes the notion of unequal participation in the same *ratio* even in connection with the term "healthy," and this because "it is the same health that the animal receives, urine signifies, medicine causes, and diet preserves, although variously participated in" (*Eadem autem sanitas est, quam animal suscipit, & urina significat, medicina facit, & dieta conservat, licet diversimode participetur*). See Dominic of Flanders, *In Duodecim Libros Metaphysicae Aristotelis* (Coloniae Agrippinae: Typis Arnoldi Kempensis, 1621), p. 144a (p. 144 is mislabeled "142"). Regarding the notion of a single *ratio*, see the discussion in the next section.

of analogy the analogy of intrinsic attribution, and a term that is in this way analogical immediately signifies a single *ratio* common to all of the analogates. Such is the analogy at work, on his view, when "being" is said of both God and creatures (*DM* 28.3.15), for "every creature is a being through some relation to God, namely, insofar as it participates in, or in some way imitates, God's *esse*" (*DM* 28.3.16).[26] It is also at work when "being" is said of substance and accident, since "the formal *ratio* of being does not altogether equally and indifferently descend to accident and substance, but rather with a certain order and relation that it *per se* requires, namely, so that it is first absolutely in substance and thereafter in accident with a relation to substance" (*DM* 32.2.14).[27]

According to Suárez, terms analogical in this way differ from specific or generic terms, such as "human being" or "animal," which are invariably said univocally of the relevant individuals or species. For the single *ratio* immediately signified by a specific or generic term is not found in one inferior in a prior way and in another in a posterior way. For example, the *ratio* of animal does not belong to one species of animal absolutely and to another by virtue of some relation that it bears to the first. As Suárez puts it, "a univocal is of itself indifferent in such a way that it descends to inferiors equally and without any order or relation of one to another" (*DM* 28.3.17).[28]

According to Suárez, then, "being" is an analogical term and signifies a single *ratio*. This position, it should be noted, has been the subject of considerable scholarly controversy: it is often asked, for example, whether being is *truly* analogical, according to Suárez.[29] But since it is

26. Francisco Suárez, *Opera Omnia*, vol. 26 (Parisiis: apud Ludovicum Vivès, 1861), p. 18b: "creatura essentialiter est ens per participationem eius esse quod in Deo est per essentiam, & ut in primo & universali fonte, ex quo ad omnia alia derivatur aliqua eius participatio: omnis ergo creatura est ens per aliquam habitudinem ad Deum, quatenus scilicet participat vel aliquo modo imitatur esse Dei, & quatenus habet esse, essentialiter pendet a Deo multo magis quam pendeat accidens a substantia. Hoc igitur modo dicitur ens de creatura per habitudinem seu attributionem ad Deum."

27. Francisco Suárez, *Opera Omnia*, vol. 26, p. 323b: "ratio formalis entis, non omnino aequaliter & indifferenter descendit ad accidens, & substantiam, sed cum quodam ordine, & habitudine, quam per se requirit, nimirum, ut prius sit absolute in substantia, & deinde in accidente cum habitudine ad substantiam."

28. Francisco Suárez, *Opera Omnia*, vol. 26, p. 19b: "univocum ex se ita est indifferens, ut aequaliter, & sine ullo ordine vel habitudine unius ad alterum ad inferiora descendat."

29. On Suárez and the analogy of being, see José Hellín, *La analogía del ser y el conocimiento de Dios en Suárez* (Madrid: Gráficas Uguina, 1947); Walter Hoeres, "Francis Suárez

only in *DM* 28.3 and *DM* 32.2 that he argues for the analogy of being, a full discussion of this controversy falls outside the scope of the introduction to the current volume. Suárez's principal aim in the first half of the Second Disputation is to prove that there is a single *ratio* or nature that all real beings share. Indeed, he thinks that the arguments in favor of this view are so strong that, if one had to choose, one would do better to deny the analogy of being rather than the unity of its objective concept (*DM* 2.2.36).

The terms of Suárez's inquiry

It will be recalled, however, that Suárez does not simply ask whether there is a single formal concept of being, nor whether there is a sin-

and the Teaching of John Duns Scotus on *Univocatio Entis*," in *Studies in Philosophy and the History of Philosophy*, vol. 3: *John Duns Scotus, 1265–1965*, ed. John K. Ryan and Bernardine M. Bonansea, 263–90 (Washington, D.C.: The Catholic University of America Press, 1965); John P. Doyle, "Suárez on the Analogy of Being" (Part I), *The Modern Schoolman* 46, no. 3 (1969): 219–49; John P. Doyle, "Suárez on the Analogy of Being" (Part II), *The Modern Schoolman* 46, no. 4 (1969): 323–41; Alain Guy, "L'Analogie de l'être selon Suárez," *Archives de philosophie* 42, no. 2 (1979): 275–94; Jean-Luc Marion, *Sur la théologie blanche de Descartes* (Paris: PUF, 1981), 70–139; Juan Roig Gironella, "La analogía del ser en Suárez," *Espíritu* 36 (1987): 5–48; Michel Bastit, "Interprétation analogique de la loi et analogie de l'être chez Suárez: De la similitude à l'identité," *Les Études philosophiques* 3/4 (1989): 429–43; Jean-François Courtine, "Différence ontologique et analogie de l'être: Le tournant suarézien," *Bulletin de la Société française de Philosophie* 83, no. 2 (1989): 41–76; E. J. Ashworth, "Suárez on the Analogy of Being: Some Historical Background"; Luigi Gentile, "Valenza logico-metafisica dell'«*analogia entis*» in F. Suárez," in *Christoph Clavius e l'attività scientifica dei gesuiti nell'età di Galileo. Atti del Convegno Internazionale (Chieti 28–30 aprile 1993)*, ed. Ugo Baldini, 209–22 (Roma: Bulzoni, 1995); Augustine Thompson, "Francisco Suárez's Theory of Analogy and the Metaphysics of St. Thomas Aquinas," *Angelicum* 72, no. 3 (1995): 353–62; Rolf Darge, "Grundthese und ontologische Bedeutung der Lehre von der Analogie des Seienden nach F. Suárez," *Philosophisches Jahrbuch* 106, no. 2 (1999): 312–33; Jean-François Courtine, *Inventio Analogiae: Métaphysique et ontothéologie* (Paris: Librairie Philosophique J. Vrin, 2005), 291–357; Benedetto Ippolito, *Analogia dell'Essere: La metafisica di Suárez tra onto-teologia medievale e filosofia moderna* (Milano: Franco Angeli, 2005); Daniel Heider, "Is Suárez's Concept of Being Analogical or Univocal?" *American Catholic Philosophical Quarterly* 81, no. 1 (2007): 21–41; Rolf Darge, "Die Transformation der aristotelischen Analogielehre bei Cajetan und Suárez," in *Der Aristotelismus an den europäischen Universitäten der frühen Neuzeit*, ed. Rolf Darge, Emmanuel J. Bauer, and Günter Frank, 57–81 (Stuttgart: W. Kohlhammer, 2010); Victor Salas, "Francisco Suárez, the Analogy of Being, and Its Tensions," in *Suárez's Metaphysics in Its Historical and Systematic Context*, ed. Lukáš Novák, 87–104 (Berlin: De Gruyter, 2014); Victor Salas, "Between Thomism and Scotism: Francisco Suárez on the Analogy of Being," in *A Companion to Francisco Suárez*, 336–62; Daniel Heider, "El concepto de ser in Suárez: ¿unívoco o análogo?" in *Suárez en perspectiva, 1617–2017*, ed. Julio Söchting Herrera, special issue of *Studium: Filosofía y Teología* 40 (2017): 99–120.

gle objective concept of being. Regarding the formal concept, he asks whether it is really and rationally one and also really and rationally prescinded from the formal concepts of being's inferiors. Regarding the objective concept, he asks whether it is rationally one and somehow prescinded from the objective concepts of all other things. The question presents itself, then: why does Suárez choose to frame his inquiry in this way? The answer, at least in part, is that by the late sixteenth century the debate over the analogy of being had become complicated enough to require more precise formulations of the questions at its very heart. The full story of this evolution has yet to be written, but a couple of points may serve to clarify the situation.

In *Ordinatio* I, d. 3, p. 1, qq. 1–2, Scotus famously argued for the univocity of being in part by noting that we must have a single mental concept of being given that we can be certain that God is a being but uncertain whether he is a finite or infinite being.[30] The idea is that we must have a formal concept of being that abstracts from both finite and infinite being if we can affirm the proposition that God is a being without affirming that he is finite or infinite. A similar argument alleged that one can be certain that something—light, say—is a being but uncertain whether it is a substance or an accident, and in this case it likewise seems necessary to posit at least a concept of finite being which abstracts from substance and accident.

In response to this last argument, however, Hervaeus Natalis, while arguing in his *Quolibet* II, q. 7, that there is no single nature or *ratio* common to all the categories, claimed that when we affirm that something is a being but do not know whether it is a categorical substance or accident, the formal concept corresponding to the proposition's predicate is a disjunctive concept, *substance or accident*. In this case, he argued, we can be certain that the thing is a being—that is, certain that it is either a substance or an accident—without being able to say which it is.[31] This is significant because later thinkers will describe Hervaeus as having denied, on the one hand, that there is a single objective concept of being while simultaneously holding, on the other, that the mind has a single formal concept of being—that is, the mental concept *substance*

30. John Duns Scotus, *Opera omnia*, vol. 3 (Vaticana), pp. 18–21 (ns. 26–34).
31. Hervaeus Natalis, *Quolibet*, fol. 45va.

or accident, the unity of which is disjunctive.[32] As a result, not only does it become necessary to distinguish between formal and objective concepts when debating the analogy of being, it also becomes necessary to ask whether any alleged single formal concept of being is prescinded or distinct from the formal concepts of being's inferiors (e.g., from the formal concepts of substance and accident). The question of distinctness or precision here is also complicated by the fact that there are two different ways of conceiving formal concepts, either as qualities of the intellect or in terms of their representational content. Thus, one might hold that the disjunctive concept *substance or accident* is a quality distinct from the two formal concepts *substance* and *accident*, but clearly, the former disjunctive concept does not represent anything other than what the latter concepts do.[33]

Further motivating the question of distinctness or precision is the view advanced by some thinkers that to an analogical term there corresponds a single "imperfect" concept which represents all of the relevant analogates, though not a truly single *ratio* common to all the analogates, since there is no such *ratio*. According to this view, the concept in question perfectly represents one of the analogates, since it is none other than the proper formal concept of that analogate, but it also imperfectly represents the remaining analogates by virtue of some sort of similarity obtaining among the various analogates.[34] For this reason too it makes sense to ask, not merely whether there is a single formal concept of being, but whether any supposed single mental concept of being abstracts or rationally prescinds from being's inferiors.

32. See Dominic of Flanders, *In Duodecim Libros Metaphysicae Aristotelis*, p. 151a.

33. At least after Fonseca, authors frequently distinguish the question of whether a formal concept is really one—i.e., numerically one quality of the intellect—from the question of whether it is rationally one—i.e., representative of a single thing or nature. Eustachius a Sancto Paulo, *Quarta pars Summae Philosophicae, Quae est Metaphysica* (Parisiis: apud Carolum Chastellain, 1609), p. 11, holds that a formal concept can be "really one but rationally many, as happens in the case of the concept of the healthy" (*reipsa unus ratione tamen multiplex, ut in conceptu sani contingit*). Implicit here, it seems, is the assumption that one can distinctly or separately represent the several analogates of the term "healthy" by means of a single mental concept.

34. See, for example, Cajetan, *Scripta Philosophica: De Nominum Analogia, De Conceptu Entis*, pp. 34–38 (ns. 36–40) and pp. 98–99 (ns. 3–4). Domenic D'Ettore, "The Fifteenth-Century Thomist Dispute over Participation in an Analogous Concept: John Capreolus, Dominic of Flanders, and Paul Soncinas," *Mediaeval Studies* 76 (2014): 241–73, argues that John Capreolus anticipates Cajetan in holding this sort of view.

A similar need arises in connection with objective concepts. If there is no single objective concept immediately signified by "being" and other analogical metaphysical terms, it is reasonable to ask whether demonstrations containing such terms can hope to avoid the fallacy of equivocation, which occurs when a single term signifies different things at different points in an argument. Partly in response to this concern, thinkers who affirmed that "being" immediately signifies several different objective concepts also frequently held that these concepts possessed a qualified similarity, unity, indistinction, or identity that is sufficient to avoid the fallacy of equivocation. A good example here is Cajetan (1469–1534), who maintains that a term analogical by attribution immediately signifies *rationes* that are in one respect the same and in another respect diverse, and that a term analogical by proportionality signifies *rationes* that are without qualification diverse but in a certain respect (i.e., proportionately) the same.[35] Holders of such views, moreover, often speak as though an analogical term signifies a single *ratio* or objective concept, although they grant that this *ratio* or concept possesses only an analogical or proportional unity (*unitas analoga vel proportionalis*), which is a qualified or imperfect unity that is to be distinguished from the unity of univocation (*unitas univocationis*) possessed by the *rationes* or objective concepts immediately signified by univocal terms.[36] This proportional unity or sameness is then

35. More specifically, in *On the Analogy of Names* Cajetan holds that things analogical by attribution are things "whose name is common but the *ratio* corresponding to that name is the same with respect to term and diverse with respect to relations directed at the term" (n. 8). For example, in the case of "healthy," there is a single term to which an animal, urine, and medicine all bear a relation—namely, health—but the things called healthy bear different relations to this term: the animal is the subject of health, urine is a sign of it, and medicine is productive of it. Things analogical by proportionality, on the other hand, have a name in common and *rationes* which are similar according to proportion or (in other words) proportionately the same (n. 23). For example, "to see" is said of both intellectual and corporeal sight, since understanding presents a thing to the soul just as seeing presents a thing to the animate body. On the notion of analogical or proportional unity or sameness, see Aristotle, *Metaph.* V, ch. 6, 1016b31–35, and Cajetan, *Scripta Philosophica: De Nominum Analogia, De Conceptu Entis*, pp. 39–50 (ns. 41–58).

36. See *DM* 2.2.1. Talk of analogical unity is common in the case of formal concepts as well and has a long history. In his *Quodlibet* I, q. 1, art. 2, Gerard of Bologna (1240s–1317), for example, says: "In regard to the unity of analogy some say 'of that which is predicated analogically of many things there can be one concept, and this concept is not univocal but analogous.' Now if they mean by the unity of this concept a unity of order, proportion, or attribution, then, in my judgment, they think correctly. But this unity is a *secundum quid*

appealed to in addressing concerns about demonstrations that make use of analogical terms. Thus Cajetan argues that in the demonstration proving that wisdom is in God, the term "wisdom," as it appears in the minor premise, does not stand for either the *ratio* of creaturely wisdom or the *ratio* of divine wisdom, "but for proportionally one wisdom, i.e., for each *ratio* of wisdom, not conjunctively or disjunctively but insofar as they are undivided [i.e., indistinct] proportionately, and one is the other proportionately, and both constitute proportionately one *ratio*."[37] Needless to say, this readiness on the part of proponents of the analogy of being to speak of a single objective concept of being—and this notwithstanding their considered view that there is, strictly speaking, no single nature or *ratio* that all beings share—is liable to muddy the waters considerably. In order to clarify what exactly is at issue in the debate over the analogy of being, therefore, it makes sense to ask not merely whether there is a single objective concept of being, but also whether this objective concept is prescinded or distinct from the objective concepts of God, substance, quality, quantity, etc.

By the late sixteenth century, then, the terms of the debate over the analogy of being had evolved considerably. Thinkers do not merely ask whether "being" immediately signifies one or more *rationes substantiae*. They often ask a more complex set of questions about both the formal and objective concepts of being. It is to be noted, however, that Suárez himself does not preface his discussion of the formal and objective concepts of being with an explanation of what exactly is involved in a thing's having a formal (or objective) concept that is one really or rationally, or what exactly is involved in its having a formal (or objective) concept that is prescinded really or rationally from the concepts of its inferiors. Fortunately, we find such an explanation in the massive commentary on Aristotle's *Metaphysics* written by Pedro da

---

unity and *simpliciter* a multitude, like every unity of a collection of things which in act are many and from which you cannot get a *per se* unit." Quoted from Stephen Brown, "Gerard of Bologna's *Quodlibet I, Quaestio 1:* On the Analogy of Being," *Carmelus* 31 (1984): 145–46.

37. Cajetan, *Scripta Philosophica: De Nominum Analogia, De Conceptu Entis*, pp. 83–84 (n. 111): "Unde, cum fit huiusmodi processus: Omnis perfectio simpliciter est in Deo; sapientia est perfectio simpliciter; ergo etc.; in minore ly sapientia non stat pro hac vel illa ratione sapientiae, sed pro sapientia una proportionaliter, idest, pro utraque ratione sapientiae non coniunctim vel disiunctim; sed in quantum sunt indivisae proportionaliter, et una est altera proportionaliter, et ambae unam proportionaliter constituunt rationem."

Fonseca. It is offered in the context of his commentary on *Metaphysics* IV, ch. 2, and more specifically in section 3 of question 2, shortly after his arguments, in question 1, for the analogy of being, and immediately prior to his discussion of the objective and formal concepts of being in question 2, sections 4 and 5.

Fonseca first notes that a concept can be called one in two ways, namely, either really or rationally (*aut re aut ratione*). For example, he explains, the objective concept of the human being—that is, the substantial nature that is multiplied in individual human beings—is not really, but only rationally, one, since it is numerically diverse in diverse human beings.[38] The assumption here is clearly that real unity is numerical unity, from which it follows, as Fonseca himself notes, that "no common nature . . . is really one."[39] That the objective concept of the human being is rationally one seems clearly to follow from the view that to be one in species—as all human beings are—is to be rationally one or one in respect of *ratio*.[40] Moreover, in accordance with his view that the analogy of being rules out a single *ratio* or nature common to all beings, Fonseca will deny, in section 4, that the objective concept of being is rationally one without qualification on the grounds that, if it were, "the univocity of being would necessarily have to be granted."[41] On the other hand, Fonseca explains, the formal concept of the human being "is one really and rationally, because it is numerically one quality and represents, in altogether one and the same way, human nature, which is multiplied in individual human beings."[42] The implication here is that the formal concept of the human being is really one

38. Pedro da Fonseca, *Commentaria in Libros Metaphysicorum Aristotelis Stagiritae*, vol. 1, col. 715: "natura humana, quae in illis existit, non est conceptus obiectivus unus re, sed ratione duntaxat, cum in diversis sit diversa numero substantia."

39. Pedro da Fonseca, *Commentaria in Libros Metaphysicorum Aristotelis Stagiritae*, vol. 1, col. 716: "nulla natura communis . . . est re ipsa una."

40. Cf. Thomas Aquinas, *ST* I–II, q. 17, art. 4, in *Opera omnia*, t. 6 (Romae: Ex Typographia Polyglotta, Sacra Congregatio de Propaganda Fide, 1891), p. 121a: "esse unum genere vel specie est esse unum secundum rationem."

41. Fonseca grants a qualified, i.e., analogical, unity to the objective concept of being, but this kind of qualified unity is a multiplicity, strictly speaking. See Pedro da Fonseca, *Commentaria in Libros Metaphysicorum Aristotelis Stagiritae*, vol. 1, col. 716.

42. Pedro da Fonseca, *Commentaria in Libros Metaphysicorum Aristotelis Stagiritae*, vol. 1, col. 715: "conceptus formalis, quem habeo de omnibus hominibus, quatenus homines sunt, est unus re, & ratione, quia & est una numero qualitas, & eodem prorsus modo repraesentat naturam humanam, quae est multiplicata in individuis hominibus."

because it is numerically one—that is, numerically one quality of the intellect. That the same formal concept is rationally one, on the other hand, is apparently understood by Fonseca to be a consequence of the fact that it represents human nature, as found in individual human beings, "in altogether one and the same way." Since Fonseca understands a formal concept to be a likeness (*similitudo*),[43] the formal concept of the human being presumably does this by being a single likeness of a single nature common to all human beings. The crucial thought here would seem to be that the rational unity of a formal concept is unity or uniqueness of *ratio*. Granted this, and granted Fonseca's view that the *ratio* of a formal concept consists in its actual representation of the corresponding objective concept,[44] it follows that a formal concept is rationally one if and only if what it represents—that is, its corresponding objective concept—is rationally one. Indeed, in section 5, Fonseca will justify his conclusion that the formal concept of being is not rationally one without qualification simply by recalling his conclusion, in section 4, that the objective concept of being is not rationally one without qualification.[45]

Fonseca also explains that a concept can be prescinded (*praecisus*) either really or rationally from other concepts. A concept is really prescinded from the concepts of its inferiors when it is really distinct from them. Thus the formal concept of the human being is really prescinded from the formal concepts of Peter, Paul, etc., since it is a quality numerically distinct from the qualities by which the intellect represents particular human beings individually and according to their proper *ra-*

43. Pedro da Fonseca, *Commentaria in Libros Metaphysicorum Aristotelis Stagiritae*, vol. 1, col. 710: "Conceptus formalis nihil est aliud, quam actualis similitudo rei, quae intelligitur, ab intellectu ad eam exprimendam producta."

44. See text quoted in the next note.

45. Pedro da Fonseca, *Commentaria in Libros Metaphysicorum Aristotelis Stagiritae*, vol. 1, col. 719: "Formalis conceptus entis, nec est unus ratione, nec item praecisus ratione ab omnibus conceptibus formalibus membrorum dividentium, nisi secundum quid. Haec conclusio facile deducitur ex secunda, & tertia, cum ratio conceptus formalis in actuali repraesentatione obiectivi consistat, ut ex supra dictis patet." (I here read "obiectivi" with the Rome edition of 1577. See Pedro da Fonseca, *Commentariorum Petri Fonsecae D. Theologi Societatis Iesu In Libros Metaphysicorum Aristotelis Stagiritae Tomus primus* [Romae: apud Franciscum Zanettum & Bartholomeum Tosium socios, 1577], p. 557. The Cologne edition of 1615 reads "obiecti.") Suárez, for his part, says that "a formal concept has its entire *ratio* and unity from its object" (*DM* 2.2.3).

tiones.[46] The objective concept of the human being, on the other hand, is not really prescinded from the objective concepts of Peter, Paul, etc., since, contrary to what Plato affirmed, there is no common human nature that is really distinct from the particular natures of individual human beings.[47] Fonseca also explains that a concept is rationally prescinded—or, equivalently, abstracted—from other concepts if nothing proper or peculiar to these other concepts is found in its *ratio*. Thus the formal concept of the human being is rationally prescinded from the formal concepts of its inferiors, since its representation includes the representation of no singular entity. The objective concept of the human being is also rationally prescinded from the objective concepts of its inferiors, because nothing that is proper or peculiar to any individual human being is included in its quiddity.[48]

Suárez, as I have said, holds that there is a single *ratio* of being common to all real beings. Given the foregoing explanations from Fonseca, his claim can now be formulated more precisely: Suárez holds that the formal concept of being is really and rationally one, and also really and rationally prescinded from the formal concepts of other things or objects (*DM* 2.1.9–12). Regarding the unity of this concept, he is prepared to grant that it is multiplied numerically in one and the same subject at different times (*DM* 2.1.12), presumably because he understands it to be an act of the intellect, and the intellect can perform the same act on different occasions. He is also willing to grant that the formal concept

46. Pedro da Fonseca, *Commentaria in Libros Metaphysicorum Aristotelis Stagiritae*, vol. 1, col. 715: "Eum conceptum intelligo praecisum re, qui est re ipsa distinctus ab iis, a quibus dicitur praecisus, qualis est conceptus formalis, quo concipimus hominem communem comparatione eorum, quibus concipimus Socratem, Platonem, & alios particulares. Est enim alia qualitas numero distincta ab iis omnibus, quibus repraesentantur homines particulares."

47. Pedro da Fonseca, *Commentaria in Libros Metaphysicorum Aristotelis Stagiritae*, vol. 1, col. 715: "Eodem modo credebat Plato hominem communem (qui est conceptus obiectivus praedicti formalis) esse praecisum a particularibus; quippe qui putabat illum esse re ipsa a particularibus distinctum."

48. Pedro da Fonseca, *Commentaria in Libros Metaphysicorum Aristotelis Stagiritae*, vol. 1, cols. 715–16: "Eum autem dico praecisum ratione (qui etiam abstractus appellatur) in cuius ratione nihil includitur eorum, quae sunt propria conceptibus, a quibus praecisus est. Hoc pacto est praecisus uterque conceptus hominis communis a particularibus. Nam neque in repraesentatione conceptus formalis, quo concipimus hominem communem, includitur repraesentatio cuiusquam particularis entitatis, nec item in quidditate ipsius hominis communis includitur quicquam, quod sit proprium & peculiare cuiquam particulari."

of being can perhaps be multiplied specifically according as one apprehends the formal *ratio* of being more or less distinctly (*DM* 2.1.12). However, neither of these concessions undermines the real and rational unity of the formal concept of being as Suárez understands it, since what he is particularly concerned to deny is the view that this concept is one only in a qualified sense, by virtue of possessing a merely analogical unity. Hence his claim that the formal concept of being is really and rationally prescinded from the formal concepts of its inferiors. As regards the objective concept of being, Suárez holds that it is both rationally one (*DM* 2.2.8–14) and rationally prescinded from the proper objective concepts of being's inferiors (*DM* 2.2.15–20), but that it is neither really one (see *DM* 2.2.8 and 2.2.14) nor (*pace* Scotus) really prescinded from the proper objective concepts of other things (*DM* 2.3.7–11).

Suárez and Scotus

Although Suárez rejects Scotus's view that "being" is univocal, the fact that he agrees with Scotus in holding that there is a single nature or *ratio* of being common to all real beings means that he must contend with some of the same problems that Scotus does. In his response to such problems he distinguishes himself rather clearly from the *doctor subtilis*.

One standard argument against Scotus and the univocity of being focuses on the question of how any alleged single nature or *ratio* of being could be contracted or determined to its inferiors—that is, to the items contained immediately under it (e.g., God or infinite being, substance, accident). In the case of a genus like *animal*, its contraction to the species contained under it (e.g., *human being*) is by way of differences (e.g., *rational*). In this case, the genus stands to each of its differences as a determinable (*determinabile*) stands to a determining element (*determinans*). The case of being, however, presents a unique problem, since it is generally held that a determinable must be outside the nature of any element that determines or contracts it to an inferior. Granted, then, that there is a single nature of being that is contracted to its inferiors, it would seem that the elements which contract it cannot themselves be beings. But this seems impossible. Indeed, this very problem was noticed as far back as Aristotle, who in *Metaph.* III, ch. 3, famously argues that being cannot be a genus because any difference of a genus must itself be a being (998b22–27). In a similar vein, Hervaeus Natalis argues that the univocity of being would require that being be contracted to any given category by "something formally diverse from every being" and so by a difference that formally signifies either nothing or something privative—neither of which, he argues, can enter into the formal *ratio* of something positive like a category.[49]

Scotus, however, was commonly read as having bitten the bullet here, and as having held that being is not predicated quidditatively or essentially of the intrinsic modes by which it is contracted to its inferiors—that (for example) it is essentially predicated neither of the mode of being *per se* (*modus essendi per se*), which is the intrinsic mode that essentially characterizes substances, nor of the mode of being in another (*modus essendi in alio*), which is the intrinsic mode that essentially characterizes accidents as such.[50] This, at least, was taken to be an implication of the arguments in *Ord.* I, d. 3, p. 1, q. 3, which purport to show that being is not predicated quidditativey of ultimate differences, that is, of differences whose concepts are unqualifiedly simple (*simpliciter simplices*).[51] What's more, Scotus was also read as having affirmed that there is some sort of distinction in reality obtaining between being and its intrinsic modes and so between being and its inferiors.[52]

As mentioned, Suárez agrees with Scotus in holding that there is a formal concept of being that is really and rationally one and really

49. Hervaeus Natalis, *Quolibeta*, fol. 45ra. Cf. *DM* 2.2.2.

50. The intrinsic modes which contract being to its inferiors are to be distinguished from the sort of mode which is said by Suárez in *DM* 7 to be modally distinct from, and outside the essence of, the thing of which it is a mode. See *DM* 7.1.17 (*Opera Omnia*, vol. 25, p. 256a), where Suárez distinguishes the latter sense of "mode" from the sense in which "every contracting or determining thing is wont to be called a mode of the thing contracted, for in this way rational can be called a mode of animal, and this word is especially wont to be applied to those modes by which being or accident is determined to the most general genera" (*omne contrahens, vel determinans solet appellari modus contracti: sic enim rationale dici potest modus animalis, & specialiter solet haec vox applicari ad illos modos, quibus determinatur ens, vel accidens ad genera generalissima*).

51. John Duns Scotus, *Opera omnia*, vol. 3 (Vaticana), pp. 81–83 (ns. 131–33) and pp. 97–100 (ns. 159–61).

52. Suárez and Scotus assume that a determinable is distinct *ex natura rei* from the determining elements that contract it to its immediate inferiors if and only if the same determinable is distinct *ex natura rei* from its immediate inferiors. See *DM* 2.3.1.

and rationally prescinded from the formal concepts of being's inferiors. Establishing this conclusion is the principal aim of *DM* 2.1 ("Whether in our mind being as being has one formal concept common to all beings"). Moreover, Suárez also agrees with Scotus in holding that there is an objective concept of being that is rationally one and rationally prescinded from the objective concepts of being's inferiors. Establishing this conclusion is the principal aim of *DM* 2.2 ("Whether being has a single objective concept, or a single objective formal *ratio*"). However, against Scotus, Suárez denies that there is any distinction in reality—or any "distinction *ex natura rei*"—between the *ratio* of being and its inferiors, or between the *ratio* of being and the intrinsic modes which contract it to these inferiors. Showing that there is no such distinction is the principal aim of *DM* 2.3 ("Whether the *ratio* or concept of being is in some way prescinded from inferiors really and antecedently to the intellect's operation"). In addition, Suárez disagrees with Scotus in holding that being is essentially predicated of both ultimate differences and the intrinsic modes which determine being to its inferiors. After explaining, in *DM* 2.4, what the *ratio* of being consists in, Suárez turns in *DM* 2.5 ("Whether the *ratio* of being transcends all *rationes* and differences of inferior beings in such a way that it is included in them intimately and essentially") to the task of showing that this is the case. Of course, this means that Suárez must explain how being can be contracted to its inferiors, given that the intrinsic modes which divide it are themselves beings. This is the principal task of *DM* 2.6 ("How being as being is contracted or determined to its inferiors"), the final section of the Second Disputation.

DM 2.1: The formal concept of being

In the first section of *DM* 2, Suárez considers and rejects three answers to the question of whether there is a formal concept of being that is really and rationally one and also really and rationally prescinded from the formal concepts of being's inferiors. The first opinion, attributed to Cajetan, affirms that there is no such concept. Suárez, however, seems to recognize that attributing this opinion to Cajetan is complicated by a pair of distinctions that Cajetan makes, the first between the perfect and imperfect formal concepts of being,[53] the second between the nominal and real formal concepts of being.[54] Suárez chooses to ignore these complications, however, apparently because he will deal with the relevant distinctions in connection with the second and third opinions, since the second distinction seems to be substantially the same as one made by Francesco Silvestri of Ferrara (1474–1528), the author of the second opinion, while the first distinction seems identical to one made by Fonseca, the author of the third opinion. In any case, the first opinion, Suárez explains, is based on the view that "being" is an analogical name, and on the further view that if there were a single formal concept of being, then "being" would be univocal, rather than analogical. The latter claim is in turn proved by appeal to the premise that an analogical name immediately signifies several *rationes* or objective concepts, and also by appeal to the premise that a name immediately signifies several objective concepts if and only if it expresses several formal concepts, since formal concepts are individuated by appeal to their corresponding objective concepts.

The second opinion, which Suárez attributes to Ferrara and characterizes as an explication or exposition (*explicatio*) of the first, distinguishes between two kinds of formal concept, one nominal (*quid nominis*), the other real (*quid rei*), and affirms that, in the particular case of being, its nominal concept can be one, but its real concept must rather be many, that is, a set consisting in the various formal concepts of being's inferiors. The foundation of this opinion is the view that analogicals generally can be conceived in either of two ways, namely, by means of several real concepts, or by means of a single nominal concept. Thus, when one hears the name "healthy thing" (*sanum*), for example, the mind either forms several real concepts—the concept of an animal, the concept of food, and the concept of urine—or it forms a single nominal concept having "more to do with the signification of the word than with some thing" (*DM* 2.1.3), which is what happens when, upon hearing the name "healthy thing," one simply conceives

53. See Cajetan, *Scripta Philosophica: De Nominum Analogia, De Conceptu Entis*, pp. 34–38 (ns. 36–40) and pp. 98–99 (ns. 3–4).

54. See Cajetan, *Scripta Philosophica: De Nominum Analogia, De Conceptu Entis*, pp. 99–100 (ns. 5–6).

what has some relation to health (*quod habet ordinem ad sanitatem*). Similarly, in the case of "being," either the mind forms the real formal concepts of its immediate significates (i.e., the categories), or it forms the nominal formal concept of something having *esse* or some relation to *esse* (*quidquid habet esse, vel habitudinem ad esse*).

The third opinion, which Suárez treats as a mere variant of the second and ascribes to Fonseca, goes further inasmuch as it distinguishes three different formal concepts of being, namely, a distinct concept, a confused concept, and an intermediate concept, this last being described as partly confused and partly distinct. Fonseca's distinct formal concept of being corresponds to what Ferrara calls the real mental concept of being and to what Cajetan calls both the real and the perfect formal concept of being. However, unlike Ferrara and Cajetan, Fonseca holds that the distinct formal concept of being is composed from or includes the formal concepts of all simple entities (i.e., entities not composed from a common nature and a contracting difference), where the list of simple entities includes not merely the categories and God, but the differences which determine or contract the categories to every subaltern genus or species of creature, including those creatures which God never actually creates.[55] Fonseca's confused formal concept of being corresponds to the nominal mental concept of being found in Ferrara and Cajetan, and it is really one, rather than many. Finally, Fonseca's intermediate formal concept of being, which is also really one, rather than many, corresponds to Cajetan's imperfect concept of being. It "represents one nature (for example, substance) determinately but the others (namely, quantity, quality, etc.) implicitly and indeterminately, insofar as they all agree with substance according to some proportion" (*DM* 2.1.4).

Suárez offers various arguments against the positions of Cajetan, Ferrara, and Fonseca. Suffice it to say that he rejects the mentioned distinctions between different formal concepts of being. The concept that Cajetan calls imperfect and Fonseca intermediate cannot prop-

55. As Suárez observes (*DM* 2.1.5), Fonseca accordingly holds that the altogether distinct formal concept of being cannot be found in a creature, since only God can understand all possible simple entities determinately and expressly. See Pedro da Fonseca, *Commentaria in Libros Metaphysicorum Aristotelis Stagiritae*, vol. 1, col. 714.

erly be called a formal concept of being, he argues, since the formal concept of substance (for example) is not rightly called a concept of being on the grounds that it also implicitly or confusedly represents accidents thanks to some proportional agreement obtaining between the categories, for the formal concept of substance is not rightly said to represent accidents at all (*DM* 2.1.7–8). The concept that is variously termed distinct, perfect, and real is not the formal concept of being, either, Suárez claims, since the formal concept of being does not determinately represent particular kinds of being insofar as they are such, but rather a single *ratio* in which all beings agree (*DM* 2.1.5–6). As regards the concept called nominal or confused, Suárez grants that the formal concept of being is confused in relation to particular types of being, just as the concept *animal* is confused in relation to the several species of animal (*DM* 2.1.6), but he denies that this concept is correctly called a concept of the name alone (*tantum nominis*). It is rather an image which naturally represents what the word "being" signifies by convention (*DM* 2.1.13).

Suárez also argues directly for the claim that the formal concept of being is really and rationally one as well as really and rationally prescinded from the formal concepts of being's inferiors (*DM* 2.1.9–11). He begins with four arguments for the real unity of the formal concept of being (*DM* 2.1.9). Especially worth noting is the first, which appeals to experience, and in particular to the claim that when we hear the word "being" our thought "is not drawn in different directions or divided into several concepts, but is rather gathered into one" (*DM* 2.1.9). The conclusion that the formal concept of being is really one entails, Suárez further argues, that it is really distinct or prescinded from the formal concepts by which the mind conceives substance as such, accident as such, and so on. And this is so even if, in a substance itself (say), there is no distinction in reality between (i) that which makes it a being and (ii) that which is proper to it and serves to distinguish it from accident. For, Suárez explains, in distinguishing what is not in reality distinct (e.g., God's mercy and his justice), the mind nonetheless forms really distinct concepts by which one and the same thing is inadequately conceived (*DM* 2.1.10).

Finally, Suárez argues that the formal concept of being is rationally one—or "one according to its formal *ratio*" (*secundum rationem formalem suam*)—and rationally prescinded or distinguished, in accordance with this *ratio*, from the formal concepts of being's inferiors. Suárez does not indicate here what exactly the formal *ratio* of a mental concept consists in, but he elsewhere states that a formal concept has its entire *ratio* and unity from its object (*DM* 2.2.3). It is therefore natural to suppose that the formal *ratio* or essential character of a mental concept is determined by, and specified by appeal to, its object. Indeed, arguing for the rational unity of being's formal concept and its rational precision from the formal concepts of being's inferiors, Suárez claims that the formal concept is the simplest objectively—that is, with respect to its object or representational content—and infers from this that it is also the simplest formally. (The thought, presumably, is that its formal simplicity guarantees its rational unity and its formal difference from other mental concepts.) Suárez also argues that when the mind confounds (*confundere*) and conjoins really different or distinct things insofar as they are similar, it unites its concept (*unit conceptum suum*), or produces a concept that is one really and according to its formal *ratio*, just as, conversely, when it distinguishes items that are not in reality distinguished, it produces really distinct concepts. The formal concept of being, therefore, is one in respect of its formal *ratio* and prescinded, according to that *ratio*, from formal concepts that represent determinate *rationes* of beings.

DM 2.2: (i) Suárez on rational precision

DM 2.2 is the longest section of the Second Disputation and arguably the most difficult to navigate. Again, Suárez's principal aim here is to argue that the objective concept of being is both rationally one and rationally prescinded from the objective concepts of being's inferiors. The unity of the objective concept of being is rational, rather than real, because the unity at issue is not numerical or entitative, but formal or fundamental (*DM* 2.2.14).[56] Indeed, according to Suárez, the unity of being's objective concept is simply an "agreement and likeness" (*convenientia et similitudo*) obtaining among all beings (*DM* 2.2.14).

56. On entitative unity, see *DM* 4.2.19.

Suárez also holds, against Scotus, that the precision of being's objective concept from its inferiors is merely rational, and not real. However, as mentioned, the task of showing that it is not real is left for *DM* 2.3.

Central to Suárez's case for the rational unity and precision of being's objective concept is his account of how the intellect rationally prescinds or abstracts this concept from the objective concepts of its inferiors. In some respects, the operation by which it does this, on his view, is like that by which it prescinds the concept of a genus from its species, or the concept of a species from its individuals. However, the case of being presents special difficulties, according to Suárez, since, as we have seen, it is unlike a genus or species in important respects.

Suárez denies that being is a proper universal, which would require that it be a genus, since a proper universal must be a predicable (i.e., a genus, species, difference, property, or accident), and a genus is the only predicable that being could plausibly be. It is not a proper universal, according to Suárez, because a proper universal must be related to its inferiors "by an equal relation and ordering" (*DM* 2.2.36), whereas he holds (as we have seen) that the *ratio* of being instead belongs to its principal analogate absolutely and to other analogates by virtue of some relation they bear to the principal analogate. Nonetheless, although Suárez denies that being is a universal, strictly so-called, he also holds that the relation of being to its inferiors is in some respects like the relation of a genus to its species, or like the relation of a lowest species to its individuals. In this last case, the intellect prescinds or abstracts a species like *human being* from various individuals by means of a partial or inadequate conception of some individual, a consideration of that individual in which it "does not grasp all that is in the object as it exists *a parte rei*, but rather [grasps the object] only in accordance with some agreement or likeness" that it has with other individuals of the same species (*DM* 2.2.16). According to Suárez, moreover, in thus forming the mental concept *human being*, the mind effects the rational precision of the corresponding objective concept from the objective concepts of Peter, Martha, and other individual human beings. For what is conceived in and by means of this formal concept just *is* the objective concept of the human being, that is, human nature. Further, Suárez stresses that in such a rational precision a "precision of things in themselves [*secundum se*] is not necessary" (*DM* 2.2.16). In other words, there need be no distinction *ex natura rei* between the human nature in Martha, on the one hand, and Martha's haecceity or individual difference, on the other. (In fact, Suárez will explicitly deny in *DM* 5 that in a singular there is any such distinction between the common nature of the species, on the one hand, and the singular's individual difference, on the other. See *DM* 5.2.9.) Rather, all that is required for a rational precision is a "certain denomination from the formal concept which represents" the objective concept (*DM* 2.2.16). That is, all that is required is that the objective concept serve as the term or adequate object of the corresponding formal concept. This is why Suárez says, in *DM* 2.2, that the objective concept of the human being is distinguished only rationally, and not really, from Peter, Paul, and other individual human beings (*DM* 2.2.16).

Much the same process occurs, according to Suárez, when the mind effects either the rational precision of being from its inferiors or the rational precision of a genus from its species. In both cases, the mind engages in the same sort of partial or inadequate consideration of some inferior, informed by a comparison of that inferior with other inferiors of the same common nature. In each of these cases as well, Suárez thinks, a rational precision is made in the absence of any distinction *ex natura rei* between the items that it rationally distinguishes.[57]

For Suárez, moreover, the rational precision of a genus or species from its inferiors necessarily involves the rational precision of that nature from the elements that contract it to those inferiors. For example, when the intellect rationally prescinds the objective concept of an animal from the objective concepts of its species, this requires a rational precision of its concept from the objective concepts of the specific differences (e.g., *rational*) that divide it and essentially constitute its species. Indeed, it is worth noting that Suárez speaks indifferently either of such a common nature's precision from its inferiors or of its precision from the items that contract it to its inferiors, and this, it seems, because wherever one of these occurs, the other must as well. Thus, in presenting an argument that he canvasses for the claim that

57. Suárez will argue in *DM* 6 that there is no distinction *ex natura rei* between a genus such as *animal* and a difference such as *rational* (*DM* 6.9.8).

the objective concept of being is not one, but many, Suárez (speaking in the voice of his opponent) argues that being cannot be prescinded from its inferiors by alleging that it cannot be prescinded from the intrinsic modes that contract it and essentially constitute these inferiors (*DM* 2.2.2). It should be noted, however, that Suárez elsewhere recognizes an important difference between these two types of rational precision. When the mind effects a rational precision in the absence of a corresponding distinction *ex natura rei*, it draws a rational distinction, and in particular, a distinction of reasoned reason (*distinctio rationis ratiocinatae*).[58] Moreover, in *DM* 7 Suárez grants that there are several modes of this rational distinction.[59] When neither of the things distinguished includes the other—as is the case with *animal* and *rational*, for example—the distinction is termed mutual (*mutua*). But when one includes the other—as is the case with *animal* and *human being*, for example—the distinction is termed non-mutual (*non mutua*). In either case, the extremes or terms are rationally distinguished—that is, reason conceives them as different or non-identical (though without affirming that they are in reality different[60])—but in the former case the distinction is between two co-parts (*duae compartes*), while in the latter it is between the included and the including (*inclusum et includens*).

Being, according to Suárez, differs importantly from genera and species especially in respect of the relation that it bears to the elements that contract it to its inferiors—for example, the mode of being *per se* (*modus essendi per se*), which is the mode of being that essentially characterizes substances, and the mode of being in another (*modus essendi in alio*), which is the mode of being that essentially characterizes accidents.[61] Such intrinsic modes, on his view, stand to being in somewhat like the way differences stand to the genus that they divide and contract. However, there is a crucial dissimilarity here, according to him, that is especially pertinent to the question of whether the objective concept of being is rationally one and prescinded from the objective concepts of its inferiors: as we have seen, Suárez holds that

58. See *DM* 7.1.4–5.
59. See *DM* 7.1.21.
60. See *DM* 7.1.6.
61. See n. 50 above.

being is predicated essentially of the modes that contract it, but that a genus or species is never predicated of the differences that contract it.[62]

This dissimilarity between being, on the one hand, and a genus or species, on the other, gives rise to the greatest problem standing in the way of the conclusion that the objective concept of being is rationally one rather than many. Indeed, as we have seen, a traditional and oft-repeated argument against the rational unity of the concept of being—a version of which Suárez himself rehearses at *DM* 2.2.2—alleges that if being is rationally prescinded from its inferiors, then it must be contracted to such an inferior by something. However, the argument continues, it cannot be so contracted, for the contracting element can be neither a being nor nothing. It cannot be nothing, since nothing cannot divide being and essentially constitute anything; nor can it be a being, since what is contracted must be outside the *ratio* of what contracts it.[63]

Suárez, as we have seen, takes Scotus to have denied that being is predicated quidditatively of either ultimate differences or the intrinsic modes that contract being. Suárez himself disagrees; he holds that being is predicated quidditatively of both, and he will devote *DM* 2.5 to refuting Scotus's position on this question. The challenge for Suárez, then, is to explain how being can be contracted by intrinsic modes of which it itself is predicated essentially. It is important to remember, however, that according to Suárez being is only rationally, and not really, prescinded from its inferiors. The challenge for him, then, is not that of explaining how the *ratio* of being could in reality be prescinded from, or in reality be contracted to, its inferiors. The challenge, rather, concerns our mental concepts: how does the mind rationally prescind the objective concept of being from its inferiors, and how does it con-

62. It was commonly held that substances are not constituted from non-substances (see Aristotle, *Phys.* I, ch. 6, 189a33), and that the differences from which items in the category of substance are constituted are therefore substances, albeit incomplete ones. However, it was also commonly held that the substance which is a highest genus or category is complete substance, and that it is therefore not predicated essentially of any substantial difference. For Suárez's discussion of this, see *DM* 33.1. For his discussion of the similar issue that arises in connection with accidents, see *DM* 39.1.

63. This argument, or a version of it, is commonly deployed against the view that being is predicated univocally of its inferiors. It is so used by Hervaeus Natalis and Pedro da Fonseca, for example. For Hervaeus, see *Quolibeta*, fol. 45ra–45rb. For Fonseca, see Pedro da Fonseca, *Commentaria in Libros Metaphysicorum Aristotelis Stagiritae*, vol. 1, col. 696. But it can also be adapted so as to target a view like Suárez's.

ceive the contraction of being to these same inferiors? Suárez does not answer this question in *DM* 2.2. In fact, as mentioned, he answers it only in *DM* 2.6, the final section of the Second Disputation. On his view, the precision cannot occur through the resolution of a concept into simpler concepts, in the way it resolves the concept *human being* into the concepts *rational* and *animal*, nor can the contraction be conceived through composition or addition, in the way the mind conceives the contraction of *living substance* to *animal* by means of a composition of the concepts *living substance* and *sensitive*. At the very least, a resolution of concepts here would open the door to an infinite regress: granted that the intrinsic modes which contract being include being itself, the formal concept of such a mode would admit of resolution into the concepts of being and some other intrinsic mode, and the formal concept of this other intrinsic mode would likewise have to be resolvable into the concepts of being and some third intrinsic mode, and so on, *ad infinitum* (*DM* 2.6.5). Moreover, although it might be alleged that such an infinite regress poses no insuperable problem, since it does not entail that in a substance itself (say) there is a real composition of infinitely many modes that are distinct *ex natura rei* from each other, nevertheless, Suárez himself rejects the view in question, in part by appeal to Aristotle's claim in *Metaph.* II, ch. 2, 994b16–25, that there can be no progression to infinity when it comes to quidditative predicates (*DM* 2.6.5). Instead, Suárez argues that the intellect conceives the contraction of being to its inferiors "by means of a more express conception of some being contained under being" (*per modum expressioris conceptionis alicuius entis contenti sub ente*) (*DM* 2.6.7). In other words, according to Suárez, the formal concept of being is not related to the formal concept of substance (say) as a simple concept is related to a composite one. Rather, the greater generality of the former is merely the product of greater confusion. More on this anon.

DM 2.2: (ii) The rational precision and unity of the objective concept of being

Suárez opens *DM* 2.2 by outlining two arguments for the view that the objective concept of being is not one, but many. The first argument alleges that if a term immediately signifies a single *ratio* or objective concept, and the unity of this objective concept is not a qualified, analogical unity, then the term must be univocal (*DM* 2.2.1). Suárez does not directly reply to this argument in *DM* 2.2 but says that he will reply to it later (*DM* 2.2.20). Presumably, he is looking forward to his discussions in *DM* 28.3 and *DM* 32.2, although he will close the section by affirming that univocity requires more than the unqualified rational unity of an objective concept (*DM* 2.2.36).

The second argument, which is more complicated, is a version of the argument mentioned above. It runs as follows. If the objective concept of being is one, it is in itself prescinded and abstracted from the proper *rationes* of determinate beings. But it is impossible for the objective concept of being to be in itself prescinded and abstracted from these inferior *rationes*. Therefore, the objective concept of being is not one. The consequence (i.e., the conditional which serves as the first premise) is justified as follows. The unity of the objective concept of being is incompatible with its actual inclusion of intrinsic modes, for since modes of this sort are opposed to each other and cannot belong to one and the same thing, their actual inclusion in the objective concept of being would generate multiplicity and undermine its rational unity. Therefore, if the objective concept of being is one, rather than many, it must prescind from such intrinsic modes. The second premise of the principal argument is defended as follows. If being prescinds from its inferiors, then it must be contracted or determined to each of its inferiors through the addition of some contracting element to it. But this item that is added to being is either itself a being or nothing. It cannot be nothing, since nothing cannot determine or contract being and constitute the *ratio* of some determinate type of being. But if this added item is a being, being cannot be prescinded from it, for "what is prescinded from another thing is not included in it" (*DM* 2.2.2). (Presumably, what Suárez *means* here is that where *A* and *B* are related as common *ratio* and contracting element, respectively, *A* cannot be included in *B*.[64]) For, the argument alleges, contraction requires addition (e.g., the addition of *rational* to *animal*), and there is addition only when what is added does not include that to which it is added, "either really or rationally, in accordance with the way it is understood to be added" (*DM* 2.2.2). Indeed, this is why Aristotle states that the genus is outside the *rationes* of the differences that divide and contract it.[65]

Immediately after presenting these two arguments against the rational unity of the objective concept of being, Suárez presents a third argument in favor of his own view (*DM* 2.2.3). This argument alleges that a formal concept has its entire *ratio* and unity from its object or corresponding objective concept, and that since the formal concept of being has been shown to be rationally one in *DM* 2.1, the objective concept of being must also be rationally one.

Together, these three arguments regarding the rational unity of the objective concept of being constitute "reasons for doubt" (*rationes dubitandi*), that is, reasons that are liable to make one hesitate or vacillate when faced with the question of whether the objective concept of being is rationally one or many. Immediately after presenting them, Suárez identifies three positions that have been taken on the issue. First, there are those who deny the rational unity and precision of the objective concept of being. These include thinkers like Cajetan and Ferrara, who deny that there is a single formal concept of being, but also thinkers who are said to have granted that there is such a single formal concept, in particular, Soncinas (aka Paulo Barbo) (ca. 1458–94), Hispalensis (aka Diego Deza) (1444–1523), Hervaeus Natalis, and Dominic of Flanders (1425–79) (*DM* 2.2.4). The second opinion is that

64. In the translation of Rábade et al., the clause in question ("*quod ab alio praescinditur, non includitur in illo*") is rendered "aquello de que algo prescinde no está incluído en él" ("that from which something prescinds is not included in it"). See Francisco Suárez, *Disputaciones metafísicas*, ed. Sergio Rábade Romeo, Salvador Caballero Sánchez, and Antonio Puigcerver Zanón, vol. 1 (Madrid: Ed. Gredos, 1960), p. 374. Assuming that "to prescind from" and "to be prescinded from" amount to the same thing, this translation seems incorrect. The translator's (or translators') choice to render the Latin in this way may betray some discomfort with Suárez's claim when strictly construed, for so understood, it implies, not only that *animal* is not included in *rational*, but also that *animal* is not included in *human being*.

65. Aristotle, *Metaph.* III, ch. 3, 998b24–26.

the objective concept of being has an unqualified rational unity, and this opinion is said to have been held by Scotus, Giovanni Crisostomo Javelli (ca. 1470–ca. 1538), Domingo de Soto (1494–1560), and John Capreolus (aka Jean Cabrol) (ca. 1380–1444). Scotus is said to differ from the others, however, in having held that the objective concept of being is prescinded *ex natura rei* from both its inferiors and the modes that contract being. Javelli, Soto, and Capreolus, on the other hand, are said to have posited the unity of this objective concept only "according to our mode of conceiving, without a precision and distinction that obtains in reality" (*DM* 2.2.5).[66] The third opinion is said to be intermediate between the first two and comes in two versions. The first is advanced by unnamed thinkers and affirms that the objective concept of being, "taken in itself and absolutely without inferiors, is one and rationally prescinded from them," but that, when "compared to inferiors and [conceived] as included in them, it is not one" (*DM* 2.2.6). This position, Suárez states, allows its holders to explain the unity of the formal concept of being, for as conceived by means of this concept, they allege, the objective concept of being is considered in itself and without any comparison to its inferiors. The position also allows them to hold that when the objective concept of being is "considered as existing in the same inferiors, it cannot have unity" (*DM* 2.2.6). And this is as it should be, for inferiors like substance and accident differ from each other "through that very thing by virtue of which they are beings, and therefore they cannot as such have unity in it, since they cannot agree and differ in the same respect" (*DM* 2.2.6). The argument here seems to be that, since a substance is both a substance and a being by virtue of the same simple nature, A, and an accident is both an accident and a being by virtue of the same simple nature, B, then necessarily $A \neq B$, since to be a substance ≠ to be an accident, and from this it follows that there is no single nature in virtue of which a substance and an accident are both termed beings. The second version of this intermediate view is attributed to Fonseca, apparently on the strength of what he has to say about the objective concept which corresponds to what he terms the confused formal concept of being. Specifically, Fonseca holds that

66. It's worth noting that it is not always clear that Suárez is correct in his assessment of his predecessors' views.

this concept is one, Suárez explains, and that "it is indeed in some way prescinded, since it does not expressly and determinately contain that which is proper to inferior members" (*DM* 2.2.6). However, Fonseca also claims that "it is not without qualification prescinded even rationally, lest it follow that it is univocal" (*DM* 2.2.6), for it "excludes those things which are proper to substance and the other simple entities in such a way that, nevertheless, its essence is not other than the essence of entities of this sort" (*DM* 2.2.6).[67]

In the remainder of *DM* 2.2, Suárez argues, first, that to the formal concept of being there corresponds a single objective concept "that does not expressly signify [*dicit*] substance, or accident, or God, or creature, but all of these in the manner of one thing, namely, insofar as they are in some way similar to each other and agree in being [*in essendo*]" (*DM* 2.2.8). (Interestingly, Suárez says that Fonseca does not disagree with this view.) Two arguments are given for this conclusion. In the first, Suárez identifies three ways in which concepts of being's inferiors might be thought to figure in the objective concept of being—copulatively, disjunctively, or without qualification—and he argues that the relevant concepts cannot be supposed related in any of these ways. This is so whether the objective concept of being is conceived to include (i) the objective concepts of substance and accident (*DM* 2.2.9–11), (ii) the objective concepts of all ten categories (*DM* 2.2.12), or (iii) one nature "determinately and expressly, and others implicitly and confusedly" (*DM* 2.2.13). In the second argument, Suárez affirms that all real beings have some "likeness and agreement in the *ratio* of *esse*,"

67. Cf. Pedro da Fonseca, *Commentaria in Libros Metaphysicorum Aristotelis Stagiritae*, vol. 1, cols. 716–18. Fonseca explains here that there is a difference between the way the objective concept of the human being excludes things proper to Socrates and Plato and the way the confused objective concept of being excludes things proper to substance and the other items immediately signified by "being." Things proper to Socrates and Plato do not pertain to the essence of the human being as such. But this is not so in the case of being: its essence is not other than the essences of the simple entities immediately signified by the word "being." Accordingly, things proper to these simple entities "are not without qualification excluded from the concept of being, even from the altogether confused one, but are rather excluded in a certain way, namely, insofar as they are conceived neither determinately nor expressly, but indeterminately and implicitly" (*non simpliciter excluduntur a conceptu entis, etiam omnino confuso, sed quodammodo*). Therefore, Fonseca says, "being is never unqualifiedly abstracted from its dividing members, but only in a certain way and in a certain respect" (*nunquam ens abstrahi simpliciter a suis membris dividentibus, sed solum quodammodo, & secundum quid*).

in part by appeal to the fact that the intellect evidently finds a greater agreement and likeness between substance and accident than it does between substance and non-being (*DM* 2.2.14). Moreover, he argues, it follows from this that all real beings "can be conceived and represented under that prescinded *ratio* in which they agree with each other," and since the unity of the objective concept of being is merely a "formal or fundamental unity, which is nothing other than the mentioned agreement and likeness," it also follows that all real beings "constitute one objective concept under that *ratio*" (*DM* 2.2.14). This objective concept can only be the objective concept of being, moreover, since it is transcendent, the simplest, and the first of all objective concepts, and all these attributes are attributes of being.

Suárez goes on to argue, in the second place, that the objective concept of being "is rationally prescinded from all particulars or members that divide being, even though they are entities that are simple in the highest degree" (*DM* 2.2.15). This conclusion, he states, "seems to me to follow necessarily from the preceding one" (namely, from the conclusion that the objective concept of being is rationally one without qualification), for the rational unity of the objective concept of being, understood as a concept in which all determinate real beings agree, presupposes its rational precision from the objective concepts of these determinate beings, since the latter are many, rather than one (*DM* 2.2.15). Sensitive, perhaps, to Fonseca's view that the rational precision at issue is only qualified or in a certain respect, Suárez nevertheless proceeds to offer several arguments for this conclusion (*DM* 2.2.17), after explaining that the rational precision of a common nature from its inferiors occurs through the intellect's production of a formal concept which represents that nature in isolation from its inferiors. That there is such a rationally prescinded formal concept of being as such, as established in *DM* 2.1, is the premise of the first argument: since the rational precision of the objective concept is effected simply by the formation of such a concept, it follows that the objective concept of being is rationally prescinded from being's inferiors.

To this argument, Suárez adds three more by way of confirmation. First, it has already been proved that the objective concept of being is, according to reason, other than the objective concepts of substance, accident or any other determinate genus. It has also been proved that it is not something aggregated from these. Therefore, it is something rationally prescinded from them. Second, it is only thanks to this rational precision of the objective concept of being from its inferiors that the propositions "a substance is a being" and "an accident is a being" are true without being identical, since what is predicated in each—namely, the objective concept of being—is common to, and rationally distinguished from, both substance and accident. It is also only for this reason, Suárez adds, that we can be certain that something is a being but uncertain whether it is a substance or accident. Finally, third, Suárez alleges that there is an objective concept of substance rationally prescinded from particular substances only because of the resemblance that all substances have, and similarly for the rationally prescinded objective concept of accident as such. The same, therefore, must be said about the concept of being.

Suárez next observes that against the view that there is a single objective concept of being, it might be objected that the view implies, falsely, that the categories are not primarily diverse, since they agree in a common *ratio*. The assumption here is that things which are primarily diverse are distinguished from each other in respect of their entire essences or by themselves (*per se* or *se ipsis*), where *A*'s being primarily diverse from *B* is contrasted with *A*'s differing essentially from *B*—in a strict sense of "differ."[68] In the latter case, but not the former, *A* and *B*

68. Cf. Collegium Complutense Sancti Cyrilli, *Artium Cursus sive Disputationes in Aristotelis Dialecticam, et Philosophiam naturalem*, p. 348a–b: "First, then, it must be noted that *to differ* or *difference*, if we attend to the force of the word, as it is taken in the present place, signifies distance, distinction, or diversity among some things. But it is taken in two ways, as Aristotle teaches in *Metaph.* V, text 15 [...]. For first, it is taken in a large sense and improperly for any distinction or diversity of things, for which it is not required that the things agree in some one thing. In this sense, we say that the categories and differences themselves differ from each other. ❡ Second, it is taken properly for the diversity of those thing which agree in some one thing, or insofar as it implies things which differ from each other not by themselves, but by some other thing. Whence also the name 'difference' is applied to signify the principle of this distinction, or that grade by which one differs from another. And it is taken in this sense in the present place." (*Primo ergo notandum est, quod* differre, *seu* differentia, *si vim nominis, ut in praesenti sumitur, attendamus, significat distantiam, distinctionem, seu diversitatem inter aliqua. Sumitur autem dupliciter, ut ex doctrina Aris. 5. Metaph. text. 15* [...]. *Primo enim sumitur late, & improprie pro quacunque diversitate, aut distinctione aliquorum, ad quod non requiritur, ut in aliquo uno conveniant. Quo sensu praedicamenta, ipsasque differentias dicimus inter se differre; cum tamen sint primo diversa, ut infra constabit.* ❡ *Secundo sumitur proprie, pro diversitate eorum, quae in aliquo uno conveniunt, seu prout*

share an essential predicate (e.g., *animal*), and the one is distinguished from the other, not by itself (*per se* or *se ipso*) or by its entire essence, but by an essential difference (e.g., *rational*). To this objection, Suárez replies that the categories are not called primarily diverse because they agree in nothing, since it is clear (for example) that the accidental categories agree in the *ratio* of accident. Rather, they are called primarily diverse because they agree in no genus, and also because they do not differ "by means of proper differences, but by themselves, as will be clear from the things to be said in section 6" (*DM* 2.2.20).

Suárez goes on to conclude, as a corollary, that "the intrinsic modes of substance and of the other members that divide being are not actually included in this objective and thus prescinded concept of being" (*DM* 2.2.21). A second corollary is that it is only mediately that the word "being" signifies particular genera or entities in which the *ratio* of being really exists, by virtue of its immediately signifying the rationally prescinded objective concept of being as such (*DM* 2.2.22–25). The remainder of the section is devoted, in large part, to considering and refuting various arguments against this second corollary (*DM* 2.2.26–33). All of these arguments are drawn from Soncinas, and they all involve appeals to passages in Aristotle. Suárez's responses involve either challenging the interpretation of Aristotle on which Soncinas's argument relies or denying a consequence drawn from the relevant passage. Finally, near the close of the section, Suárez rejects the first of the mentioned ways of explaining what he earlier termed the third, intermediate opinion regarding the unity of the objective concept of being (*DM* 2.2.34–35). That is, he argues against the view that this concept is rationally one and rationally prescinded from inferiors only when considered absolutely, and not when compared to its inferiors.

---

importat ea, quae non se ipsis, sed aliquo alio inter se differunt. Unde etiam nomen differentiae *applicatum est ad significandum principium huius distinctionis, seu gradum illum per quem unum differt ab alio; & sic sumitur in praesenti.)*

DM 2.3: Against the real precision of the objective concept of being from its inferiors

In *DM* 2.3 Suárez asks whether there is a distinction *ex natura rei* between the *ratio* of being, on the one hand, and the objective concepts of its inferiors, on the other. This question is equivalent, in his view, to the question of whether there is a distinction *ex natura rei* between the *ratio* of being, on the one hand, and each of the intrinsic modes which contract being to its inferiors, on the other. Much the same question, Suárez remarks, can be asked in the case of a genus in relation to its species, or in the case of a lowest species in relation to its individuals. However, he notes, the case of being presents special difficulties on account of its transcendence, which (he will argue in *DM* 2.5) requires that being be quidditively included in the items that contract it to its inferiors.

Suárez opens his discussion by explaining that in what follows he will be assuming that, "in addition to the perfect real distinction, which obtains between entities that are mutually separable, there can be found in reality, before any operation of the intellect, another lesser distinction of the sort that normally obtains between a thing and a mode of that thing" (*DM* 2.3.1). Suárez is here anticipating, in part, the results of his discussion in *DM* 7.1, where he argues that, in addition to the distinction of reason and the so-called "distinction of thing from thing" (*distinctio rei a re*), there is a third distinction, "which is not as great as the distinction between two things or altogether distinct entities" (*quae non sit tanta, quanta est inter duas res, seu entitates omnino distinctas*) (*DM* 7.1.16). This distinction is real in the sense that it is not a distinction of reason, but a distinction *ex natura rei*, and it is termed the modal distinction because it normally obtains, according to Suárez, between a thing and a mode of that thing, where the mode in question is not an intrinsic mode of the sort that contracts being to the categories, but rather something that stands outside the essence of the thing to which it belongs.[69] Here in *DM* 2.3, however, Suárez merely

69. Suárez offers, as an example of such a mode, a given quantity's inherence in a substance (*DM* 7.1.17). This inherence adds no new entity to the quantity, he insists, since it "has a mode of being that is such that it can by no power exist unless actually conjoined to that form of which it is the inherence" (*habet talem modum essendi, ut per nullam potentiam esse possit, nisi actu coniuncta ei formae cuius est inhaerentia*) (*DM* 7.1.18). Regarding Suárez's

assumes that there is some distinction, less than the distinction of thing from thing, which is found in reality independently of any operation of the intellect. And taking for granted that the distinction between the *ratio* of being and the intrinsic mode of substance (for example) is not a distinction of thing from thing, he asks whether this distinction is merely a distinction of reason or rather an instance of this lesser real distinction. As mentioned, his conclusion will be that it is a mere distinction of reason.

After introducing the subject and terms of his inquiry, Suárez presents four arguments for the view that there is a distinction *ex natura rei* between the objective concept of being and its inferiors (*DM* 2.3.2–5). The first affirms that the *ratio* of being in reality is the same as the *ratio* of being that is conceived in the mind, notes that the latter does not include either the intrinsic mode of substance or the intrinsic mode of accident, and concludes that in reality the *ratio* of being does not include either mode. It adds that these modes are, on the other hand, included in the *rationes* of substance and accident, and further concludes that in reality, therefore, the *ratio* of being is distinct from the *rationes* of substance and accident (*DM* 2.3.2). Suárez rejects this argument, in part by noting that although God's wisdom is the same as the divine wisdom conceived in the mind, nevertheless, as conceived in the mind the divine wisdom does not include justice, from which, nevertheless, it is not in reality distinct (*DM* 2.3.13). The second, third, and fourth arguments all invoke the agreement of substance and accident in respect of the *ratio* of being and their simultaneous disagreement in respect of their proper *rationes*. The second affirms that separability in reality and

conception of this sort of mode, see José Ignacio Alcorta, *La teoría de los modos en Suárez* (Madrid: Consejo Superior de Investigaciones Científicas, 1949); Juan Francisco Yela Utrilla, "Modo y límite en Suárez," in *Actas del Congreso Internacional de Filosofía, Barcelona, 4–10 octubre 1948, con motivo del Centenario de los filósofos Francisco Suárez y Jaime Balmes,* vol. 3, 533–46 (Madrid: Instituto "Luis Vives" de Filosofía, 1949); José Hellín, "La teoría de los modos en Suárez," *Pensamiento* 6 (1950): 216–26; Stephen Menn, "Suárez, Nominalism and Modes," in *Hispanic Philosophy in the Age of Discovery*, ed. Kevin White, 226–56 (Washington, D.C.: The Catholic University of America Press, 1997); Guillermo Hurtado, "Entes e modos en las *Disputationes Metafísicas,*" in *Francisco Suárez (1548–1617): Tradição e modernidade,* ed. Adelino Cardoso, António Manuel Martins, and Leonel Ribeiro dos Santos, 99–117 (Lisbon: Colibri, 1999); Jean-Pascal Anfray, "A Jesuit Debate about the Modes of Union: Francisco Suárez vs. Pedro Hurtado De Mendoza," *American Catholic Philosophical Quarterly* 93, no. 2 (2019): 309–34.

distinctness in reality go hand in hand, and then alleges that the *ratio* of being is separable from the *ratio* of substance, since it is also found in an accident, and likewise separable from the *ratio* of accident, since it is found in a substance. Therefore, the argument concludes, the *ratio* of being is in reality distinct from both the *ratio* of substance and the *ratio* of accident (*DM* 2.3.3). To this argument, Suárez replies that the *ratio* of being in a substance is not in fact separable from the substance, and similarly in the case of accident. To the retort that the *ratio* of being in a substance must indeed be separable, since it is found in an accident, Suárez responds that the *ratio* of being found in a substance is not really the same as that found in an accident; rather, "it is only the same according to reason, that is, according to a certain agreement and similarity that reason can conceive precisely in the manner of one thing" (*DM* 2.3.14). The third argument alleges that *a parte rei* what makes a substance a substance is not the same as what makes it a being, since what makes a substance a being is the same as what makes an accident a being, since substance and accident are one in respect of the *ratio* of being. Therefore, the argument concludes, there is some distinction *ex natura rei* between the objective concept of being and the objective concept of substance (*DM* 2.3.4). To this Suárez replies, first, that the argument's initial premise is false: that by virtue of which a substance is a being is in reality the same as that by virtue of which it is a substance. Second, he again affirms that what makes a substance a being is not in reality the same as what makes an accident a being: it is only according to reason that both a substance and an accident are constituted in the *ratio* of being by the same thing (*DM* 2.3.15). Finally, the fourth argument targets the claim that what makes a substance a substance is in reality the same as what makes it a being. It alleges that it is impossible for *A* to both agree with, and differ from, *B* by virtue of the same thing or in the same respect (*secundum idem*), and it further claims that in reality substance and accident agree in the *ratio* of being but differ in respect of their proper *rationes*. It follows, the argument concludes, that the *ratio* of being and the *ratio* of substance are somehow distinguished *ex natura rei* (*DM* 2.3.5). Suárez replies, in part, by claiming that the first premise of the argument is not in fact true when "the distinction and the agreement belong to diverse orders," as they do in the present case, for the distinction between substance and accident is real, whereas the agreement between them is according to reason only (*DM* 2.3.16). He also gives several examples of things which, he claims, similarly agree and differ in the same respect (*DM* 2.3.16).

Suárez offers three arguments in favor of his claim that the objective concept of being is not distinguished *ex natura rei* from the objective concepts of its inferiors (*DM* 2.3.8–11). The first alleges that if the *rationes* of being and substance are distinct *ex natura rei*, then they must be related as part and whole, that is, as included and including. But, it claims, they cannot be so related, for there are insuperable problems standing in the way of the view that in any singular substance there is a distinction *ex natura rei* between the *ratio* of being and the intrinsic mode constitutive of substance. For example, one can ask of the being that is supposed distinct *ex natura rei* from this intrinsic mode, Is it being in general abstracted from every singularity, or is it determined to singular being? Suárez takes the former option to be a non-starter, since he holds that being which is existent *a parte rei* and produced must be intrinsically determined and singular. However, the second option is also rejected by him, since one can ask of this singular being whether there is a distinction *ex natura rei* between it and the *ratio* of being. If there is no need for such distinction, then neither is there any need for such a distinction in the determination of being to substance. On the other hand, if we posit such a distinction, then we can again ask of the *ratio* of being whether it is being in general abstracted from every singularity or rather determined to singular being, and in this way we will be led into an infinite regress (*DM* 2.3.8). Suárez's second argument begins by pointing out that the concept of being is prescinded not only from creatures, but also from God, and it alleges that if the objective concept of being is distinct *ex natura rei* from the objective concepts of the categories, then it must also be distinct *ex natura rei* from the concept of the uncreated or infinite being. But this, he claims, is impossible for a variety of reasons, not least because it is inconsistent with divine simplicity (*DM* 2.3.10). Finally, Suárez's third argument alleges that when we conceptually distinguish a common nature from one of its inferiors (e.g., *animal* from *human being*), the distinction of formal concepts that this involves is insufficient to establish a distinction *ex natura rei* between the nature and its inferior. It follows that neither does it establish a distinction *ex natura rei* in the case of the concept of being in relation to its inferiors, since "the ground of distinction is less in the case of being, on account of its transcendence" (*DM* 2.3.11). Therefore, there is no such distinction, for such distinctions are not to be multiplied without cause, "and especially and particularly this one, which can hardly be conceived by the mind" (*DM* 2.3.11). Moreover, that a distinction *ex natura rei* cannot be established merely on the strength of a conceptual distinction between a common nature and an inferior is clear (i) in the case of things pertaining to God alone, (ii) in the case of *rationes* common to God and creatures, and (iii) in the case of *rationes* common only to created beings (*DM* 2.3.11). For the concept of a divine person is common to the three divine persons, but the *ratio* of divine person and the *ratio* of this or that divine person are clearly not distinct *ex natura rei*; to suppose that they are is inconsistent with divine simplicity. Likewise, the *ratio* of wisdom is common to created and uncreated wisdom, but the perfect simplicity of uncreated wisdom precludes a distinction *ex natura rei* between the *ratio* of wisdom and the *ratio* of uncreated wisdom. Finally, a concept of sense perceptive of color can be abstracted from sight and the common sense, and a concept of sense perceptive of sound can likewise be abstracted from hearing and the common sense, but it is absurd to suppose that in the common sense the power to perceive color is distinguished *ex natura rei* from the power to perceive sound, or that in it there is a distinction *ex natura rei* between the power of sensing in general and the power to perceive color.

DM 2.4: The *ratio* of being and its agreement with inferior beings

Having argued that the objective concept of being is only rationally, and not really, prescinded from its inferiors, Suárez turns to the task of explaining being's formal or essential *ratio*, although he cautions that since this *ratio* is the simplest and most abstract, it can only be described, not defined (since only species of a genus admit of being defined). Suárez begins by explaining that Avicenna (ca. 970–1037) was of the opinion that "being" (*ens*) signifies the being (*esse*) of actually existing things, which he took to be an accident, since it can be given to them and also taken away from them. This opinion, Suárez further explains, is based on the signification of the word "being" (*ens*), which is the participle of the verb "*esse*," for "*esse*," when predicated absolutely of something (e.g., "Peter is"), signifies the act of being or existing (*actus essendi seu existendi*), since to be and to exist are one and the same thing, "as is clear from the common use and signification of these words" (*DM* 2.4.1). This is why Aristotle frequently uses the expression "that which is" in lieu of the term "being." According to this opinion, then, "being" formally signifies *esse* or existence, which is outside the essence or quiddity of things.

Suárez's own view is that "being" (*ens*) is used in either of two senses, in accordance with a distinction customarily made between "being" taken as a participle and "being" taken as a noun. In the former sense, it signifies, as Avicenna would have it, the act of being as exercised (*actum essendi ut exercitum*), and it is used to refer to actually existent things. In the latter sense, it signifies "the essence of a thing that has or can have *esse*" (*DM* 2.4.3), and in this sense it can also be said to signify *esse* "in potency or aptitude" (*in potentia vel aptitudine*) (*DM* 2.4.3). Suárez further observes that it is in this second sense that being is both the object of metaphysics and divided into the ten categories. Moreover, he explains that when "being" is taken as a participle its *ratio* "consists in this, that it is something actually existing, or something having a real act of being [*habens realem actum essendi*], or something having actual reality, which is distinguished from potential reality, which is actually nothing" (*DM* 2.4.4). On the other hand, when "being" is taken as a noun, its *ratio* "consists in this, that it is something having a real essence, that is, not a fictitious or chimerical essence, but one that is true and suited to really existing" (*DM* 2.4.5).

With a view to further explaining the latter *ratio*, Suárez undertakes to explain, first, what an essence is, and second, what its being real consists in. Regarding an essence, he affirms that it must be explained either in relation to a thing's effects and passions, or in relation to our mode of conceiving and speaking. Explained in the former way, the essence of a thing is correctly described as "that which is the first, fundamental, and innermost principle of all the actions and properties that agree with the thing" (*DM* 2.4.6). In other words, a thing's essence is the ultimate internal source of its operations and properties. So conceived, moreover, it is termed the thing's nature. Explained in relation to our mode of conceiving and speaking, a thing's essence is rightly described as what its definition purports to explain, or what is first conceived about a thing, where by "first" we mean, not what we initially grasp about a thing when we first become acquainted with it (for this normally falls outside its essence), but rather what is first "in order of excellence and the object's primacy" (*ordine nobilitatis potius & primitatis objecti*) (*DM* 2.4.6). In this sense, what we first conceive about a thing is that which agrees primitively or immediately with it, and that which is first constituted in real being or existence (*in esse rei*). A thing's essence is also called its quiddity in reference to our manner of speaking, since we specify a thing's essence in response to the question, What is it (*Quid est*)?

As regards an essence's being real, Suárez states that this can be explained either by negation or by affirmation. Explained in negative terms, an essence is said to be real when it "involves no impossibility in itself and is not wholly fabricated by the intellect" (*DM* 2.4.7). When it comes to explaining by affirmation what an essence's being real consists in, this can be done either *a posteriori* or *a priori*—that is, either by appeal to what is posterior in the order of explanation or by appeal to what is prior in the order of explanation. When explained *a posteriori*, an essence's being real is said to consists in its being "the principle or root of real operations or effects," whether it gives rise to these effects as an efficient cause, a formal cause, or a material cause (*DM* 2.4.7). When it comes to the *a priori* explanation of an essence's being real, this can be done only in the case of a created essence, since there is nothing prior in the order of explanation to the divine essence, and in accordance with this way of explaining it, we say that a created essence is real if it can really be produced by God and constituted in the *esse* of an actual being. Here, the appeal is necessarily to an extrinsic cause, since an essence "is itself the first and simplest intrinsic cause or *ratio* of a being" (*DM* 2.4.7).

Having thus explained what we are to understand when it is said that a being is something having a real essence, Suárez notes that a more precise understanding of the matter must wait until three questions are answered—namely, What sort of entity does a real essence have when it does not actually exist? What is actual existence, and for what is it necessary in things? and, How is existence distinguished from essence? These are questions that Suárez will answer only in *DM* 31, since they arise, according to him, in connection with finite beings, and it is only in this disputation that he first takes up the consideration of created being, after having discussed the existence and essence of God in *DM* 29 and *DM* 30.[70]

In the remainder of *DM* 2.4, Suárez does two things. First, he explains that "being," understood as both a participle and a noun, does not signify two *rationes* falling under some common *ratio*. The claim,

70. Inspired in part by Étienne Gilson's claim, in *L'Être et l'Essence*, 2nd ed. (Paris: J. Vrin, 1962), 144–55, that Suárez champions a metaphysics which privileges essence at the expense of existence, some scholars have argued that in Suárez's hands metaphysics becomes the science of the logically possible, a development which reaches its climax in Christian Wolff's conception of the science of being as the science of possibles (*scientia possibilium*). Other interpreters have challenged both this reading and Gilson's reading of Suárez as an "essentialist." On this issue, see José Hellín, "Existencialismo escolástico suareciano: La existencia, constitutivo del ente," *Pensamiento* 12 (1956): 157–78; José Hellín, "Existencialismo escolástico suareciano: La existencia es lo principal en el ente," *Pensamiento* 13 (1957): 21–38; Marius Schneider, "Der angebliche philosophische Essentialismus des Suárez," *Wissenschaft und Weisheit* 24 (1961): 40–68; John P. Doyle, "Suárez on the Reality of the Possibles," *The Modern Schoolman* 45, no. 1 (1967): 29–48; John P. Doyle, "Heidegger and Scholastic Metaphysics," *The Modern Schoolman* 49, no. 3 (1972): 201–20; Jean-François Courtine, "Le projet suarézien de la métaphysique," *Archives de Philosophie* 42, no. 2 (1979): 235–74; Jean-François Courtine, "Le statut ontologique du possible selon Suárez," *Cuadernos salmantinos de filosofía* 7, no. 1 (1980): 247–67; Jean-François Courtine, "Ontologie ou métaphysique?" *Giornale di metafisica* 7, no. 1 (1985): 3–24; Jean-François Courtine, *Suárez et le système de la métaphysique* (Paris: PUF, 1990); Ludger Honnefelder, *Scientia transcendens: Die formale Bestimmung der Seiendheit und Realität in der Metaphysik des Mittelalters und der Neuzeit* (Hamburg: F. Meiner, 1990); Pierre Aubenque, "Suárez et l'avènement du concept d'être," in *Francisco Suárez (1548–1617): Tradição e modernidade*, 11–20; Rolf Darge, "«Ens in quantum ens»: Die Erklärung des Subjekts der Metaphysik bei F. Suarez," *Recherches de théologie et de philosophie médiévales* 66, no. 2 (1999): 335–61; Rolf Darge, *Suárez' transzendentale Seinsauslegung und die Metaphysiktradition* (Leiden & Boston: Brill, 2004); José Pereira, *Suárez: Between Scholasticism and Modernity* (Milwaukee: Marquette University Press, 2007), 97–139; Rolf Darge, "Suárez on the Subject of Metaphysics," in *A Companion to Francisco Suárez*, 91–123. Cf. Pedro da Fonseca, *Commentaria in Libros Metaphysicorum Aristotelis Stagiritae*, vol. 1, col. 739: "In order that we might explain that [opinion], four things must be noted beforehand. One is that by the name 'being' we understand in this place only real being, since this alone is what has a true quiddity and essence, that is, one which can truly and positively exist in the nature of things" (*Eam [sententiam] ut explicemus, quatuor ante praemittenda sunt. Unum est, nomine entis intelligi a nobis hoc loco solum ens reale; quoniam hoc solum est, quod veram habet quidditatem & essentiam, quae scilicet vere ac positive existere in rerum natura possit*).

in other words, is that there is no common concept of being that is divided into being understood as an actually existent thing and being understood as a thing possessed of a real essence. Rather, "being," understood as a noun, signifies that which has a real essence, prescinding from, but not denying, actual existence. In other words, it is "being," understood as a noun, which signifies a common *ratio*, and it is this common *ratio* which is divided into two members—that is, into being in act (i.e., the actually existent) and being in potency (i.e., that which can exist but does not in fact exist) (*DM* 2.4.8–12).

Second, Suárez affirms that this common *ratio* of being is an essential predicate, or (in other words) that it is predicated quidditatively of its inferiors (*DM* 2.4.13–15). In this respect it differs from the significate of the participle "being," which is predicated quidditatively of God alone. That the former *ratio* is an essential predicate, he argues, is clear in the first place because "having a real essence agrees with each real being and is most of all essential to it" (*DM* 2.4.14). It is also clear, in the second place, because to be a being (something with a real essence) agrees with a creature even if it does not exist, for which reason a proposition affirming that some creature is a being (in this sense) counts as an eternal truth. But in a proposition of this sort, the predicate must hold of the subject *per se*, and where a predicate holds of its subject *per se*, it must be predicated either in the first mode of perseity—that is, essentially—or in the second mode—that is, as a property.[71] But to be something possessed of a real essence cannot belong to a creature as a property, for a property must emanate from something in the subject which is prior to the property itself, and there is nothing prior from which being something possessed of a real essence could emanate. For to be a being (in this sense) "is rather the first concept of any given real being" (*DM* 2.4.14). Therefore, this most common *ratio* of being is predicated quidditatively of its inferiors.

71. See Aristotle, *Post. An.* I, ch. 4, 73a34–b4.

DM 2.5: The inclusion of being in all *rationes* and differences

Scotus famously argues in *Ord.* I, d. 3, q. 3 that being is not predicated quidditatively of either ultimate differences or the proper passions of being (namely, one, good, true).[72] By the seventeenth century, those who discuss this thesis, Suárez included, typically claim that Scotus likewise denies that being is predicated quidditatively of the intrinsic modes by which it is contracted to the categories. The reasons for this interpretation of Scotus's thesis are not clear. Suárez, for one, merely notes that Scotus's first argument for the claim that being is not predicated quidditatively of ultimate differences "can be applied in the same way to the intrinsic modes by which being is contracted to the ten primary genera" (*DM* 2.5.3).

Be that as it may, Suárez's principal aim in *DM* 2.5 is to argue that being is in fact included essentially in all differences and intrinsic modes. Regarding the proper passions of being, in *DM* 3.1 he will argue against Scotus that being cannot have "true and altogether real, positive passions that are distinct *ex natura rei* from itself" (*non posse habere veras, & omnino reales passiones positivas ex natura rei ab ipso distinctas*) (*DM* 3.1.8). In his view, what such a passion adds to being is either a mere negation (one) or a mere extrinsic denomination (good, true). He accordingly grants that being is not predicated quidditatively of that which is added to being when it is said to be one, good, or true.

Early in *DM* 2.5, Suárez complains that Scotus does not clearly explain what he means by an ultimate difference (*differentia ultima*). He is not alone in finding the notion unclear. The obscurity is due in part to the fact that Scotus never gives an example of an ultimate difference. Rather, he notes that a difference is called ultimate "because it does not have a difference, since it is not resolved into a quidditative concept and a qualitative one, [i.e., into] a determinable concept and a determining one."[73] Accordingly, a difference is ultimate if its concept is without

72. John Duns Scotus, *Opera omnia*, vol. 3 (Vaticana), pp. 81–85 (ns. 131–36) and pp. 97–100 (ns. 159–61).

73. John Duns Scotus, *Opera omnia*, vol. 3 (Vaticana), p. 81 (n. 131): "Differentia ultima dicitur quia non habet differentiam, quia non resolvitur in conceptum quiditativum et qualitativum, determinabilem et determinantem, sed est tantum conceptus eius qualitativus, sicut ultimum genus tantum quiditativum habet conceptum."

qualification simple (*simpliciter simplex*). Scotus also notes that a difference fails to be ultimate if it is taken "from an ultimate essential part which is a thing other than, and a nature other than, that from which the concept of the genus is taken."[74] By way of example, he explains that if, in accordance with the doctrine of the plurality of forms,[75] the intellective soul is distinct from the sensitive soul in a human being (the genus *animal* being taken from the latter and the difference *rational* from the former), then the difference *rational* is not ultimate. In this case, Scotus explains, just as being will be predicated quidditatively of the intellective soul, so will it be predicated quidditatively of rationality.[76] Moreover, such a difference is not ultimate because "in such a difference several realities are contained that are in some way distinct [. . .], and so such a nature can be conceived in some respect, that is, in terms of some reality and perfection, and also be unknown in some respect, and therefore the concept of such a nature is not without qualification simple."[77] In other words, in a non-ultimate difference there are multiple realities or formalities—one purely determinable, the others determining or perfecting—which correspond to different

74. John Duns Scotus, *Opera omnia*, vol. 3 (Vaticana), pp. 97–98 (n. 159): "Et ad videndum quomodo hoc verum sit—cum tamen praedictum sit quod ens non praedicatur 'per se primo modo' de differentiis ultimis—distinguo de differentiis, quod aliqua potest sumi a parte essentiali ultima, quae est res alia et natura alia ab illo a quo sumitur conceptus generis, sicut si ponatur pluralitas formarum, et genus dicatur sumi a parte essentiali priori et differentia specifica a forma ultima. Tunc sicut ens dicitur in 'quid' de illa parte essentiali a qua sumitur differentia talis specifica, ita dicitur in 'quid' de tali differentia in abstracto, ita quod sicut haec est in 'quid' 'anima intellectiva est ens'—accipiendo eundem conceptum entis secundum quem dicitur de homine vel de albedine—ita haec est in 'quid' 'rationalitas est ens', si 'rationalitas' sit talis differentia. Sed nulla talis differentia est ultima, quia in tali continentur realitates plures, aliquo modo distinctae (tali distinctione vel non-identitate qualem dixi in quaestione prima distinctionis secundae esse inter essentiam et proprietatem personalem, vel maiore, sicut alias explanabitur), et tunc talis natura potest concipi secundum aliquid, hoc est secundum aliquam realitatem et perfectionem, et secundum aliquam ignorari,—et ideo talis naturae conceptus non est simpliciter simplex. Sed ultima realitas sive 'perfectio realis' talis naturae, a qua ultima realitate sumitur ultima differentia, est simpliciter simplex; ista realitas non includit ens quiditative, sed habet conceptum simpliciter simplicem."

75. On the doctrine of the plurality of forms, see Robert Pasnau, "Form and Matter," in *The Cambridge History of Medieval Philosophy*, ed. Robert Pasnau and Christina van Dyke (Cambridge: Cambridge University Press, 2010), 644–46, and Roberto Zavalloni, *Richard de Mediavilla et la controverse sur la pluralité des formes: Textes inédits et étude critique* (Louvain: Éditions de l'Institut Supérieur de Philosophie, 1951).

76. See n. 74.

77. See n. 74.

essential grades in it. Presumably these essential grades are none other than those found in the nature or form from which the difference is taken (e.g., the ones found in the intellective soul, according to the doctrine of the plurality of forms). Scotus further explains that, on the other hand, "the ultimate reality or real perfection of such a nature, from which ultimate reality the ultimate difference is taken, is without qualification simple; this reality does not include being quidditatively, but has a concept that is without qualification simple."[78] The claim here seems to be that, although (according to the theory of the plurality of forms) neither the difference *rational* nor the intellective soul has a concept that is without qualification simple, since there are several realities distinguishable in this soul, nevertheless, the ultimate reality of this soul *does* have a concept that is without qualification simple, and the difference derived from this reality, which is presumably the difference of the difference *rational*, is therefore ultimate.

Some such reading, at any rate, is likely behind Suárez's claim that Scotus "calls ultimate that difference which is taken from the ultimate reality of a form, but he calls non-ultimate that difference which is taken from a whole form" (*DM* 2.5.2). In Scotus's own example, after all, the difference *rational* is taken from a whole form—namely, the intellective soul—whereas the intellective soul's own difference seems to be taken from its ultimate reality. On Suárez's reading of Scotus, however, a necessary, though not sufficient, condition for being an ultimate difference is that it immediately constitute, together with the relevant genus, a lowest species. An odd consequence of this reading, which Suárez himself will exploit, is that there are differences which are neither ultimate nor non-ultimate, namely, all such differences as are immediately constitutive of a subaltern genus but are not taken from a whole form. This perhaps fails to do justice to Scotus's claim that a difference "is called ultimate *because* [*quia*] it does not have a difference." The qualification "ultimate," it might be thought, is applied to it because it does not admit of resolution, not because it constitutes a lowest species.[79]

78. See n. 74.

79. Bartolomeo Mastri (1602–73) faults unnamed fellow Scotists for thinking that a difference is called ultimate "either because it is of ultimate specification [*ultimatae*

Be that as it may, Suárez begins his discussion of Scotus's thesis regarding ultimate differences by rehearsing the two arguments that Scotus offers for it in *Ord.* I, d. 3, p. 1, q. 3.[80] The first argument begins with the observation that one difference is not another. It follows that a given difference, d_1, either agrees with another in the quidditative concept of being, or it does not. If one affirms that it does not, then one grants Scotus's thesis. If one affirms that it does, then d_1 must differ from other things through another difference, d_2, in accordance with Aristotle's doctrine that things which agree with each other must differ from each other by means of differences,[81] in which case d_1 is not an ultimate difference. Regarding d_2, then, we can likewise ask whether it includes the quidditative concept of being. If it does, then it too will have to differ from other beings by means of some difference, d_3. Evidently, either we shall continue in this way to infinity, or we shall have to stop at some ultimate difference that does not quidditatively include being and differs from all other things and concepts *per se* (by or through itself), and not by means of some further difference (*DM* 2.5.3).

After noting that much the same argument can be applied to the intrinsic modes which contract being to the categories, Suárez presents Scotus's second argument, which alleges a parallel between metaphysical composition (of genera and differences) and physical composition (of matter and form, in the case of composite substances). In the case of physical composition, the argument alleges, a final resolution must be made to (i) an ultimate determinable potency that includes nothing of form or determining act and (ii) an ultimate form or determining act that includes nothing of determinable potency. Therefore, the argument alleges, in the case of metaphysical composition as well, a resolu-

specificationis], namely, when the thing constituted by it is not further divisible by essential differences"—i.e., is a lowest species—"or of ultimate determination [*ultimatae determinationis*], namely, when the thing constituted by it is incommunicable"—i.e., is an individual. Mastri thinks this is wrong on two counts: first, because Scotus is clearly prepared to call the difference proper to a lowest species a non-ultimate difference, and second, because Scotus thinks any difference, including an intermediate one, is ultimate if it and the genus are both taken from different realities distinguishable in the same nature. See Bartolomeo Mastri de Meldula, *Philosophiae ad mentem Scoti cursus integer tomus quartus: Metaphysicorum pars prior* (Venetiis: apud Nicolaum Pezzana, 1708), p. 76a (n. 184).

80. For these arguments, see John Duns Scotus, *Opera omnia*, vol. 3 (Vaticana), pp. 81–83 (ns. 132 and 133).

81. Aristotle, *Metaph.* V, ch. 9, 1018a9–15, and *Metaph.* X, ch. 3, 1054b22–31.

tion of all beings to ultimate determinable and determining concepts must be made, neither of which includes the other. But the ultimate determinable concept is the concept of being. Therefore, the other concept, which is the concept of an ultimate difference, will not include the concept of being.

Suárez first replies to this argument by alleging that Scotus's distinction or division between ultimate and non-ultimate differences both assumes a false foundation and is insufficient. It assumes a false foundation because there is no difference that is taken from a whole form, since the doctrine of the plurality of forms is false. Moreover, even if this doctrine were true, there would be no difference taken from a whole form. If, for example, the rational soul in the human being were distinct from the sensitive soul, two differences, and not one, would be taken from this form, one distinguishing intellectual beings (humans and angels) from non-intellectual living things, and another—namely, rational—distinguishing human beings from angels (*DM* 2.5.5).[82]

That the division is insufficient follows, according to Suárez, from the fact that there are differences which are taken neither from a whole form nor from the ultimate reality of a form, but from a higher reality. For example, if there is only one soul in the human being, the difference *sensitive* will be neither ultimate nor non-ultimate. The same is true in the case of an accidental form, since in the case of whiteness (for example), two differences—one immediately constitutive of the genus *color*, the other immediately constitutive of the species *whiteness*—are taken from the same form. Regarding such subaltern differences, then, Suárez observes that it must be asked whether they quidditatively include being or not. If not, then "there are no real differences whatsoever that include being" (*DM* 2.5.6). This, Suárez alleges, is denied even by Scotus, and it is also evidently absurd, since it implies that "there are no real differences in things, and consequently real essences are not constituted or essentially distinguished by them" (*DM* 2.5.6). On the other hand, if such subaltern differences do include being, the same must be

82. It was commonly held that angels do not reason, but grasp the consequences of first principles immediately. See, e.g., Thomas Aquinas, *ST* I, q. 58, art. 3, in Thomas Aquinas, *Opera omnia*, t. 5 (Romae: Ex Typographia Polyglotta, Sacra Congregatio de Propaganda Fide, 1889), p. 83.

said of ultimate differences that are not taken from a whole form, for if subaltern differences include being even though they are not taken from a whole form, then the same must be said of ultimate differences.

That this is so Suárez endeavors to prove by two arguments. The first alleges that, if an ultimate difference and a subaltern one are taken from the same form, albeit according to different grades, and the subaltern difference intrinsically and essentially includes being, then so must the ultimate difference, since it is taken from a real grade that is lower and more perfect. Implicitly assumed here, perhaps, is the claim advanced at *DM* 2.5.11 that where things differ in their degree of perfection, they must both have entity, where having entity is equated with intrinsically and essentially including being. The second argument alleges that there is no greater reason for being to be included in a subaltern difference, since the concept of the difference *sensitive* (for example) is as simple as the concept of the difference *rational*, "since the one does not formally include the other, or vice versa" (*DM* 2.5.6). For as Scotus himself concedes, Suárez explains, the difference *rational* does not differ from other things through another difference, but rather *per se*, "since, while it is itself that through which another thing differs, it is at the same time also different by itself, lest we proceed to infinity and make the difference itself a species, as consisting in a genus and another difference" (*DM* 2.5.6). But the same goes for the subaltern difference *sensitive*. If, Suárez continues, it is replied that subaltern differences are determinable by ultimate differences,[83] this is irrelevant to the question of whether subaltern differences, rather than ultimate ones, include being. In fact, the second of Scotus's arguments implies that a subaltern difference will not include either lower differences that determine it or a higher difference that is determined by it, and therefore, that such a subaltern difference will be as simple as an ultimate difference is. Moreover, according to Scotus's own opinion, ultimate differences are determinable by individual differences.

83. That a subaltern difference is determinable by a lower difference seems to be implied by Aristotle in *Metaph.* VII, ch. 12, 1037b27–1038a15, where he claims that when we take the genus *footed animal*, we must find a difference of it "*qua* footed" (ᾗ ὑπόπουν) (1038a11). E.g., of footed animals we should say that some are cloven footed and some uncloven, "since these are differences of foot, for cloven-footedness is a kind of footedness" (αὗται γὰρ διαφοραὶ ποδός· ἡ γὰρ σχιζοποδία ποδότης τις) (1038a14–15).

After noting that, consistently with his own position, Scotus ought to have held that only individual differences are ultimate, and after further arguing that individual differences too must include being (*DM* 2.5.7), Suárez offers four arguments for the claim that the intrinsic modes which contract being to the categories likewise intrinsically and essentially include being (*DM* 2.5.8–11). In the first, he alleges that Scotus himself grants that these modes are both positive and real, and he goes on to argue that if they are to constitute a real essence, they must themselves have some real essence, in which case they must be intrinsically and essentially beings, in accordance with the conclusion of *DM* 2.4 that to be a real being is to be something having an essence; failing that, they will be nothing and therefore incapable of constituting a real essence (*DM* 2.5.8). Second, Suárez argues that just as a subaltern difference includes being because it is taken from a form according to some grade of its reality, so must an intrinsic mode include being, since it too is taken from a form according to some grade of its reality. For example, in a substance, the mode of being *per se* (*modus essendi per se*) is taken from the reality of any substantial nature insofar as it agrees with other substantial natures in the aptitude to subsist (*DM* 2.5.9). In the third place, Suárez argues that, if being is not predicated essentially of any intrinsic mode, then such a mode has everything required to be a difference, and being has everything required to be a genus, "particularly since Scotus supposes that being is univocal" (*DM* 2.5.10), for being fails to be a genus insofar as it is predicated essentially of all things that contract it, as Aristotle proves in *Metaph.* III, ch. 3 (998b22–27). Being, however, is *not* a genus. Therefore, it *is* predicated essentially of intrinsic modes. Fourth, the intrinsic modes which contract being to substance and accident differ with respect to their entitative perfection, and from this it follows that they are beings, "for perfection without real entity cannot be conceived, since either these are the same, or perfection presupposes entity and is a property of it" (*DM* 2.5.11). Moreover, that intrinsic modes are unequal in entitative perfection is clear from the fact that substance must be more perfect than accident thanks to that by virtue of which it is distinguished from accident. But that by virtue of which it is distinguished from accident is the mode of being *per se*. Therefore, the mode of being *per se* is itself more perfect than the mode of being in another (*modus essendi in alio*), the intrinsic mode of accident.

In response to all this, Suárez notes, one might allege that when Scotus denies that being is predicated essentially of intrinsic modes and differences, it is because these modes and difference are incomplete beings, and that what he means to deny is merely that they are complete beings. In much the same way, the category of substance is commonly held not to be predicated of the differences that contract it only because these differences are incomplete substances, whereas the category of substance is the genus of complete substance (*DM* 2.5.12). Suárez replies that this account "is neither in accord with the thought of Scotus nor true in itself" (*DM* 2.5.13). That it is not Scotus's view is clear in part from the fact that Scotus himself grants that being is predicated essentially of non-ultimate differences, even though no difference is a complete being. That the opinion is also false is clear in part from the fact that there can be no concept which is common only to complete beings, since incomplete substances are more perfect than accidents placed directly in some accidental category, and this implies that any concept common to complete substances and such accidents must also be common to incomplete substances, and indeed to anything having entity, "for only this agreement"—namely, having entity—"can be observed between substance and accident" (*DM* 2.5.15).

It follows, Suárez now concludes, "that being as being is intrinsically included in every being and in every concept of a positive difference or mode of real being" (*DM* 2.5.16). This, he thinks, is clear from the things said against Scotus. As for Scotus's first argument, Suárez replies that one difference can be primarily diverse from another even if they agree in the *ratio* of being, just as the categories are primarily diverse notwithstanding their agreement in this *ratio* (see *DM* 2.2.20). Of course, if one thing is primarily diverse from another, then it does not differ from that other by means of a difference. Suárez adds, however, that he will explain in the next and final section of *DM* 2 how one should understand the claim that the categories are primarily diverse. As regards Scotus's second argument, Suárez rejects the parallel between physical and metaphysical composition, for since there is no form that includes matter, nor (contrary to the doctrine of the plurality of forms) any matter that includes form, the parallel would require that no genus or determinable concept include a difference, and that no difference include being, the first determinable. Moreover, if one understands the alleged parallel more narrowly, as implying only that a genus does not include a difference that contracts it, and vice versa, then it can be granted, Suárez says. However, this mutual exclusion will not hold in the case of a simple concept (i.e., one not composed from a genus and a difference) and a higher transcendental predicate, since the determination of the latter to the former does not occur through metaphysical composition. How this determination occurs is the topic of the final section of *DM* 2.

DM 2.6: The contraction of being to its inferiors

Suárez begins the final section of *DM* 2 by observing that the great difficulty of explaining how being is contracted to its inferiors explains why some reject a prescinded concept of being. After all, if there is no such concept, then no contraction of it is necessary. And indeed, it seems that being can be contracted to inferiors in no way, since it can be contracted neither by non-beings, as was shown against Scotus, nor by any contracting elements that include being, since in positing such an element one already presupposes a contraction of being to some inferior. Suárez, for his part, grants that this opinion is true if it is understood merely to be denying a concept of being that is distinct *ex natura rei* from its inferiors, "but if it is understood to concern only an abstraction according to reason, it is not true [...], and therefore it must be explained how this contraction or determination occurs even according to reason" (*DM* 2.6.1).

After noting that Scotus erred in two ways—first by positing a distinction *ex natura rei* between being and its inferiors, and second by positing modes and differences that are not beings—Suárez observes that Soncinas agrees in some way with Scotus when he claims that the intrinsic mode which contracts being to substance—that is, the mode of being *per se* (*modus essendi per se*)—is only a negation or being of reason. Suárez confesses to finding this puzzling, since Soncinas rejects an objective concept of being prescinded from the disjunctive concept *substance or accident* and therefore should feel no need to posit that substance is intrinsically and essentially constituted by something that contracts being. Still, he argues that Soncinas is wrong to think that substance can be intrinsically constituted by a negation or a being of reason, in part by noting that it follows from this view that "the concept of substance would formally be privative, or made up by reason, and not real" (*DM* 2.6.2).

A third opinion considered by Suárez neither rejects a concept of being that is rationally prescinded from its inferiors nor supposes these inferiors constituted by something that is not a being. Rather, it grants a contraction of being to inferiors through the composition of being and certain positive, real modes, and this composition, it alleges, is not one from genus and difference, since it involves the inclusion of the determinable in the concept of the determining, which is thought not to be problematic where the composition is according to reason only. Moreover, it further alleges that a concept is simple when it is not resolvable into two concepts neither of which includes the other, and that for this reason the concepts of the categories count as simple, notwithstanding their composition from being and some real, positive mode.

If, Suárez observes, one objects that on this view the resolution of the concept of substance (say) paradoxically gets one nowhere, since the concept of the mode of being *per se* (*modus essendi per se*) will include both being and itself (just as the concept of substance does), holders of the view will reply with two claims. First, being is included in the concept of the mode of being *per se* and in the concept of substance in different ways, since it is included in the latter as in a complete and perfect being, while it is included in the mode only as in an incomplete being. Second, the concept of the mode of being *per se* can be said to include itself, but not as a part of itself, since it is rather the same as itself. For this reason, it is false to say that on this view the resolution of the concept of substance gets one nowhere.

To this, Suárez says, one can still demand an explanation of how being is contracted to the mode of being *per se*. After all, if it is composed from the concept of being and some other mode, we can ask of this further mode whether it is a being or not. If one replies that it is not, one errs as Scotus did. If one replies that it is, one can ask how being is contracted to it. Of course, an infinite regress looms here.

Suárez explains that there are two ways of replying to this objection. First, one can bite the bullet and grant the infinite regress while yet alleging that it is not a problem, and this because the relevant concepts are only rationally distinct. After all, to grant an infinite regress here is not to grant that in a substance there are infinitely many modes that are distinct *ex natura rei*. Nonetheless, as I mentioned earlier, Suárez rejects this solution, in part because it seems incompatible with Aristotle's claim that there is no progression to infinity in the resolution of quidditative predicates. The second reply alleges that the mode of being *per se* is not resolvable into two concepts and is thus distinguished *per se* or by itself from every other being, whether complete or incomplete. For, one might claim, in the resolution of the constituted into its constituents, a stop must be made at that "by which" (*in eo quo*), lest one proceed to infinity. Suárez is not unsympathetic to this reply, judging it plausible or arguable (*probabilis*). And indeed, an appeal to simple concepts will figure in his own solution to the problem. Nevertheless, he rejects the second reply on the grounds that it is not "advanced with sufficient consistency and does not sufficiently clarify the issue" (*DM* 2.6.6).

Suárez's own opinion is that the contraction or determination of being to its inferiors does not occur by means of composition,

> but only by means of a more express conception of some being contained under being, and this in such a way that both concepts—for example, the concepts of being and substance—are simple and irresolvable into two concepts and differ only because one is more determinate than the other. (*DM* 2.6.7)

On Suárez's view, the formal concept of substance is not composed from the formal concepts of being and some intrinsic mode. Both the formal concept of substance and the formal concept of being are simple, and they differ from each other primarily, if not exclusively, because the concept of being more confusedly represents what the concept of substance represents more expressly or determinately. In other words, the rational precision of the objective concept of being from its inferiors, which is the result of the mind's forming a mental concept of being in general, occurs not by means of a resolution of the formal concept of substance into the formal concepts of being and an intrinsic mode, but by the introduction of a higher degree of confusion into the concept of one of being's inferiors. Suárez, moreover, seems particularly concerned to argue that on this account, one can still understand the concept of being to be included in the concept of substance, and this because "everything that is confusedly conceived in that prescinded concept is found conceived more expressly in the other object, and in all of it" (*DM* 2.6.7).

Suárez next aims to prove that this sort of intellectual abstraction and determination is indeed possible. He does so by appeal to examples. In particular, he notes that when we divide the genus of quantity into two-cubit, three-cubit, and so on, it cannot be the case that the concept of a two-cubit quantity is resolved into the concepts of quantity and two-cubit, since the latter concept must include the concept of quantity. This, he says, "is a sign that these two concepts are distinguished only as express and confused" (*DM* 2.6.9). Much the same is true of the concept of heat and the concept of eight degrees of heat (*in conceptu caloris & caloris ut octo*). As a third example, he cites the determination of being to infinite being, for infinity, he says, "cannot be conceived as some mode added to being, or as something less than infinite being itself" (*DM* 2.6.9). In this case, too, then, the concept of the infinite being can only be a "more express and determinate concept of some most simple being" (*DM* 2.6.9). This, moreover, explains how being can be more abstract than God in respect of how it is conceived without, however, being simpler than him.

Granted, Suárez now argues, that this mode of contraction is possible, and that it is sufficient to account for the contraction of being to its inferiors, this, he argues, is how it should be understood to occur. For, in the first place, we can in this way resolve the difficulty under consideration and explain how, without any sort of infinite regress, "being" can signify a rationally prescinded objective concept that is determined to inferiors while yet being intimately included in them all, even intrinsic modes. Second, we can in this way explain how the categories can have concepts that are without qualification simple (*simpliciter simplices*) while yet holding that the concept of being can be abstracted from them by means of a precision of the intellect. Again, this precision does not involve a separation of one grade from another, but depends on a cognition that is in some way confused, "by means of which the object is considered, not distinctly and determinately as it is in reality, but according to some similarity or agreement that it has with other things" (*DM* 2.6.10). Moreover, this agreement in the concept of being "is in things with respect to their whole entities and real modes" (*DM* 2.6.10). In other words, the foundation of similarity in the *ratio* of being that one thing, *A*, bears to another, *B*, is not some proper part of *A*, but *A*'s entire entity. Finally, that this is how being is contracted to its inferiors is also proved by appeal to the fact that no third way of effecting a rational precision is possible. Granted, then, that a formal precision of one grade from another is impossible in the case of being, and this because of being's limitlessness (*illimitatio*) and the fact that the similarity of all beings is in respect of everything they contain, the precision can only occur through confusion.

Finally, Suárez closes *DM* 2 by noting that it follows from his account of being's contraction to its inferiors that the concept of substance and the concept of its intrinsic mode are not distinguished objectively (*obiective*) or in the object, but only according to our mode of conceiving, since the mind cannot explain simple things except in the way it explains composite things. This is why he granted that it is true to say that each intrinsic mode is distinguished *per se* or by itself from another thing or mode. The same, however, must be said of the categories, which are constituted by such modes, since they are not constituted by way of composition. Nor, he adds, is there any reason why the intrinsic mode of substance should be thought distinguished *per se* from another mode to a greater degree than substance is, since an intrinsic mode, like a category, is immediately under being and includes it totally. This, Suárez notes, is why the categories are said to be primarily diverse—not because they agree in no common concept, but because they have no determinate difference that does not fall under being. They are diverse by themselves, "even though they also have an imperfect similarity in the *ratio* of being" (*DM* 2.6.12). For, as Suárez earlier argued, it is not impossible for two simple things to be both similar and diverse (see *DM* 2.3.16).

REMARKS ON THE LATIN TEXT AND ENGLISH TRANSLATION

My starting point in the preparation of the Latin text appearing in this edition was the electronic version of the Second Disputation prepared by Michael Renemann and Salvador Castellote.[1] This version is based on a scan of the Latin text that appears together with the Spanish translation of Sergio Rábade et al.[2] The latter text, moreover, is substantially the same as the one that appears in volumes 25 and 26 of the Vivès edition of Suárez's works, although Rábade and his colleagues do sometimes make corrections to the text of the Vivès edition—without drawing attention to that fact—on the strength of readings found in earlier editions.[3] I have, however, made changes to Renemann and Castellote's text in order to bring it into line with the text of the first edition.[4] Where the text of the Vivès edition differs from that of the first edition, I have signaled that fact in a footnote, and I have also given the readings found in various early editions, which are listed in the bibliography of this volume.[5]

1. Renemann and Castellote have since made a number of corrections to their text of *DM* 2, partly as a result of my suggestions. See "Francisco Suárez, *Disputationes Metaphysicae*," prepared by Michael Renemann and Salvador Castellote, last updated June 12, 2020, http://homepage.ruhr-uni-bochum.de/Michael.Renemann/suarez/index.html.

2. Francisco Suárez, *Disputaciones metafísicas*, ed. and trans. S. Rábade Romeo, Salvador Caballero Sánchez, and Antonio Puigcerver Zanón, 7 vols. (Madrid: Ed. Gredos, 1960–66).

3. Francisco Suárez, *Opera Omnia*, vols. 25 and 26 (Parisiis: apud Ludovicum Vivès, 1861).

4. Francisco Suárez, *Metaphysicarum Disputationum, in quibus et universa naturalis theologia ordinate traditur, & quaestiones omnes ad duodecim Aristotelis libros pertinentes accurate disputantur, Tomus Prior* (Salmanticae: apud Ioannem & Andream Renaut Fratres, 1597).

5. My procedure in establishing the Latin text of *DM* 2 is the same as that used in my preparation of the Latin text of *DM* 1. For more on this procedure and my reasons for it, see "Remarks on the Latin Text and English Translation" in Francisco Suárez, *Metaphysical*

For ease of reference, I have retained the numbering of paragraphs found in the Vivès edition, which differs in spots from that of the first edition. I have also inserted into the Latin text bracketed page numbers that reproduce the paginations of both the first edition and the Vivès edition. The numbers appearing in square brackets—for example, "[38a]"—refer to the pagination of the first edition, while the letters "a" and "b" immediately following these numbers refer to the first and second columns (respectively) appearing on that page. The numbers appearing in angled brackets—for example, "⟨64a⟩"—refer to the pagination of the Vivès edition, and the letters which appear there refer (again) to columns.

Most of the notes on the English translation of *DM* 2 serve to clarify, or bring additional specificity to Suárez's references to other authors. These notes are an important tool for the reader, in part because Suárez's ways of citing other authors frequently differ from our own. This is often the case with his references to Aristotle's works, since the chapter divisions of these works in Suárez's day often differ from the ones we are familiar with. (There were even different and competing chapter divisions current at the time.) Accordingly, if Suárez refers to (say) *Posterior Analytics* I, ch. 7, but my note refers to *Posterior Analytics* I, ch. 9, 76a15–25, the reader should not assume that I am endeavoring to correct Suárez's citation. I am rather recasting it so as to bring it into line with our modern editions of Aristotle's works. (Any corrections I make to Suárez's citations are explicitly identified as corrections.) The reader will also see that Suárez often refers to a numbered text in a particular book of (say) Aristotle's *Metaphysics*. This was a common way of citing a passage in Aristotle and is based on a division of books into numbered texts, which is a division that existed alongside their division into chapters. This division into numbered texts is not reproduced in recent translations of Aristotle's works, or even in recent editions of medieval Latin translations of them.

Other notes on Suárez's citations refer the reader to various editions of works by other authors. A complete list of these editions will be found in the bibliography. I do not always refer the reader to a recent

Disputation I: On the Nature of First Philosophy or Metaphysics, trans. Shane Duarte (Washington, D.C.: The Catholic University of America Press, 2021), xci–xcii.

edition of such a work, or to a recent reproduction of some early edition. My choice of which edition to cite has been guided, for the most part, by considerations of reliability and availability. Having looked through a good number of scans of early modern editions, I have found that such editions vary significantly in quality and reliability. Scans of most of the editions I have used are available for download from various sites, such as the HathiTrust Digital Library (https://www.hathitrust.org), the Internet Archive (https://archive.org), the Bavarian State Library (https://www.bsb-muenchen.de), the Post-Reformation Digital Library (http://www.prdl.org/index.php), and Google Books (https://books.google.com).

I have aimed for some measure of consistency in my rendering of key Latin words. The following are worth noting:

cognitio	cognition
cognoscere	to cognize
dicere	to signify$_d$ (in some contexts)
esse	being$_e$, existence$_e$, to exist$_e$ (in some contexts)
essendi	being$_e$, existing$_e$
existentia	existence
existere	to exist
notitia	knowledge$_n$
notus, -a, -um	known$_n$
ratio	account$_r$, argument, aspect$_r$, basis$_r$, character$_r$, concept$_r$, conception$_r$, consideration$_r$, essence$_r$, ground$_r$, kind$_r$, method$_r$, nature$_r$, notion$_r$, rationale$_r$, reason
res	thing$_r$
scientia	knowledge, science
scire	to know

Those familiar with Latin know that it is frequently necessary to supply the English word "thing" when rendering Latin terms—for example, *album*, "white thing." This can be problematic in the context of scholastic philosophy, where *res*, "thing," is a technical term. In order to spare the reader the need to look repeatedly over at the Latin text, I have, by means of a subscript "r," indicated where "thing" renders *res*.

As regards the Latin word *ratio*, it is not always possible or desirable to use one and the same English word to render it, even across instances where it is employed in pretty much the same sense—for example, to mean something like *nature* or *essence*. (To do so leads to some rather strange-sounding expressions and can also lead to confusion—e.g., if one were to render *ratio* in *ratio formalis* as "concept.") Therefore, since I have used various terms to render *ratio*, I have (for the most part) clearly indicated to the reader when one of these terms is being so used, again by means of a subscript "r." (I do not, however, use a subscript "r" when I render *ratio* as "reason" or "argument.") In many instances, readers should feel free to replace one of these terms with another, according as they see fit (e.g., "character$_r$" with "nature$_r$," or vice versa).

LATIN ABBREVIATIONS

Please note: as regards the abbreviation of Latin words, I give one form of the word corresponding to the abbreviation, normally the nominative form, unless the case of the word can be inferred from the abbreviation. But of course, in many instances Suárez would have the reader understand the word to be in some case other than the nominative. For example, when citing a text, "cap." should be understood to mean "capite."

&	et
&c.	et caetera
Alex. Alens.	Alexander Alensis
Alexan.	Alexander (Aphrodisiae)
Algazel.	Algazelus
Antepraed.	Antepraedicamenta
Anton. And.	Antonius Andreae
Anton. Trombeta	Antonius Trombeta
ar.	articulus
arg.	argumentum
Aris.	Aristoteles
Arist.	Aristoteles
Aristot.	Aristoteles
Aristotel.	Aristoteles
art.	articulus
artic.	articulus
Avic.	Avicenna
Avicen.	Avicenna

c.	caput
c. ult.	caput ultimum
cap.	caput
Caie.	Caietanus
Caiet.	Caietanus
Caieta.	Caietanus
capit.	capite
Capreol.	Capreolus
cit. locis	citatis locis
comm.	commentus
commen.	commentus
conclu.	conclusio
conseq.	consequens or consequentia
cont. gent.	Summa Contra Gentiles
cont. Gent.	Summa Contra Gentiles
d.	distinctio
D.	Divus
de analog. nomin.	De nominum analogia
de analo. nom.	De nominum analogia
de Interpr.	De Interpretatione
in 2. d. 3	In secundum librum Sententiarum, distinctio 3
de pot.	De potentia
de veri.	De veritate
de verit.	De veritate
dict.	dictus
disp.	disputatio
dist.	distinctio
Ferrar.	Ferrariensis
Ferrarien.	Ferrariensis
Flandr.	Flandria or Flandrensis

Greg.	Gregorius Ariminensis
Hispal.	Hispalensis
Iavell.	Iavellus
lect.	lectio
li.	liber
lib.	liber
Met.	Metaphysica
Meta.	Metaphysica
Metap.	Metaphysica
Metaph.	Metaphysica
Metaphys.	Metaphysica
opusc.	opusculum
p.	pars
part.	parte
Phys.	Physica
Physic.	Physica
Posterior.	(Analytica) Posteriora
Prior.	(Analytica) Priora
q.	quaestio
quaest.	quaestio
quodl.	quodlibet
quodlib.	quodlibet
rat.	ratio
responsionib.	responsionibus
S.	Sanctus
Scot.	Scotus
sect.	sectio
sect. praeced.	sectio praecedens
sect. seq.	sectio sequens
sect. sequent.	sectione sequente

section. praeced.	sectione praecedente
Soncin.	Soncinas
t.	tomus
tex.	textus
text.	textus
Th.	Thomas
Tho.	Thomas
Thom.	Thomas
Topic.	Topica
tract.	tractatus
v. g.	verbi gratia

ENGLISH ABBREVIATIONS

Abbreviations for titles of works and books

Cat.	*Categories*
DM	*Disputationes Metaphysicae* (*Metaphysical Disputations*)
DM 2.1.4	Metaphysical Disputation II, section 1, paragraph 4
De Int.	*On Interpretation*
Metaph.	*Metaphysics*
Ord.	*Ordinatio*
Phys.	*Physics*
Post. An.	*Posterior Analytics*
Pr. An.	*Prior Analytics*
Quodl.	*Quodlibet*
Sent.	*Sentences*
ST	*Summa Theologiae*
Top.	*Topics*

Other abbreviations

art. / arts.	article / articles
bk.	book
ca.	circa
cf.	confer
ch. / chs.	chapter / chapters

col. / cols.	column / columns
fasc.	fascicle
fol. / fols.	folio / folios
ll.	lines
n. / ns.	number / numbers
p. / pp.	page / pages
plur.	plural
Ps.	Pseudo
q.	question
r	recto
sing.	singular
t. / ts.	tome / tomes
v	verso
vol. / vols.	volume / volumes

LATIN TEXT AND ENGLISH TRANSLATION

[47b] ⟨64a⟩

DISPUTATIO II.[1]

DE RATIONE ESSENTIALI SEU CONCEPTU ENTIS.

His suppositis, quae de obiecto seu subiecto huius scientiae tradidimus, necessarium in primis est, eius propriam, & adaequatam rationem, ac deinde proprietates eius, & causas exponere, & haec erit prior principalis pars huius operis. In posteriori praecipuam eius partitionem proponemus, atque ita res omnes, quae sub ente continentur, & illius rationem includunt, ut sub obiectiva ratione huius scientiae cadunt, & a materia in suo esse abstrahunt, quantum ratione naturali attingi possunt, investigabimus, & explanabimus. Ut enim maiori compendio ac brevitate utamur, & conveniente methodo universa tractemus, a textus Aristotelici prolixa explicatione abstinendum duximus, resque ipsas, in quibus haec sapientia versatur, eo doctrinae ordine ac dicendi ratione, quae ipsis magis consentanea sit, contemplari. Nam, quod spectat ad Philosophi textum in his Metaphysicae libris, nonnullae partes eius parum habent utilitatis, vel quod varias quaestiones ac dubitationes proponat, easque insolutas relinquat, ut in toto tertio libro, vel quod in antiquorum placitis referendis, & refutandis immoretur: ut ex primo fere libro, & ex magna parte aliorum constare facile potest: vel ⟨64b⟩ denique quod eadem, quae in prioribus libris dicta fuerant, vel repetat, vel in summam redigat, ut patet ex libro undecimo, & aliis. Quae vero utilia sunt, scituque di[48a]gna, & necessaria, insudarunt satis in eis

Ordo ratioque doctrinae in hoc opere servanda.

1. Regarding my procedure for establishing the Latin text that appears here, see "Remarks on the Latin Text and English Translation," pp. lxxiii–lxxiv.

DISPUTATION II.

ON THE ESSENTIAL CONCEPT$_R$ OR CONCEPT OF BEING.

Supposing the things that we have taught about the object or subject of this science, we must explain, in the first place, this object's proper and adequate nature$_r$, and thereafter its properties and causes, and this will be the first principal part of this work.[1] In the second part,[2] we shall present this object's chief division,[3] and we shall also investigate and explain, insofar as they can be reached by natural reason, all those things$_r$ which are contained under being and include its nature$_r$ in such a way that they fall under the objective character$_r$ of this science and abstract from matter in their existence$_e$. For in order that we might proceed more briefly and profitably, and treat of everything according to a fitting method, I have thought it best to abstain from lengthy explanations of the Aristotelian text, and to consider the very things$_r$ with which wisdom is concerned in accordance with that order of teaching and manner$_r$ of exposition which is more in agreement with them. For, as regards the text of the Philosopher in these books of the *Metaphysics*, some parts of it are of little use, either because they present various questions and doubts and leave them unsolved, as is the case with the entire third book, or because they dwell on relating and refuting the opinions of the ancients, as can easily be seen in al-

The order & method$_r$ of teaching to be observed in this work.

1. I.e., *DM* 2–27.
2. I.e., *DM* 28–53.
3. See *DM* 28, "On the First Division of Being, into the Infinite without Qualification and the Finite, and Other Divisions Equivalent to This One."

explicandis, prout in litera Aristotelis continentur, varii expositores Graeci, Arabes, & Latini, ex quibus nos praecipue utemur Alexan. Aphrodisaei, Averrois, & maxime omnium D. Thomae expositione. Rerum vero ipsarum examinationem in sequentibus disputationibus trademus, simulque curabimus Arist. mentem ac sensum, & singula testimonia, in quibus fere quaestiones omnes fundari solent, accuratius declarare. Ut vero Aristotelis studiosis omni ex parte satisfaciamus, in initio[2] huius operis indicem quaestionum omnium, quae circa textum Aristotelis, & servato eius ordine tractari solent, vel nobis occurrerunt, praemisimus,[3] & loca, in quibus nos eas disputamus, designavimus. Quod si fortasse sententiae aliquae Aristotel. quarum cognitio ad alias scientias utilis est, in his libris occurrant, quae in nostris disputationibus, servato doctrinae ordine quem instituimus, tractari non possint, in eodem indice breves circa textum Arist. annotationes tradimus, in quibus, quidquid in disputationibus tactum non est, & aliquid difficultatis, vel utilitatis habet, declaramus. In praesente ergo disputatione explicanda nobis est quaestio, quid sit ens in quantum ens: nam, quod ens sit, ita per se notum est, ut nulla declaratione indigeat. Post quaestionem autem, an est, quaestio quid res sit, est prima omnium, quam in initio cuiuscunque scientiae de subiecto eius praesupponi, aut declarare, necesse est. Haec autem scientia, cum sit omnium naturalium prima atque suprema, non potest ab alia sumere, vel probatam, vel declaratam subiecti sui rationem, & quidditatem: & ideo ipsam statim in initio tradere, & declarare oportet.

2. Reading "initio" here with S, V_1, and V_2. The following read "fine" instead: C_1, C_2, G_2, M_1, M_2, M_3, M_4, P_1, P_2, V_3, V_4, V_5, and Vivès.

3. Reading "praemisimus" here with S, V_1, and V_2. The following read "posuimus" instead: C_1, C_2, G_2, M_1, M_2, M_3, M_4, P_1, P_2, V_3, V_4, V_5, and Vivès.

most the whole first book and in a good number of others, or finally because the same things that were mentioned in earlier books they either return to or summarize, as is clear in the case of book XI and others. Moreover, with respect to things that are useful, worthwhile, and necessary to know, various Greek, Arab, and Latin expositors have sufficiently labored to explain them as they are contained in the text of Aristotle. Of these, we shall especially make use of the expositions of Alexander of Aphrodisias, Averroes, and most of all St. Thomas. But we shall provide an examination of the things$_r$ themselves in the following disputations, and we shall at the same time take care to explain exactly Aristotle's thought and meaning, as well as the individual testimonies on which nearly all questions are usually founded. However, in order to satisfy students of Aristotle entirely, at the beginning of this work we have placed an index of all the questions that are usually discussed in connection with Aristotle's text, with their order preserved, or that have presented themselves to us, and we have indicated the places where we have discussed them.[4] But in case there are certain opinions of Aristotle in these books that we are not able to deal with in our disputations because of the order of teaching that we have established, and cognition of these opinions is useful for other sciences, we shall provide in the same index brief annotations on the text of Aristotle, annotations in which we explain whatever has not been touched on in the disputations and is difficult or useful. In the present disputation, then, we must settle the question, What is being as being? For *that* being is is so known$_n$ *per se* that it requires no elucidation. But after the question of whether a thing$_r$ is, the question of *what* it is is the first of all, which it is necessary to presuppose or explain at the beginning of any science whatsoever in connection with its object. And since this science is the first and highest of all the natural sciences, it cannot take the nature$_r$ and quiddity of its subject as proved or explained by another science, and therefore it is necessary to hand it down and explain it immediately at the beginning.

4. This is the so-called *Index locupletissimus in Metaphysicam Aristotelis*, or "A Most Ample Index to the *Metaphysics* of Aristotle." For an English translation, see Francisco Suárez, *A Commentary on Aristotle's* Metaphysics, trans. John P. Doyle (Milwaukee: Marquette University Press, 2004).

Sectio I.

Utrum ens in quantum ens, habeat in mente nostra unum conceptum formalem omnibus entibus communem.

Conceptus formalis, & obiectivus quid sint, & in quo differant.

1. Supponenda in primis est vulgaris distinctio conceptus formalis, & obiectivi: conceptus formalis dicitur actus ipse, seu (quod idem est) verbum quo intellectus rem aliquam seu communem rationem concipit, qui dicitur conceptus, quia ⟨65a⟩ est veluti proles mentis, formalis autem appellatur, vel quia est ultima forma mentis, vel quia formaliter repraesentat menti rem cognitam: vel quia re vera est intrinsecus & formalis terminus conceptionis mentalis, in quo differt a conceptu obiectivo, ut iam[4] dicam. Conceptus obiectivus dicitur res illa, vel ratio, quae proprie & immediate per conceptum formalem cognoscitur seu repraesentatur, ut verbi gratia, cum hominem concipimus, ille actus quem in mente efficimus ad concipiendum hominem, vocatur conceptus formalis, homo autem cognitus, & repraesentatus illo actu dicitur conceptus obiectivus, conceptus quidem per denominationem extrinsecam a conceptu formali, per quem obiectum eius concipi dicitur: & ideo recte dicitur obiectivus: quia non est conceptus, ut forma intrinsece terminans conceptionem, sed ut obiectum & materia circa quam versatur formalis conce[48b]ptio, & ad quam mentis acies directe tendit, propter quod ab aliquibus ex Averroe *intentio intellecta* appellatur: & ab

4. Reading "iam" here with C_1, C_2, G_2, M_1, M_2, M_3, P_1, P_2, S, V_1, V_2, V_3, and V_4. The following have "ita" instead: M_4, V_5, and Vivès.

Section 1

Whether in Our Mind Being as Being Has One Formal Concept Common to All Beings.

What formal & objective concepts are, & how they differ.

1. First of all, the commonplace distinction between formal and objective concepts must be assumed. The act itself, or (what is the same thing) the word by means of which the intellect conceives some thing$_r$ or common nature$_r$, is called a formal concept. And it is called a concept because it is, as it were, an offspring of the mind,[5] and it is called formal either because it is an ultimate form of the mind, or because it formally represents the thing$_r$ cognized to the mind, or because really it is the intrinsic and formal term of a mental conception,[6] in which respect it differs from an objective concept, as I shall now say. That thing$_r$ or nature$_r$ is called an objective concept which properly and immediately is cognized or represented by a formal concept. For example, when we conceive the human being, that act which we produce in the mind in order to conceive the human being is called a formal concept, but what is cognized or represented by that act, the human being, is called an objective concept, and indeed it is called a concept by extrinsic denomination from the formal concept through

5. The Latin noun "*conceptus*" (here rendered "concept") can also mean the "action of conceiving in the womb, conception" or "that which is conceived, embryo, foetus" (v. "conceptus," in *Oxford Latin Dictionary*, ed. P. G. W. Glare [Oxford: Clarendon Press, 1996]).

6. See Francisco Suárez, *De anima*, bk. III, ch. 5, esp. ns. 4–5, in Francisco Suárez, *Opera Omnia*, vol. 3 (Parisiis: apud Ludovicum Vivès, 1856) pp. 630b–37a, esp. p. 631a–b.

aliis dicitur *ratio obiectiva*. Unde colligitur differentia inter conceptum formalem, & obiectivum, quod formalis semper est vera ac positiva res & in creaturis qualitas menti inhaerens, obiectivus vero non semper est vera res positiva, concipimus enim interdum privationes, & alia, quae vocantur entia rationis, quia solum habent esse obiective in intellectu. Item conceptus formalis semper est res singularis, & individua, quia est res producta per intellectum, eique inhaerens: conceptus autem obiectivus interdum quidem esse potest res singularis, & individua, quatenus menti obiici potest, & per actum formalem concipi, saepe vero est res universalis, vel confusa & communis, ut est homo, substantia, & similia. In hac ergo disputatione praecipue intendimus explicare conceptum obiectivum entis ut sic secundum totam abstractionem suam, secundum quam diximus esse Metaphysicae obiectum: quia vero res[5] est valde difficilis, multumque pendens ex conceptione nostra, initium sumimus a conceptu formali, qui, ut nobis videtur, notior esse potest.

Variae sententiae referuntur.

2. Prima sententia absolute negat dari unum conceptum formalem entis, qui re vera sit in se unus, & praecisus ac distinctus ab aliis conceptibus particularium entium. Ita sentit Caieta. opusc. de analog. nomin. capit. 4. & 6. Licet enim obscure loquatur, & ⟨65b⟩ distinguat de conceptu perfecto, vel imperfecto, tamen illa distinctio coincidit cum alia Fonsecae statim tractanda: unde si attente legatur, hoc re vera sentit, eumque veritatem attigisse, aut propius ad illam accessisse, dixit

5. Reading "res" here with S, V_1, and V_2. The following omit "res": C_1, C_2, G_2, M_1, M_2, M_3, M_4, P_1, P_2, V_3, V_4, V_5, and Vivès.

which its object is said to be conceived. And therefore it is rightly called objective, since it is not a concept in the sense of a form intrinsically terminating a conception, but in the sense of the object and subject matter with which the formal conception is concerned, and to which the attention of the mind directly tends, for which reason it is called by some, following Averroes, an "intellected intention,"[7] and by others it is called an "objective character$_r$." And from this is inferred a difference between formal and objective concepts, namely, that a formal concept is always a true and positive thing$_r$ and, in creatures, a quality inhering in the mind, whereas an objective concept is not always a true, positive thing$_r$, for we sometimes conceive privations and other things that are called beings of reason because they only have being$_e$ objectively in the intellect. Further, a formal concept is always a singular and individual thing$_r$, since it is a thing$_r$ produced by the intellect and inhering in it, whereas an objective concept, to be sure, can sometimes be a singular and individual thing$_r$, insofar as [a singular thing] can be an object of the mind and can be conceived through a formal act, but it is often a thing$_r$ that is universal, or confused and common, as are human being, substance, and the like. In this disputation, then, we intend especially to explain the objective concept of being as such according to its entire abstraction, in accordance with which, we have said, it is the object of metaphysics. But since the question is very difficult, and very much dependent on our conception, we shall take our start with the formal concept, which, as it seems to us, can be better known$_n$.

Various opinions are presented.

2. The first opinion absolutely denies that there is a single formal concept of being that is in itself really one and really prescinded or distinct from other concepts of particular beings. This is Cajetan's view in his short work, *On the Analogy of Names*, chs. 4 and 6.[8] For although he speaks obscurely and draws a distinction between perfect

7. See Averroes, *Aristotelis De Anima Libri Tres cum Averrois Commentariis* (Venetiis: apud Junctas, 1562), fol. 146D (*antiqua translatio*), fol. 147B (*Mantini translatio*), fol. 148E (*antiqua translatio*), fol. 152B (*antiqua translatio*), fol. 159C, fol. 188E.

8. Cajetan, *Scripta Philosophica: De Nominum Analogia, De Conceptu Entis* (Romae: apud Institutum «Angelicum», 1952) pp. 34–38 (ns. 36–40) and pp. 54–55 (ns. 66–68).

Fonseca 4. Metaph. capit. 2. quaest. 2. sect. 3. Fundamentum est, quia alias ens esset univocum, & non analogum, quod infra videbimus esse falsum. Sequela probatur, quia univoca sunt quorum nomen est commune, ratio vero[6] substantiae nomini accommodata est eadem, teste Arist. initio Praedicam. sed omnibus entibus commune est nomen entis, ergo vel ratio nominis est una & eadem, & sic ens erit univocum: vel non est una: & sic nec conceptus formalis entis poterit esse unus: quia conceptus formalis habet suam unitatem ex aliqua una re, vel ratione concepta, quam adaequate respicit. Unde, si ille conceptus est etiam voci seu nomini entis adaequatus, non potest magis esse unus, quam sit una ratio entis illo nomine significata.

3. Secunda opinio, quae potius est praecedentis explicatio, est Ferrar. 1. cont. gent. cap. 34. qui distinguit duplicem conceptum, unum appellat quid nominis, alium quid rei: priorem dicit posse esse unum in conceptu entis: posteriorem vero minime: utrumque vero fundat in analogia entis. Et explicatur in hunc modum ex communi ratione analogorum: dupliciter enim concipi possunt, uno modo proprio conceptu reali significato per nomen, & hoc modo, quatenus analoga sunt, non habent unum conceptum realem, sed plures, ut patet, tam in analogis proportionalitatis, quam proportionis seu attributionis: nam si audito hoc nomine, *ridens*, proprius conceptus [49a] rei significatae formetur, non unus, sed duplex conceptus formatur: unus hominis, qui proprie ac formaliter ridens est: alius prati,[7] quod solum per quandam proportionalitatem sic appellatur. Quod si non uterque horum conceptuum, sed alter tantum formatur, non concipitur illa vox secundum totam analogiam, seu communem significationem ad res illas, sed vel

6. Reading "commune, ratio vero" here with all the older editions. Vivès reads "commune. Ratio vero" instead.

7. Reading "prati" here with S, V_1, and V_2. The following read "bruti" instead: C_1, C_2, G_2, M_1, M_2, M_3, M_4, P_1, P_2, V_3, V_4, V_5, and Vivès.

and imperfect concepts,[9] nevertheless, that distinction coincides with another distinction of Fonseca's that is to be discussed presently. For this reason, if he is read carefully, he really thinks this, and Fonseca, *Metaph.* IV, ch. 2, q. 2, sect. 3,[10] says that he has arrived at the truth or very closely approached it. The foundation is: because otherwise being would be univocal, and not analogical, which we shall see below to be false.[11] The consequence is proved because univocals are things which have a name in common and the essential account$_r$ corresponding to the name is the same, as Aristotle attests at the beginning of the *Categories.*[12] But the name "being" is common to all beings. Therefore, either the account$_r$ corresponding to the name is one and the same, and so "being" will be univocal, or it is not one, and so neither will the formal concept of being be able to be one. For a formal concept has its unity from some one conceived thing$_r$ or nature$_r$ to which it is adequately related. For this reason, if that concept is also adequate to the word or name "being," it cannot be one to a greater degree than the single nature$_r$ of being signified by that name is.

3. The second opinion (which is, rather, an explication of the previous one) is that of Francesco Silvestri of Ferrara in *Summa Contra Gentiles* I, ch. 34.[13] Ferrara distinguishes two concepts: one he calls nominal, the other real. He says that, in the case of the concept of being, the former can be one, but the second not at all, and he founds both [claims] on the analogy of being. And it is explained in this way by appeal to the common character$_r$ of analogicals, for analogicals can be conceived in two ways: in one way, by means of the proper real concept that is signified by the name, and in this way, insofar as they are analogical, they do not have a single real concept, but several, as is clear

9. Cajetan, *Scripta Philosophica: De Nominum Analogia, De Conceptu Entis*, pp. 34–38 (ns. 36–40) and pp. 98–99 (ns. 1–4).

10. Pedro da Fonseca, *Commentariorum Petri Fonsecae Lusitani, Doctoris Theologi Societatis Iesu, In Libros Metaphysicorum Aristotelis Stagiritae Tomi Quatuor. Continet hic Tomus Primus quatuor priorum librorum explicationem* (Coloniae: Sumptibus Lazari Zetzneri Bibliopolae, 1615), col. 714.

11. See *DM* 28.3 and *DM* 32.2.

12. Aristotle, *Cat.* 1, 1a6–12.

13. Thomas Aquinas, *Sancti Thomae Aquinatis opera omnia*, t. 13 (Romae: Typis Riccardi Garroni, 1918), pp. 107b–109b. Cf. Cajetan, *Scripta Philosophica: De Nominum Analogia, De Conceptu Entis*, pp. 99–100 (ns. 5–6).

solum prout univoca est respectu hominum, vel solum prout translata est, & metaphorice pratum[8] significat. Et simile est in analogis attributionis, v. g. *sanum*: nam si proprius rei significatae conceptus formetur, non est unus, sed multiplex: unus animalis, quod formaliter, & proprie sanum est, alii aliarum rerum, quae per varias habitudines, seu denominationes a sa⟨66a⟩nitate animalis extrinsecus sanae appellantur. In utroque autem ex his analogis potest unus conceptus valde confusus formari, qui magis est de vocis significatione, quam de aliqua re, ut si, audito nomine *sani*, concipias quod habet ordinem ad sanitatem. Sic igitur in praesenti, audito nomine entis, potest formari conceptus confusus comprehendens quidquid habet esse, vel habitudinem ad esse: sed hic tantum est conceptus quid nominis, tamen, si re vera concipiantur res illo nomine significatae, non formatur unus conceptus, sed plures.

Sententia Fonsecae huic proxima.

4. Nec multum ab hac sententia differt Fonseca supra distinguens triplicem conceptum entis, scilicet distinctum, confusum, & medium, id est, partim confusum, partim distinctum. Distinctus est, qui determinate & expresse repraesentat omnes entitates simplices, quas ens immediate significat, & hic non est unus, sed plures. Confusus est, qui repraesentat omnia confuse, & indeterminate, & hic est unus. Medius vero qui partim confusus, partim distinctus est, qui determinate repraesentat unam naturam, v. g. substantiam, caeteras vero, scilicet quantitatem, qualitatem, &c. implicite & indeterminate, quatenus

8. Reading "pratum" here with S, V_1, and V_2. The following read "brutum" instead: C_1, C_2, G_2, M_1, M_2, M_3, M_4, P_1, P_2, V_3, V_4, V_5, and Vivès.

both in the case of things analogical by proportionality and in the case of things analogical by proportion or attribution. For if, when the name "laughing thing"[14] is heard, the proper concept of the thing$_r$ signified is formed, not one, but two concepts are formed: one the concept of the human being, who properly and formally is laughing, the other the concept of the meadow, which is so called only through a certain proportionality. And if only one, but not both, of these concepts is formed, that word is not conceived in accordance with the entire analogy or signification common to those things$_r$, but either only insofar as it is univocal with respect to the human being, or only insofar as it is transferred and metaphorically signifies the meadow. And likewise in the case of names that are analogical by attribution, for example, "healthy thing."[15] For if the proper concept of the thing$_r$ signified is formed, it is not one, but several: one the concept of the animal, which is formally and properly healthy, and the others the concepts of other things$_r$ which, by virtue of various relations or denominations, are extrinsically called healthy from the health of the animal. But in either case, from such analogicals a single very confused concept can be formed, one which has more to do with the signification of the word than with some thing$_r$—for instance, if, having heard the name "healthy thing," you were to conceive what has a relation to health. In this way, then, in the present case, when the name "being" is heard, a confused concept can be formed, comprehending whatever has being$_e$ or a relation to being$_e$, but this is only a nominal concept. Still, if the things$_r$ signified by that name are really conceived, one concept is not formed, but several.

Fonseca's opinion is close to this one.

4. Fonseca does not depart much from this opinion, going further by distinguishing three concepts of being, namely, a distinct one, a confused one, and an intermediate one, that is, one that is partly confused and partly distinct.[16] Distinct is that concept which determinately and explicitly represents all the simple entities that "being" immediately signifies, and this concept is not one, but several. Confused is that concept which represents all things confusedly and indeterminately, and

14. The words "laughing thing" here translate a single Latin word, "*ridens*."

15. The words "healthy thing" here and elsewhere translate a single Latin word, "*sanum*."

16. Pedro da Fonseca, *Commentaria in Libros Metaphysicorum Aristotelis Stagiritae*, vol. 1, cols. 714–15, 718.

omnes cum substantia proportione quadam conveniunt, & hic etiam unus esse dicitur.

Tot distinctionum diversitatem obesse potius, quam prodesse claritati.

5. Sed huiusmodi distinctiones mihi videntur sine causa multiplicari, remque potius confundere, quam explicare. Nam de conceptu formali entis loqui debemus, non iuxta id, quod de rebus omnibus, quae sub hac voce comprehenduntur, cognosci & comprehendi potest, prout in se sunt, sed prout hac voce significantur: alioqui non erit sermo de conceptu entis in quantum ens, sed de conceptu rerum omnium tum existentium, tum etiam possibilium, quatenus tales sunt, & inter se distinguuntur: quomodo a nemine possunt uno conceptu formali distincte concipi, nisi a solo Deo, ut recte idem autor notavit. Hoc autem sensu etiam conceptus substantiae, aut viventis, si illo modo sit explicitus, & distinctus, erit tantum ille, quo omnes substantiae vel viventia omnia, quatenus talia[9] sunt, distincte concipiantur, quomodo solus etiam Deus poterit habere eorum formalem conceptum distinctum substantiae, viventis, &c.

6. Dices, substantiam, vivens, & similia nomina non significare immediate has vel ⟨66b⟩ illas naturas substantiales, aut viventes, sed rationem substantiae, viventis, &c. & ideo ad formandum conceptum distinctum respondentem significato talis vocis, non esse necessarium ad particulares naturas descendere, secus vero esse de ente, quia imme[49b]diate significat entitates, saltem simplices, id est non compositas ex natura communi & differentia contrahente. Sed hoc re vera falsum est, ut fusius constabit ex sectione sequente, & nunc breviter patet ex communi modo concipiendi. Quis enim dicat, ens immediate significare Deum ut Deus est, etiam si Deus simplicissimus sit, & non compositus ex natura communi & differentia contrahente? Denique idem interrogari potest de substantia, accidente, & aliis generibus, vel conceptibus simplicibus. Item, cur magis dicetur ens significare im-

9. Reading "talia" here with the older editions. Vivès omits this word.

this concept is one. However, the intermediate concept, which is partly confused and partly distinct, represents one nature (for example, substance) determinately but the others (namely, quantity, quality, etc.) implicitly and indeterminately, insofar as they all agree with substance according to some proportion, and this concept also is said to be one.[17]

That the variety of so many distinctions undermines, rather than promotes, clarity.

5. But such distinctions seem to me to be multiplied without cause, and to confuse matters, rather than clarify them. For we should speak of the formal concept of being, not according to what can be cognized and grasped about all the things$_{r}$ contained under this word as they are in themselves, but insofar as they are signified by this word. Otherwise the discussion will not be about the concept of being as being, but about the concept of all things$_{r}$, both existent and possible, insofar as they are items of particular kinds and are distinguished from each other—in which way they can be distinctly conceived by means of a single formal concept by no one but God alone, as the same author has rightly noted.[18] And in this sense the concept of substance or living thing[19] also, if it is made explicit and distinct in this way, will merely be that concept by which all substances or living things, insofar as they are substances or living things of particular kinds, are distinctly conceived—in which way, once again, God alone will be able to have, with respect to them, a distinct formal concept of substance, living thing, etc.

6. You will say that "substance," "living thing," and similar names do not immediately signify these or those substantial or living natures, but the nature$_{r}$ of substance, of living thing, etc., and that it is not, therefore, necessary to descend to particular natures in order to form a distinct concept corresponding to the significate of such a word, but that it is otherwise with "being," since it immediately signifies entities, at least simple ones, that is, entities not composed of a common nature and a contracting difference. But this is in fact false, as will be established more fully in the next section. And for now, briefly, this is clear from the common mode of conceiving. For who would say that "being" immediately signifies God insofar as he is God, even if God is most simple

17. Cf. Cajetan, *Scripta Philosophica: De Nominum Analogia, De Conceptu Entis*, pp. 34–35 (n. 36).

18. See Pedro da Fonseca, *Commentaria in Libros Metaphysicorum Aristotelis Stagiritae*, vol. 1, col. 714.

19. The words "living thing" here and elsewhere translate a single Latin word, "*vivens*."

mediate entitates simplices quam compositas ex natura communi & differentia contrahente, ut est animal, habitus, &c? nam ens ut sic, generatim omnia sub se comprehendit, &, sicut in conceptu substantiae, vel qualitatis nihil includitur quod non sit ens, ita neque in conceptu animalis, vel habitus. Quod autem conceptus compositus possit resolvi in plures, quorum neuter alterum includat, non autem conceptus simplex, parum refert ad mediatam, vel immediatam significationem. Quis enim credat ens immediate significare rationale, & non hominem, quia rationale dicit simplicem conceptum, & homo compositum? Itaque sistendo proprie ac praecise in conceptu formali entis ut sic, non pertinet ad ipsum, ut per eum concipiantur distincte particularia entia secundum proprias & determinatas rationes: ideoque conceptus entis ut sic, si in eo sistatur, semper est confusus respectu particularium entium, ut talia sunt. Et ideo D. Tho. 1. part. q. 14. art. 6. dicit, quod si Deus tantum cognosceret alia a se, in quantum sunt entia, tantum cognosceret in communi, confuse, & imperfecte: unde concludit, non tantum ea cognoscere secundum quod communicant in ratione entis, sed etiam secundum quod unum ab alio distinguitur: sentit ergo conceptum entis ut sic, praecise in eo sistendo semper esse confusum respectu cuiuscunque determinatae rationis entis, prout in se talis est, & ab aliis distinguitur, sive composita sit, sive simplex.

7. Quapropter etiam illud membrum de conceptu partim confuso, partim distincto, est supervacaneum ad rem praesentem explican⟨67a⟩dam. Primo quidem, quia conceptus substantiae improprie dicitur, implicite vel confuse esse conceptus accidentis: & in universum conceptus proprius primi analogati impropriissime dicitur esse confusus conceptus caeterorum analogatorum, quae secundaria sunt, quanvis multi ita loquantur dicentes, sicut idem nomen, licet immediate significet prim-

and is not composed of a common nature and a contracting difference? Moreover, the same thing can be asked about substance, accident, and other genera or simple concepts. Further, why is "being" said to immediately signify simple entities rather than entities composed of a common nature and a contracting difference, such as animal, habit, etc.? For being as such generally comprehends all things under itself, and just as nothing is included in the concept of substance or quality that is not a being, so neither [is anything that is not a being included] in the concept of animal or habit. And that a composite concept can be resolved into several concepts neither of which includes the other, while a simple concept cannot, matters little to mediate or immediate signification. For who would believe that "being" immediately signifies rational, and not the human being, on the grounds that "rational" signifies$_d$ a simple concept and "human being" a composite one? And so, stopping properly and precisely at the formal concept of being as such, it does not pertain to it that particular beings are distinctly conceived by means of it in accordance with their proper and determinate natures$_r$. And therefore, the concept of being as such, if one stops with it, is always confused with respect to particular beings insofar as they are items of particular kinds. And therefore, St. Thomas, *ST* I, q. 14, art. 6, says that if God only cognized things other than himself insofar as they are beings, he would only cognize them in a common way, confusedly, and imperfectly.[20] For this reason, he concludes that God does not merely cognize them insofar as they agree in the nature$_r$ of being, but also insofar as one is distinguished from the other. He believes, therefore, that the concept of being as such, stopping precisely at it, is always confused in relation to any given determinate nature$_r$ of a being, insofar as it is in itself such and is distinguished from other things, whether it be composite or simple.

7. For this reason, that other kind of concept which is partly confused and partly distinct is also unnecessary for explaining the present matter. First, indeed, because the concept of substance is improperly said to be implicitly or confusedly a concept of accident, and in general the proper concept of a primary analogate is most improperly said to be a confused

20. Thomas Aquinas, *Sancti Thomae Aquinatis opera omnia*, t. 4 (Romae: Ex Typographia Polyglotta, Sacra Congregatio de Propaganda Fide, 1888), p. 176a.

um analogatum, secundario significat caetera: ita conceptum formalem primi analogati, confuse repraesentare caetera, quatenus illi primo similia sunt, vel proportionalia: nam quod repraesentat distincte aliquid, consequenter videtur repraesentare, saltem confuse, alia illi similia. Sed hoc quanvis sit parvi momenti, & fortasse de modo loquendi, mihi non probatur, quia huiusmodi conceptus proprius & distinctus primi analogati tantum est unus, & formaliter tantum repraesentat ipsum primum analogatum: in quo non recte cum nomine comparatur, quia nomen significat per impositionem tantum, & ideo idem nomen, quod primario ac proprie unum significat, potest per translationem imponi ad alia secundario significanda: conceptus autem rei tantum naturaliter repraesentat rem ipsam, & ideo si est proprius & adaequatus conceptus primi analogati secundum propriam rationem [50a] eius non potest repraesentare reliqua, unde nec per se facit illa cognoscere, sed ad summum esse potest veluti origo, seu occasio, ut alia concipiantur, & denominentur secundum aliquam proportionem, vel habitudinem ad primum analogatum: quod non est satis, ut conceptus specialis & proprius primi analogati dicatur implicitus vel confusus reliquorum. Deinde interrogo an ille conceptus primi analogati sit idem omnino cum conceptu, qui respondet proprio nomini eiusdem rei seu naturae, v. g. substantiae, an vero sit diversus. Hoc posterius dici non potest, quia, si uterque est proprius conceptus substantiae, intelligi non potest, in quo sit diversitas, ut alter dicatur repraesentare accidentia & non alius. Si vero dicatur prius, ergo non magis potest ille conceptus dici repraesentare accidentia, quam conceptus proprius hominis alia animalia, imo minus id dici poterit, cum sit minor similitudo. Item quia alioqui dicendum esset, substantiam habere unum conceptum formalem aliquo modo communem substantiae, & accidenti, quod re vera impropriissimum est, & in rigore falsum, quia licet accidens dicat habitudinem ad substantiam, tamen conceptus substantiae nullo modo reprae⟨67b⟩sentat illam habitudinem, sed solum terminum eius, & illum non formaliter sub ratione termini, sed secundum absolutam rationem suam: ergo hoc non satis est, ut ille conceptus dicatur implicitus, vel confusus conceptus accidentis. Atque idem considerari facile potest in caeteris analogatis, seu conceptibus eorum; nam conceptus formalis hominis ridentis ut sic, nullo modo est conceptus confusus

Modus loquendi aliorum non probatur.

concept of the other analogates which are secondary—although many speak in this way, saying that, just as the same name, even if it immediately signifies the primary analogate, secondarily signifies the others, so also does the formal concept of the primary analogate confusedly represent the others insofar as they are similar or proportional to that primary analogate, for that which distinctly represents something seems as a consequence to represent, at least confusedly, other things similar to it. But this, even if it is of little importance, and perhaps concerns a manner of speaking, is to my mind not proved, since such a proper and distinct concept of the primary analogate is only one, and it formally represents only the primary analogate itself, in which respect it is not rightly compared to the name, since the name signifies only by imposition, and therefore the same name that primarily and properly signifies one thing can by transference be imposed to signify other things secondarily. However, the concept of a thing$_r$ naturally represents only the thing$_r$ itself, and therefore, if it is a proper and adequate concept of the primary analogate in accordance with its proper nature$_r$, it cannot represent the other analogates. For this reason, neither can it *per se* make one cognize them, but at most it can be a motive, as it were, or occasion for the others to be conceived and denominated according to some proportion or relation to the primary analogate. And this is not a sufficient reason to call a special and proper concept of the primary analogate an implicit or confused concept of the other analogates. Second, I ask whether that concept of the primary analogate is altogether the same as the concept that corresponds to the proper name of the same thing$_r$ or nature—for example, the name "substance"—or is it diverse? The latter cannot be said, because if each of the two concepts is a proper concept of substance, it cannot be understood in what respect they differ so that the one, but not the other, might be said to represent accidents. If, however, the former is said, then that concept can no more be said to represent accidents than the proper concept of the human being can be said to represent other animals. In fact, it can less rightly be said, since the similarity is less. Further: because otherwise it would have to be said that substance has a single formal concept that is in some way common to substance and accident, which is really most improper, and strictly false, since although "accident" signifies$_d$ a relation to substance, never-

The manner of speaking employed by others is not approved.

prati, nec conceptus proprius animalis sani est conceptus medicinae, & sic de aliis. Et ratio est, quia id, quod fundat huiusmodi analogiam, vel est aliqua realis convenientia seu similitudo inter analogata, ut de ente infra dicemus: & illa non repraesentatur per conceptum proprium alicuius analogati: vel non est propria similitudo, sed solum proportio quaedam, vel attributio, & haec etiam non satis est, ut conceptus proprius unius analogati, ut tale est repraesentet aliquo modo reliqua, sed solum formam illam, per ordinem ad quam reliqua talia denominantur, quae absolute & prout in se talis est, & non cum habitudine ad reliqua, per talem conceptum repraesentatur.

8. Addo ulterius. Quidquid sit de hoc loquendi modo, quod determinatus conceptus substantiae dicatur confusus reliquorum generum entium, seu accidentium; tamen adhuc ille dici non potest conceptus formalis entis ut sic, tum quia ille est proprius conceptus formalis substantiae, ut substantia est, conceptus autem proprius entis esse debet diversus a conceptu substantiae, quandoquidem ens recte dividitur in substantiam & accidens; tum etiam, quia ens non significat immediate substantiam, ut infra ostendam: ergo nec immediate exprimit proprium formalem conceptum substantiae. Relinquitur ergo, conceptum formalem entis ut sic comparatum ad determinata entia, ut talia sunt, semper esse conceptum confusum & indistinctum in repraesentando hoc, vel illud ens. Dico autem, respectu particularium entium, ut talia sunt, quia respectu eius obiecti quod immediate & proprie repraesentat (quodcunque illud sit[10]) dici potest, & revera est proprius & distinctus conceptus, sicut idem conceptus anima[50b]lis, qui respectu hominis

10. Reading “sit” here with the older editions. Vivès has “sic” instead.

theless, the concept of substance in no way represents that relation, but only its term, and not formally under the aspect$_r$ of a term, but in accordance with its own absolute nature$_r$. Therefore, this is not a sufficient reason for that concept to be called an implicit or confused concept of accident. And the same thing can easily be observed in the case of other analogates or their concepts, for the formal concept of the laughing human being as such is in no way a confused concept of the meadow, nor is the proper concept of the healthy animal a concept of medicine, and likewise in other cases. And the reason is: because what founds such an analogy is either some real agreement or similarity among the analogates, as we shall say below about being, and that agreement or similarity is not represented by the proper concept of some analogate; or it is not a proper similarity, but only some proportion or attribution, and this proportion or attribution also does not suffice for the proper concept of the one analogate, insofar as it is such, to represent the others in some way, but it suffices only for it to represent that form in relation to which the others are denominated such, which form is represented by such a concept absolutely and insofar as it is in itself such, and not with some relation to the other analogates.

8. I further add: Whatever might be the case regarding this manner of speaking—that the determinate concept of substance is called a confused concept of the remaining genera of beings, i.e., of accidents—nevertheless, it still cannot be called a formal concept of being as such, both because it is the proper formal concept of substance insofar as it is substance, and the proper concept of being must be diverse from the concept of substance, since being is rightly divided into substance and accident; and also because "being" does not immediately signify substance, as I will show below, and therefore, neither does it immediately express the proper formal concept of substance. It remains, therefore, that the formal concept of being as such, with respect to determinate beings insofar as they are such, is always a confused and indistinct concept in representing this or that being. And I say "in relation to particular beings insofar as they are such," because in relation to that object which it immediately and properly represents (whatever it is), it can be called, and it really is, a proper and distinct concept, just as one and the same concept of animal, which is confused in relation to the

est confusus, respectu animalis ut sic, est proprius & distinctus, quanvis sub hac eadem comparatione idem conceptus simplex soleat dici confusus, respectu illius conceptus compositi, quo animal per suam definitionem concipitur. Atque simili modo ⟨68a⟩ potest, vel in diversis hominibus, vel in uno diversis temporibus, unus conceptus entis esse distinctior alio, & e contrario unus potest vocari confusus respectu alterius distinctioris, quatenus contingit ipsammet rationem seu quidditatem entis ut sic magis vel minus perfecte cognosci: quae distinctio conceptuum formalium nihil ad propositum refert: quia magis est ex parte concipientis, & ex perfecto vel imperfecto lumine, vel modo concipiendi, quam ex habitudine ad obiectum, quam hic praecipue consideramus.

Vera sententia.

9. His ergo distinctionibus praetermissis, dicendum est conceptum formalem proprium & adaequatum entis ut sic esse unum, re & ratione praecisum ab aliis conceptibus formalibus aliarum rerum vel[11] obiectorum. Haec est communis sententia, ut fatetur Fonseca supra; tenent eam Scotus & omnes eius discipuli, ut videbimus sect. sequent. Capreol. in 1. d. 2. q. 1. conclu. 1. & 9. & in responsionib. ad arg. contra illas; & Caiet. de ente & essen. c. 1. q. 2. qui citat D. Tho. q. 7. de pot. artic. 5. & 6. Soncin. 4. Metaph. q. 1. Iavell. q. 1. Flandria. q. 2. ar. 6. Hervaeus quodlib. 2. q. 7. Soto in praedicam. c. 4. q. 1. & plane colligitur ex D. Thom. locis citandis sect. seq. Et probatur primo experientia, audito enim nomine entis, experimur mentem nostram non distrahi neque dividi in plures conceptus, sed colligi potius ad unum, sicut cum concipit hominem, animal, & similia. Secundo, quia, ut Arist. dixit 1. de Interpr. per voces exprimimus nostros formales conceptus: sed haec[12] vox, *ens*, non solum materialiter est una, sed etiam unam habet significationem ex primaeva impositione sua, ex vi cuius non significat immediate naturam aliquam sub determinata, & propria ratione,

11. Reading "vel" here with S, V_1, and V_2. The following have "&": C_1, C_2, G_2, M_1, M_2, M_3, M_4, P_1, P_2, V_3, V_4, V_5, and Vivès.

12. Reading "haec" here with the older editions. Vivès omits this word.

human being, is proper and distinct in relation to animal as such, even if, under the latter relation, the same simple concept is usually called confused in comparison with that composite concept by means of which animal is conceived through its definition. And likewise, either in diverse human beings or in the same human being at different times, one concept of being can be more distinct than another, and conversely, one can be called confused in comparison with another more distinct one, insofar as it happens that the same nature$_r$ or quiddity of being as such is cognized more or less perfectly, which distinction of formal concepts is irrelevant to the matter at hand, since it has more to do with the one who conceives and his perfect or imperfect light, or mode of conceiving, than it does with that relation to the object which we are here especially considering.

The true opinion.

9. With these distinctions set aside, it must be said that the proper and adequate formal concept of being as such is one and prescinded really and rationally from other formal concepts of other things$_r$ or objects. This is the common view, as Fonseca acknowledges above.[21] Scotus and all of his disciples hold it, as we shall see in the following section,[22] as does Capreolus, *Sent.* I, d. 2, q. 1, in conclusions 1 and 9,[23] and in the replies to the arguments against them,[24] and also Cajetan, in *On Being and Essence*, ch. 1, q. 2,[25] who cites St. Thomas, *On the Power of God*, q. 7, arts. 5 and 6.[26] And it is also held by Soncinas, *Metaph.* IV,

21. Pedro da Fonseca, *Commentaria in Libros Metaphysicorum Aristotelis Stagiritae*, vol. 1, col. 711.

22. See *DM* 2.2.5.

23. John Capreolus, *Defensiones Theologiae Divi Thomae Aquinatis*, vol. 1 (Turonibus: Sumptibus Alfred Cattier, Bibliopolae Editoris, 1900), p. 117a–b and pp. 124a–25b.

24. John Capreolus, *Defensiones Theologiae Divi Thomae Aquinatis*, vol. 1, pp. 132b–35b and pp. 141a–44a. Cf. John Capreolus, *Defensiones Theologiae Divi Thomae Aquinatis*, vol. 2, p. 175b.

25. Cajetan, *In De Ente et Essentia D. Thomae Aquinatis Commentaria* (Taurini: Marietti, 1934), pp. 25–27 (n. 14). Cf. Cajetan, *Scripta Philosophica: De Nominum Analogia, De Conceptu Entis*, pp. 97–100 (ns. 2–6).

26. Thomas Aquinas, *Quaestiones Disputatae*, 9th ed., vol. 2 (Taurini & Romae: Marietti, 1953), pp. 196b–202b.

sub qua ab aliis distinguitur. Unde nec significat plura ut plura sunt, quia non significat illa secundum quod inter se differunt, sed potius ut inter se conveniunt, vel similia sunt: ergo signum est huic voci respondere etiam in mente unum conceptum formalem, quo immediate & adaequate concipitur quod per hanc vocem significatur. Vel potius e contrario hoc signo colligimus, ex tali modo concipiendi res uno conceptu, talis nominis impositionem processisse. Tertio argumentari possumus ex conceptu existentiae: videtur enim per se evidens, dari unum conceptum formalem exi⟨68b⟩stentiae ut sic, quia, quoties hoc modo de existentia loquimur & disputamus tanquam de uno actu, re vera non formamus plures conceptus, sed unum: ergo etiam conceptus formalis existentis[13] ut sic unus est, quia sicut concipitur abstractum per modum unius, ita & concretum ut sic praecise constitutum: ergo similiter enti ut sic unus conceptus formalis respondet: nam ens vel est idem quod existens, vel, si sumatur ut aptitudine existens, conceptus eius habet eandem rationem unitatis. Hinc etiam conceptus entis, non solum unus, sed etiam simplicis[51a]simus dici solet, ita ut ad eum fiat ultima resolutio caeterorum, per alios enim conceptus concipimus tale, vel tale ens; per hunc autem praescindimus omnem compositionem & determinationem, unde hic conceptus dici etiam solet ex se esse primus qui ab homine formatur, quia, caeteris paribus, facilius de quacunque re concipi potest, quae omnia tradit D. Thom. q. 1. de veri. artic. 1. & q. 21. art. 1. & Avic. 2. Meta. Quapropter de unitate huius conceptus communissimi, & confusi, fere nullus est, qui dubitet: ostendimus autem nullum alium posse vere ac proprie dici conceptum entis ut sic, qui non sit confusus respectu particularium entium, ut talia sunt. Tandem, si conceptus formalis entis non est unus; erunt ergo plures: quot ergo erunt? non est maior ratio de duobus, quam de tribus, vel quolibet alio numero: quia, si multiplicantur hi conceptus, necesse est multiplicari iuxta aliquam diversitatem rerum, vel entitatum sub latitudine entis comprehensarum: hae autem entitates in infinitum possunt multiplicari, & secundum proprias rationes distingui, & si semel ponitur, conceptum vel conceptus entis ut sic repraesentare determinatas naturas entis, etiam ut distinctas, non est ulla ratio, cur sistendum sit in duabus

13. Reading "existentis" here with C_1, C_2, G_2, M_1, M_2, M_3, M_4, P_1, P_2, S, V_1, V_2, V_3, and V_4. The following read "existentiae" instead: V_5 and Vivès.

q. 1,[27] Javelli, q. 1,[28] Flanders, q. 2, art. 6,[29] Hervaeus, *Quodl.* II, q. 7,[30] and Soto, *Categories*, ch. 4, q. 1.[31] And it is plainly inferred from St. Thomas, in the passages to be cited in the next section.[32] And it is proved, first, by experience, for when the name "being" is heard, we experience that our thought is not drawn in different directions or divided into several concepts, but is rather gathered into one, just as when we conceive human being, animal, and the like. Second: because, as Aristotle says in *On Interpretation* 1, we express our formal concepts by means of words.[33] But this word, "being," not only is materially one, but also has a single signification from its original imposition, by virtue of which it does not immediately signify some nature under that determinate and proper character$_r$ in accordance with which it is distinguished from other things. For this reason, neither does it signify several things insofar as they are several, since it does not signify them insofar as they differ from each other, but rather insofar as they agree among themselves or are similar. This is a sign, therefore, that to this word there corresponds in the mind also a single formal concept by means of which what is signified by this word is immediately and adequately conceived. Or rather, conversely, from this sign we infer that the imposition of such a name came from such a way of conceiving things$_r$ by means of a single concept. Third, we can argue from the concept of existence, for it seems *per se* evident that there is a single formal concept of existence as such, since, whenever we speak or treat in this way of existence as of a single act, we really do not form several concepts, but one. Therefore, the formal concept of the existent as such is also one, since, where the abstract is conceived in the

27. Paul Soncinas, *Quaestiones Metaphysicales acutissimae* (Lugduni: apud Carolum Presnot, 1579), pp. 2a–3b. (Question 1 is mislabeled "Question 2.")

28. Giovanni Crisostomo Javelli, *Chrysostomi Iavelli Canapicii, ordinis Praedicatorum, Philosophi & Theologi nostrae aetatis eruditissimi omnia, quotquot inveniri potuerunt, Opera, quibus quicquid ad Rationalem, Naturalem, Moralem ac Divinam Philosophiam pertinet* [...], *tomus primus* (Lugduni: apud Antonium de Harsy, 1580), pp. 731b–33b.

29. Dominic of Flanders, *In Duodecim Libros Metaphysicae Aristotelis* (Coloniae Agrippinae: Typis Arnoldi Kempensis, 1621), pp. 159b–60b. See also pp. 154a–59b.

30. Hervaeus Natalis, *Quolibeta* (Venetiis: Heredes Octaviani Scoti, 1513), fols. 43ra–46vb, and especially fol. 44va ("Primo sic...") and fol. 45va ("Tertio ad idem...").

31. Domingo de Soto, *In Dialecticam Aristotelis Commentarii* (Salmanticae: Excudebat Andreas à Portonariis. S. C. M. Typographus, 1564), fols. 40rb–42rb, and especially fol. 40va–b.

32. See *DM* 2.2.8 below.

33. Aristotle, *De Int.* 1, 16a3–8.

potius, quam in tribus vel quatuor &c. ut evidentius constabit ex his, quae sect. sequente dicemus de conceptu obiectivo: nam, licet formalis, quatenus a nobis, & in nobis fit, videatur esse posse experientia notior, tamen exacta cognitio unitatis eius multum pendet ex unitate obiecti, a quo solent actus suam unitatem & distinctionem sumere.

manner of one thing, so also is the concrete, when precisely constituted as such. Likewise, therefore, to being as such there corresponds a single formal concept, for a being either is the same as an existent, or, if being is taken as existent in aptitude, its concept has the same kind$_r$ of unity. For this reason also the concept of being is usually called not only one, but also the simplest, so that the ultimate resolution of other concepts is to the concept of being. For through other concepts we conceive a being of this or that kind, while through this one we prescind from all composition and determination, for which reason this concept is also normally said to be of itself the first that is formed by a human being, since, other things being equal, it can more easily be conceived of any thing$_r$ [that it is a being]. And all of this St. Thomas teaches in *On Truth*, q. 1, art. 1,[34] and q. 21, art. 1,[35] as does Avicenna, *Metaph.* II.[36] For this reason, there is almost no one who doubts the unity of this confused and most common concept. And we have shown that no other concept that is not confused in relation to particular beings, insofar as they are such, can truly and properly be called the concept of being as such. Finally, if the formal concept of being is not one, it will therefore be several. How many will it be, then? There is no greater reason to posit two than there is to posit three, or any other number, since, if these concepts are multiplied, it is necessary that they be multiplied in accordance with some diversity of the things$_r$ or entities comprehended under the breadth of being. But these entities can be multiplied and distinguished according to their proper natures$_r$ to infinity, and if once it is posited that the concept or concepts of being as such represent determinate natures of being, and also represent these natures as distinct, there is no reason why a stop should be made at two rather than three or four, etc., as will be established more evidently from the things that we shall say in the following section regarding the objective concept. For although the formal concept, insofar as it is made by us and in us, seems to admit of

34. Thomas Aquinas, *Sancti Thomae de Aquino opera omnia*, t. 22, vol. 1, fasc. 2 (Romae: ad Sanctae Sabinae, 1970), pp. 3a–8a.

35. Thomas Aquinas, *Sancti Thomae de Aquino opera omnia*, t. 22, vol. 3, fasc. 1 (Romae: ad Sanctae Sabinae, 1973), pp. 591a–595b.

36. I believe Suárez means to refer to book I, ch. 5, of Avicenna's *Metaphysics*. See Avicenna, *Liber de philosophia prima, sive scientia divina I–IV* (Louvain & Leiden: Peeters & Brill, 1977), pp. 31ff.

10. Ex quo intelligitur primo, quo sensu qua ve ratione hic conceptus formalis dicatur secundum rem ipsam praecisus ab aliis conceptibus, scilicet quia a parte rei est realiter distinctus a conceptu substantiae ut sic, accidentis, qualitatis, & caeteris similibus: loqui⟨69a⟩mur enim in intellectu humano, qui dum ea etiam, quae in re distincta non sunt, mente dividit, in se ipso conceptus partitur, conceptus realiter distinctos formando eiusdem rei secundum diversam praecisionem, vel abstractionem rei conceptae, quomodo conceptus formales iustitiae, & misericordiae divinae in nobis sunt realiter praecisi, seu distincti, quanvis misericordia & iustitia in se non distinguantur. Sic igitur conceptus entis ut sic cum in repraesentando praescindat a propria ratione substantiae ut sic, accidentis, & omnium aliarum, necesse est ut in se sit realiter praecisus, & distinctus a conceptibus propriis talium rationum vel naturarum ut tales sunt; & hoc etiam facile omnes fatentur.

11. Secundo colligitur ex dictis, hunc formalem conceptum entis, sicut in se est unus secundum rem, ita etiam secundum rationem formalem suam, & secundum eam etiam esse ratione praecisum a conceptibus formalibus particularium rationum. Patet primo, quia hic conceptus in se est simplicissimus, sicut obiective, ita etiam formaliter: ergo in se habet unam simplicem rationem formalem adaequatam: ergo secundum eam praescinditur ab aliis conceptibus formalibus. Secundo, quia, sicut mens nostra praescindendo ea quae in re non distinguuntur, in se ipsa realiter distinguit conceptus formales suos, ita e converso confundendo, & coniungendo ea, quae in re distinguuntur, quatenus in se similia sunt, unit conceptum suum, formando illum re & ratione formali unum: hoc au[51b]tem modo concipiuntur entia hoc formali conceptu entis: sumit enim mens illa omnia solum ut inter se similia in ratione essendi, & ut sic format unam imaginem unica repraesentatione formali repraesentantem id, quod est, quae imago est ipse conceptus formalis: est ergo ille conceptus simpliciter unus re & ratione formali,

being better known$_n$ by experience, nevertheless, exact cognition of its unity depends very much on the unity of its object, from which acts normally derive their unity and distinction.

10. From this it is understood, first, in what sense or for what reason this formal concept is said to be really prescinded from other concepts, namely, because *a parte rei* it is really distinct from the concept of substance as such, from the concept of accident, from the concept of quality, and from other similar concepts. For we are speaking about the human intellect, which, even when it mentally distinguishes those things which are not in reality distinct, divides concepts in itself, forming really distinct concepts of the same thing$_r$ in conformity with diverse precisions or abstractions of the conceived thing$_r$, just as the formal concepts of the divine justice and mercy are really prescinded or distinguished in us even though divine mercy and justice are not in themselves distinguished. In this way, therefore, since the concept of being as such prescinds in its representation from the proper nature$_r$ of substance as such, from the proper nature$_r$ of accident, and from the proper natures$_r$ of all other things, it is necessary that it be in itself really prescinded and distinguished from the proper concepts of such essences$_r$ or natures insofar as they are such. And this also everyone readily concedes.

11. Second, it is gathered from what has been said that, just as this formal concept of being is in itself one in reality, so also is it one in respect of its formal character$_r$, and that, in accordance with this character$_r$, it is also rationally prescinded from the formal concepts of particular natures$_r$. This is clear, first, because just as this concept is in itself the simplest objectively, so also is it in itself the simplest formally. Therefore, in itself it has one adequate simple formal character$_r$. Therefore, in accordance with this character$_r$, it is prescinded from other formal concepts. It is also clear, second, because, just as our mind, when it prescinds things that are not in reality distinguished, really distinguishes in itself its formal concepts, so also, conversely, when it confounds and conjoins those things which are in reality distinguished, insofar as they are in themselves similar, it unites its concept, making it one really and in respect of its formal character$_r$. But it is in this way that beings are conceived by means of this formal concept of being, for the mind takes all those things only insofar as they are similar to each other in the

& secundum eam praecisus ab his conceptibus, qui distinctius repraesentant particularia entia seu rationes eorum.

Formalis conceptus entis ut sic non multiplicatur secundum multitudinem obiectorum particularium.

12. Tertio sequitur, hunc conceptum formalem entis non solum esse unum, sed etiam non posse esse plures secundum habitudinem ad obiecta magis determinata, seu distinctius concepta ex parte obiectorum. Possunt quidem hi conceptus formales multiplicari, vel secundum numerum in diversis subiectis, vel in eodem diversis temporibus, forte etiam secundum speciem ⟨69b⟩ ex parte concipientis altiori modo, vel cum maiori claritate, & distinctiori apprehensione ipsius rationis formalis entis ut sic (quanvis fortasse tota haec distinctio sit solum secundum magis & minus intra eandem speciem, maxime sistendo in conceptibus, qui ab homine naturaliter formari possunt) at vero ex maiori vel minori determinatione obiecti non potest conceptus entis ut sic multiplicari: quia, ut ostensum est, hoc ipso, quod non sistitur in communi conceptione entis ut sic, sed descenditur ad hoc & illud ens ut talia sunt, licet multiplicentur conceptus formales, non tamen conceptus entis ut sic; sed adiungendo conceptum substantiae, vel accidentis, &c.

Hic conceptus non est tantum nominis, sed etiam rei.

13. Quarto colligitur ex dictis, falso vocari hunc conceptum tantum nominis, & non rei significatae nomine entis, & secundum eam rationem, qua per illud significatur. Primo, quia, ut dixi, hic conceptus prior est voce, & impositione eius ad res tali modo significandas. Nam, licet quoad nos conceptus saepe formentur, mediis vocibus: tamen secundum se, & simpliciter, prior est conceptus, qui ex se parit vocem, qua exprimitur, & est origo impositionis eius: ergo talis conceptus est simpliciter & absolute conceptus rei secundum se, & non tantum in ordine ad significationem vocis, ut hac ratione dicatur conceptus nominis, seu quid nominis. Secundo, quia hic conceptus est per modum cuiusdam simplicis imaginis naturaliter repraesentantis id quod per vocem ad placitum significatur; sed in hoc tantum consistit, quod sit conceptus

character$_r$ of being$_e$, and as such forms a single image that represents, by means of a single formal representation, that which is, and this image is the formal concept itself. That concept, therefore, is one without qualification really and according to its formal character$_r$, and it is prescinded, in accordance with that character$_r$, from these concepts which more distinctly represent particular beings or their natures$_r$.

The formal concept of being as such is not multiplied in accordance with the multitude of particular objects.

12. Third, it follows not only that this formal concept of being is one, but also that it cannot be several in relation to objects that are more determined, or in relation to things that are conceived more distinctly in respect of objects.[37] These formal concepts can indeed be multiplied, either numerically in diverse subjects, or in the same subject at diverse times, and perhaps also specifically on the part of one who conceives in a higher way, or with a greater clarity and a more distinct apprehension of the formal character$_r$ of being as such (although perhaps this whole distinction is only according to a greater or lesser degree within the same species, especially if we stop at concepts that can naturally be formed by the human being). But the concept of being as such cannot be multiplied by means of a greater or lesser determination of the object, since, as has been shown, by virtue of the very fact that a stop is not made at the common concept of being as such, but rather a descent is made to this being and that one insofar as they are beings of particular kinds, even if formal concepts are thereby multiplied, nevertheless, the concept of being as such is not. Rather, one adds the concept of substance, or the concept of accident, etc.

This concept is not merely nominal, but also real.

13. Fourth, it is gathered from the things that have been said that this concept is falsely called a concept of the name alone, rather than a concept of the thing$_r$ signified by the name "being," and according to that concept$_r$ by means of which it is signified by that name.[38] First:

37. See *DM* 2.1.8 above, where Suárez distinguishes between two senses in which something is conceived confusedly or distinctly. On the one hand, I conceive something (e.g., the human being) distinctly or confusedly when I cognize the same *ratio* (e.g., the *ratio* of the human being) more or less perfectly. This variation is due to the one who conceives (*ex parte concipientis*). On the other hand, I am said to conceive a species (e.g., the human being) confusedly when I conceive the proper *ratio* of its genus (e.g., the *ratio* of animal), and I am said to conceive the same species distinctly when I conceive its proper *ratio* (e.g., the *ratio* of the human being). In this case, the confusion or distinctness is on the side of, or in respect of, the objects (*ex parte obiectorum*).

38. I suspect that the Latin "*qua*" here is a mistake, and that "*quae*" should be read

rei, quanquam, quia conceptus ille simplicissimus est, & ideo obiectum eius non potest propria definitione declarari, ad illud explicandum uti solemus descriptionibus, quae solum videntur nominis significationem distinctius declarare; & hoc modo potest in bono sensu dici conceptus ille esse quid nominis, dummodo non excludatur, quin ille sit proprius, & adaequatus conceptus rei immediate significatae per illam vocem.

Quorum analogorum detur una ratio communis.

14. Fundamentum primae sententiae (nam de secunda iam satis dictum est) tangit materiam de analogia entis infra tractandam, & pendet etiam ex dicendis de conceptu obiectivo, nam multi existimant unitatem conceptus formalis non repugnare analogiae, sed unitatem conceptus obiectivi, de qua re postea. Nunc breviter dicitur ex D. Tho. in 1. d. 19. q. 5. art. 2. ad 1. inter ⟨70a⟩ analoga attributionis quaedam esse, quae significant formam, quae intrinsece tantum est in principali analogato; in aliis vero solum per habitudinem, vel denominationem extrinsecam: ut sanum, & similia, & his repugnat unitas [52a] conceptus formalis: quia analogata non habent inter se propriam similitudinem & convenientiam. Alia vero esse, quae significant formam seu naturam intrinsece inventam in omnibus analogatis: & huiusmodi est ens, ut infra videbimus, nam accidentia non sunt entia per extrinsecam[14] denominationem, sed per intrinsecam naturam seu rationem entis, quam participant; & in huiusmodi analogis non est inconveniens

14. Reading "extrinsecam" here with the older editions. Vivès reads "intrinsecam" instead.

because, as I have said, this concept is prior to the word and to the word's being imposed to signify things$_{r}$ in such a way. For, although with respect to us concepts are often formed by means of words, nevertheless, in itself and without qualification, that concept is prior which, of itself, both gives rise to the word by which it is expressed and is the source of that word's imposition. Therefore, such a concept is without qualification and absolutely the concept of the thing$_{r}$ in itself—and not only in relation to the word's signification, so that it might be called, for this reason, a nominal concept or a concept of the name. Second: because this concept exists$_{e}$ as a kind of simple image that naturally represents what the word signifies by convention. But in this alone does its being a concept of the thing$_{r}$ consist, although, since that concept is the simplest, and its object cannot, therefore, be explained by means of a proper definition, in order to explain it we normally use descriptions which seem only to explain the signification of the name more distinctly. And in this way, that concept can in a correct sense be called nominal, provided that one does not deny that it is a proper and adequate concept of the thing$_{r}$ immediately signified by that word.

Which analogicals have a single common nature$_{r}$.

14. The foundation of the first opinion (for about the second opinion enough has already been said) touches upon the analogy of being, which is to be dealt with below,[39] and it depends also on things to be said about the objective concept, for many hold that the unity of the formal concept is not incompatible with analogy, but that the unity of the objective concept is, which is something that shall be discussed hereafter. For now it is briefly said, in conformity with St. Thomas, *Sent.* I, d. 19, q. 5, art. 2, ad 1,[40] that among names analogical by attribution there are some that signify a form which is intrinsically in the principal analogate alone and in the other analogates only by an extrinsic relation or denomination, such as "healthy thing" and the like. And the unity of the formal concept is incompatible with these, since the analo-

instead. If so, this sentence might be translated as follows: "Fourth, it is gathered from the things that have been said that this concept is falsely called a concept of the name alone, rather than a concept of the thing$_{r}$ signified by the name 'being,' and in accordance with that nature$_{r}$ which is signified by that name."

39. See *DM* 28.3 and *DM* 32.2.

40. Thomas Aquinas, *S. Thomae Aquinatis opera omnia*, vol. 1 (Stuttgart-Bad Cannstatt: Frommann-Holzboog, 1980), p. 56a.

dari unum conceptum formalem simpliciter & absolute in se unum re & ratione formali adaequata; in quo autem eius analogia consistat, infra explicabitur.

gates do not have a proper similarity and agreement with each other. But there are others that signify a form or nature found intrinsically in all the analogates, and of this sort is "being," as we shall see below, for accidents are not beings by extrinsic denomination, but by virtue of the intrinsic nature or character$_r$ of being, in which they participate. And in the case of such analogical names it is not problematic that there should be a single formal concept that is without qualification and absolutely one in itself, really and in respect of its adequate formal character$_r$. In what its analogy consists will be explained below.

Sectio II.

Utrum ens habeat unum conceptum seu rationem formalem obiectivam.

Ratio dubitandi prima. 1. Ratio dubitandi duplex est. Prima tacta est sect. praeced. fundaturque in analogia entis, quia, si conceptus eius obiectivus est unus, vel unitate univocationis, & sic tollitur analogia: vel unitate tantum analoga, & sic vel re vera non est unus; vel est repugnantia in terminis, quia analogia intrinsece includit vel plures rationes habentes tantum inter se proportionem, vel plures habitudines ad unam formam, ratione quarum conceptus obiectivus nominis analogi non potest esse unus. Quod declaratur, & confirmatur, quia ut ens habeat unum conceptum obiectivum, necesse est ut omnia entia conveniant in una ratione formali entis, quae per nomen, *ens*, immediate significetur, quia unitas conceptus obiectivi requirit unitatem rei, vel saltem rationis formalis; si autem omnia entia conveniunt in una ratione formali: ergo ut sic habent unam, & eandem definitionem, sicut unum conceptum obiectivum: quia, si conceptus obiectivus unus est, etiam definitio eius potest esse una: ergo nihil deest enti ad perfectam univocationem.

Secunda. 2. Secunda ratio dubitandi est, quia, si conceptus obiectivus entis est unus, ergo secundum se est praecisus & abstractus ab omnibus inferioribus, seu determinatis entium rationibus: consequens est impossibile: ergo & antecedens. Sequela patet, ⟨70b⟩ quia si conceptus entis

Section 2

Whether Being Has a Single Objective Concept, or a Single Objective Formal Character$_{R}$.

The first reason for doubt.

1. There are two reasons for doubt. The first was touched upon in the preceding section and is founded on the analogy of being, since, if the objective concept of being is one, either it is one with the unity of univocation, and so analogy is removed, or it is one with a merely analogical unity, and so either it is not really one or there is a contradiction in terms, since analogy intrinsically involves either several natures$_{r}$ having only a proportion between them or several relations to one form, by reason of which relations the objective concept of the analogical name cannot be one. This is explained and confirmed: because, in order for being to have a single objective concept, it is necessary that all beings agree in one formal character$_{r}$ of being which is immediately signified by the name "being," for the unity of the objective concept requires the unity of the thing$_{r}$, or at least the unity of the formal character$_{r}$. But if all beings agree in one formal character$_{r}$, then as such they have one and the same definition, just as they have one objective concept, since, if the objective concept is one, its definition also can be one. Therefore, being is lacking in nothing for perfect univocation.

Second reason for doubt.

2. The second reason for doubt is: because, if the objective concept of being is one, it is in itself prescinded and abstracted from all inferior or determinate natures$_{r}$ of beings. But the consequent is impossible. Therefore, so also is the antecedent. The consequence is clear, since if

est unus, ergo formaliter & actualiter non includit in se determinatos modos entium: illi enim intrinsece opponuntur, & distinctionem efficiunt: unde impossibile est ut in uno conceptu obiectivo actu includantur: ergo ut conceptus entis sit unus, necesse est ut ab his omnibus praescindat: hoc autem esse impossibile sic ostendo, quia si ens ut sic praescindit a determinatis rationibus entium: ergo ut ad eas contrahatur seu determinetur, aliquid ei addi necesse est: ergo vel id quod additur, est ens, vel nihil; si nihil, quomodo potest ens realiter determinare, & propriam aliquam rationem entis constituere? si vero est ens: ergo non potest ens ut sic ab eo praescindi, nam quod ab alio praescinditur, non includitur in illo. Neque enim intelligi potest quod ens praescindatur a modis quibus contrahitur; & quod nihilominus in eis intrinsece includatur: neque e contrario quod modus contrahens ens, nihil includat nisi ens, & tamen quod illud determinet ad specialem rationem entis. Nam contractio, & determinatio non intelligitur sine additione: non potest autem intelligi additio, nisi id quod additur tale sit, ut non includat id cui additur, aut secundum rem, aut secundum rationem, iuxta modum quo addi in[52b]telligitur. Et confirmatur, nam ob hanc causam dixit Arist. 3. Metap. tex. 10. genus esse extra rationem differentiarum, scilicet, quia abstrahit, & praescindit ab illis: ergo, si conceptus obiectivus entis est praecisus & unus, necesse est, ut in contrahentibus non includatur.

Ratio difficultatis in contrarium.

3. In contrarium autem est, quia uni conceptui formali unus conceptus obiectivus necessario respondet: sed ostensum est dari unum conceptum formalem entis: ergo necessario dandus est unus obiectivus. Maior constat, quia conceptus formalis habet totam suam rationem & unitatem ab obiecto: ergo ut sit unus, necesse est ut tendat in obiectum aliquo modo unum: sed conceptus obiectivus nihil aliud est, quam obiectum ipsum ut cognitum vel apprehensum per talem conceptum formalem: ergo si conceptus formalis est unus, necesse est ut obiectivus etiam unus sit.

the concept of being is one, it does not formally and actually include in itself determinate modes of beings, for these are intrinsically opposed and produce distinction. For this reason, it is impossible that they should be actually included in one objective concept. Therefore, in order for the concept of being to be one, it is necessary that it prescind from all of these. But that this is impossible I prove in the following way: because, if being as such prescinds from determinate natures$_r$ of beings, then in order for it be contracted or determined to them, it is necessary that something be added to it. Therefore, either that which is added is a being or it is nothing. If nothing, how can it really determine being and constitute some proper nature$_r$ of a being? But if it is a being, then being as such cannot be prescinded from it, since what is prescinded from another thing is not included in it. For it cannot be understood that being is prescinded from the modes by which it is contracted, and that, nevertheless, it is intrinsically included in them—nor, conversely, that a mode which contracts being includes nothing except being but nevertheless determines it to the special nature$_r$ of a being. For contraction and determination are not understood without addition, and addition cannot be understood unless that which is added is such that it does not include that to which it is added, either really or rationally, in accordance with the way it is understood to be added. And this is confirmed, for this is why Aristotle says in *Metaph.* III, text 10, that the genus is outside the nature$_r$ of its differences,[41] namely, because it abstracts and prescinds from them. Therefore, if the objective concept of being is prescinded and one, it is necessary that it not be included in the things that contract it.

A ground$_r$ of difficulty pointing to the opposite conclusion.

3. But to the contrary: because to one formal concept there necessarily corresponds one objective concept. But it has been shown that there is one formal concept of being. Therefore, there must necessarily be one objective concept of being. The major is clear, since a formal concept has its entire nature$_r$ and unity from its object. Therefore, in order for it to be one, it is necessary that it tend to an object that is in some way one. But the objective concept is nothing other than the object itself as cognized or apprehended by such a formal concept.

41. Aristotle, *Metaph.* III, ch. 3, 998b24–26.

Variae sententiae referuntur.

Prima sententia. *Caiet.* *Soncin.* *Hispal.* *Hervaeus.* *Flandr.* *Pereira. 2. phys. c. 2. in fine.*

4. In hac quaestione, qui negant dari unum conceptum formalem ⟨71a⟩ entis, consequenter etiam negant dari obiectivum. Et ita sentit Caiet. locis cit. sect. praecedente; in prima opinione, & Ferr. loco citato. Ex his vero qui admittunt unum conceptum formalem entis, negant unum obiectivum Soncinas, 4. Metaph. q. 2. & 3. & Hispal. in 1. d. 3. q. 1. Hervaeus & Flandria locis cit. sect. praecedenti. Tribuitur etiam Capreolo, sed re vera id non docet, ut infra dicam. Citatur etiam pro hac sententia D. Tho. 1. p. q. 13. art. 5. q. 7. de potentia, art. 7. q. 2. de verit. art. 11. quibus locis significat, vocibus quae communes sunt Deo, & creaturis, non respondere unam rationem conceptam seu significatam, sed plures. Fundamenta huius opinionis tacta sunt in principio: nam licet plura argumenta ab his autoribus afferantur, tamen vis omnium in duabus difficultatibus tactis posita est. Non conveniunt autem praedicti autores in explicando conceptum, vel potius conceptus obiectivos, qui enti correspondent. Quidam enim aiunt, immediate repraesentari per conceptum formalem entis omnia genera entium, quatenus inter se habent aliquam proportionem vel habitudinem, ut Ferrarien. & idem sentit Caiet. Alii vero dicunt, per conceptum formalem entis immediate repraesentari hoc disiunctum, *substantia, vel accidens*, ut Soncinas, Hervaeus, & alii. Rursus alii dicunt repraesentari absolute omnia genera, seu rationes, vel conceptus simplices, non copulative, nec disiunctive, sed[15] simpliciter, ut Fonseca 4. Metaph. c. 2. q. 2. sect. 4. & 7.

15. Reading "sed" here with S, V_1, and V_2. The following read "vel" instead: C_1, C_2, G_2, M_1, M_2, M_3, M_4, P_1, P_2, V_3, V_4, V_5, and Vivès. (But Charles Berton, who edited the *Disputationes Metaphysicae* in the Vivès edition of Suárez's works, suggested reading "sed" in lieu of the "vel" he found in his sources. See Francisco Suárez, *R. P. Francisci Suarez, E Societate Jesu, Opera Omnia*, vol. 27 [Parisiis: Apud Ludovicum Vivès, 1878], p. 368a.)

Therefore, if the formal concept is one, it is necessary that the objective concept be one as well.

Various opinions are presented.

The first opinion.
Cajetan.
Soncinas.
Diego Deza.
Hervaeus.
Flanders.
Pereira, 2 Phys., ch. 2, at the end.[48]

4. On this question, those who deny that there is a single formal concept of being consequently also deny that there is a single objective concept. Cajetan thinks this in the passages cited in the previous section in connection with the first opinion,[42] and also Ferrara, in the cited passage.[43] But among those who admit a single formal concept of being, the following deny that there is a single objective one: Soncinas, *Metaph.* IV, q. 2 and q. 3,[44] Deza, *Sent.* I, d. 3, q. 1,[45] Hervaeus,[46] and Dominic of Flanders,[47] in the passages cited in the preceding section. This view is also attributed to Capreolus, but he does not really teach it, as I shall say below. St. Thomas is also cited in support of this opinion, *ST* I, q. 13, art. 5,[49] *On the Power of God*, q. 7, art. 7,[50] and *On Truth*, q. 2, art. 11,[51] in which places he indicates that to words common to God and creatures there does not correspond a single conceived or signified nature$_{r}$, but several. The foundations of this opinion were touched on at the outset, for although more arguments are brought forth by these authors, nevertheless, the force of them all is situated in the two difficulties touched on. But the mentioned authors do not agree in explaining the objective concept, or rather concepts, that correspond to "being." For some say that all the genera of being, insofar as they have among

42. See n. 8 above.
43. See n. 13 above.
44. Paul Soncinas, *Quaestiones Metaphysicales acutissimae*, pp. 3b–7a, and especially p. 4a.
45. Diego Deza, *Novarum defensionum doctrine angelici doctoris beati Thomae de aquino super primo libro sententiarum quaestiones profundissime ac utilissime* (Hispali: Arte et ingenio Iacobi Kronberger Alemani, 1517), fols. 37ra–41va, and especially fols. 39vb–40ra.
46. See n. 30 above.
47. See n. 29 above.
48. Benedict Pereira, *Benedicti Pererii Societatis Iesu, De Communibus omnium rerum naturalium Principiis & Affectionibus, Libri Quindecim* (Parisiis: apud Micaëlem Sonnium, 1579), pp. 69–70.
49. Thomas Aquinas, *Sancti Thomae Aquinatis opera omnia* (Leonina), t. 4, pp. 146a–47b.
50. Thomas Aquinas, *Quaestiones Disputatae*, vol. 2, pp. 202b–205b.
51. Thomas Aquinas, *Sancti Thomae de Aquino opera omnia* (Leonina), t. 22, vol. 1, fasc. 2, pp. 77a–80b.

Secunda sententia. Scotus. Iavell. Sotus. Capreol.

5. Secunda sententia omnino contraria est, dari conceptum obiectivum entis simpliciter unum. Hanc tenet Scotus in 1. d. 3. q. 1. & 3. d. 8. q. 1. & in 2. d. 3. q. 3. & 6. Iavell. 4. Metap. q. 1. Soto in praedicam. c. 4. quaest. 1. & in eadem opinione est Capreolus in 1. d. 2. q. 1. Est tamen diversitas inter hos autores: nam Scotus ponit hunc conceptum ex natura rei praecisum ab inferioribus naturis, & modis contrahentibus ens: Alii vero solum ponunt hanc unitatem conceptus obiectivi ex modo concipiendi nostro, absque praecisione & distinctione quae sit in rebus: de qua diversitate opinionum dicemus sect. seq. De alia vero differentia quae etiam est inter hos autores quoad univocationem, vel analogiam, dicemus inferius. ⟨71b⟩

themselves some proportion or relation, are immediately represented by the formal concept of being—for instance, Ferrara.[52] And Cajetan thinks the same.[53] But others say that this disjunction, *substance or accident*, is immediately represented by the formal concept of being—for example, Soncinas,[54] Hervaeus,[55] and others. Again, others say that absolutely all simple genera, natures$_{r}$, or concepts are represented, not copulatively, nor disjunctively, but without qualification—for instance, Fonseca, *Metaph.* IV, ch. 2, q. 2, sect. 4 and 7.[56]

The second opinion.

Scotus. Javelli. Soto. Capreolus.

5. The second opinion is altogether contrary—namely, that the objective concept of being is without qualification one. This view is held by Scotus, *Sent.* I, d. 3, q. 1 and q. 3,[57] d. 8, q. 1,[58] and *Sent.* II, d. 3, q. 3 and q. 6,[59] and Javelli, *Metaph.* IV, q. 1,[60] and Soto, on the *Categories*, ch. 4, q. 1.[61] And Capreolus is of the same opinion, *Sent.* I, d. 2, q. 1.[62] There is, nevertheless, disagreement among these authors, for Scotus posits that this concept is prescinded *ex natura rei* from inferior natures and from the modes that contract being,[63] while the others only posit this unity of the objective concept according to our mode of conceiving, without a precision and distinction that obtains in reality. Of this difference of opinion we shall speak in the following section. However, we shall speak later of another difference that also exists$_{e}$ among these authors, regarding univocity or analogy.[64]

52. Thomas Aquinas, *Sancti Thomae Aquinatis opera omnia* (Leonina), t. 13, p. 108b.

53. Cajetan, *Scripta Philosophica: De Nominum Analogia, De Conceptu Entis*, pp. 31–34 (ns. 32–35).

54. Paul Soncinas, *Quaestiones Metaphysicales acutissimae*, p. 6a–b.

55. Hervaeus Natalis, *Quolibeta*, fol. 45va ("Tertio ad idem...").

56. Pedro da Fonseca, *Commentaria in Libros Metaphysicorum Aristotelis Stagiritae*, vol. 1, cols. 716–18, cols. 721–24.

57. John Duns Scotus, *Opera omnia*, vol. 3 (Civitas Vaticana: Typis Polyglottis Vaticanis, 1954), pp. 18–38 (ns. 26–55), pp. 94–103 (ns. 152–66).

58. Suárez would seem, rather, to have *Sent.* I, d. 8, p. 1, q. 3, in mind. Scotus argues here that it is compatible with God's simplicity that there should be a concept common to him and creatures. See John Duns Scotus, *Opera omnia*, vol. 4 (Civitas Vaticana: Typis Polyglottis Vaticanis, 1956), pp. 171–89 (ns. 44–79) and pp. 198–216 (ns. 95–127).

59. John Duns Scotus, *Opera omnia*, vol. 7 (Civitas Vaticana: Typis Polyglottis Vaticanis, 1973), pp. 418–21 (ns. 59–65), pp. 463–94 (ns. 142–211).

60. Giovanni Crisostomo Javelli, *Opera*, t. 1, pp. 731b–33b.

61. Domingo de Soto, *In Dialecticam Aristotelis Commentarii*, fol. 40vb.

62. See ns. 23 and 24 above.

63. See *DM* 2.3.6.

64. See *DM* 28.3 and 32.2.

6. Tertia opinio media inter praedictas, utitur distinctione, & variis modis explicatur. Quidam enim dicunt, conceptum entis obiectivum in se & absolute sumptum sine inferioribus, esse unum, & ratione [53a] praecisum ab illis, tamen comparatum ad inferiora, & ut inclusum in illis, non esse unum; & ita conciliant rationes dubitandi in principio adductas: nam, quia per conceptum formalem entis concipitur ens secundum se, & sine ulla comparatione ad inferiora, necesse est ut sub hac saltem consideratione conceptus ille obiectivus habeat unitatem. Quando vero hic conceptus consideratur, ut in ipsis inferioribus existens, non potest habere unitatem: differunt enim ipsa inferiora, v. g. substantia & accidens, per id ipsum quo entia sunt: ergo non possunt in illo ut sic habere unitatem, quia non possunt secundum idem convenire & differre: & hanc etiam posteriorem partem confirmant rationes dubitandi in principio positae. Aliter Fonseca supra, supposita illa distinctione de conceptu confuso, distincto, & medio, seu partim confuso, partim distincto, de hoc tertio conceptu dicit posse quidem esse unum, non tamen praecisum ab inferioribus, sed esse conceptum substantiae, v. g. de conceptu autem distincto similiter dicit non esse unum adaequatum enti, nisi fortasse in Deo, in nobis vero includere conceptum substantiae, qualitatis, &c. Sed, ut dixi, hi re vera non sunt conceptus entis ut sic. Tandem de conceptu confuso entis, qui ad rem spectat, ait quodammodo esse unum & praecisum, non tamen simpliciter, sed secundum quid. Esse quidem aliquo modo praecisum quia non expresse & determinate continet id, quod est proprium inferiorum membrorum, non esse autem simpliciter praecisum, etiam secundum rationem, ne sequatur illum esse univocum. Declarat autem, hanc praecisionem esse secundum quid, & non simpliciter, quia hic conceptus confusus entis ita excludit ea quae sunt propria substantiae, & caeterarum entitatum simplicium, ut tamen eius essentia non sit alia, quam essentia huiusmodi entitatum.

6. The third opinion, which is intermediate between the ones mentioned, makes use of a distinction and is explained in various ways. For some say that the objective concept of being, taken in itself and absolutely without inferiors, is one and rationally prescinded from them, but that, nevertheless, when compared to inferiors and as included in them, it is not one. And in this way they reconcile the reasons for doubt adduced at the beginning, for since being is conceived through the formal concept of being by itself and without any comparison to inferiors, it is necessary that, at least considered in this way, the objective concept have unity. But when this concept is considered as existing in the same inferiors, it cannot have unity, for the inferiors themselves—for example, substance and accident—differ through that very thing by virtue of which they are beings, and therefore they cannot as such have unity in it, since they cannot agree and differ in the same respect. And the reasons for doubt laid down at the beginning confirm this second part also. Fonseca, cited above,[65] [thinks] otherwise: supposing that distinction among the confused, distinct, and intermediate (i.e., partly confused and partly distinct) concepts, regarding this third concept he says that it can indeed be one, though it is not prescinded from inferiors, but is the concept of substance, for example. Regarding the distinct concept, he likewise says that it is not one concept adequate to being, except, perhaps, in God's case, but that in ours it includes the concept of substance, the concept of quality, etc. However, as I have said, these are not really concepts of being as such. Finally, regarding the confused concept of being, which is relevant to the matter at hand, he says that it is in a certain way one and prescinded, though not without qualification, but rather in a certain respect. [For he says] that it is indeed in some way prescinded, since it does not expressly and determinately contain that which is proper to inferior members, but that it is not without qualification prescinded even rationally, lest it follow that it is univocal. And he explains that this precision is in a certain respect, and not without qualification, because this confused concept of being excludes those things which are proper to substance and the other simple entities in such a way that, nevertheless, its essence is not other than the essence of entities of this sort.

65. Pedro da Fonseca, *Commentaria in Libros Metaphysicorum Aristotelis Stagiritae*, vol. 1, cols. 716–18.

7. Sed hae distinctiones, ut praecedente sectione attigi, mihi non videntur deservire ad rem explicandam; sed quo amplius multiplicantur, eo magis res videtur obscurari, & confundi. Omissis ergo conceptibus distinctis seu particularibus substantiae, & aliorum generum seu membrorum dividentium ens in communi, hic solum agimus de eo conceptu ⟨72a⟩ obiectivo, qui immediate, & adaequate respondet illi conceptui formali, quem diximus sect. praecedenti correspondere in mente huic voci, *ens*, & rei immediate significatae per illam: caeteri enim conceptus particulares secundum se sumpti non sunt conceptus entis in quantum ens, sed ut sunt talia, vel talia entia.

Prior assertio.

Datur una ratio entis obiectiva.

8. Dico ergo primo, conceptui formali entis respondere unum conceptum obiectivum adaequatum & immediatum, qui expresse non dicit substantiam, neque accidens, neque Deum, nec creaturam, sed haec omnia per modum unius, scilicet quatenus sunt inter se aliquo modo similia, & conveniunt in essendo. In hac conclusione conveniunt autores secundae sententiae, & Fonseca non dissentit, & plurimum favet *D. Thom.* D. Tho. locis supra cit. de veritate q. 1. art. 1. q. 21. art. 1. quatenus dicit, conceptum entis esse simplicissimum, & primum omnium, determinarique ad substantiam, quantitatem, &c. per quandam determinationem, & expressionem talis modi entis, ubi necesse est esse sermonem de conceptu obiectivo; nam formalis non determinatur, nec contrahitur. Unde apertius 1. p. q. 5. art. 3. ad 1. ait D. Tho. *Substantia, quantitas, & qualitas contrahunt ens, applicando ens ad aliquam quidditatem, seu naturam*: contractio autem intelligi non potest sine [53b] aliqua unitate, & communitate conceptus obiectivi. Atque eodem modo favet huic sententiae Arist. 4. Met. text. 7. ubi inquit, Metaphysicam considerare ens inquantum ens, sub quo alia genera continentur; ubi D. Th. ait, primam Philosophiam considerare ens commune, & ea, quae sunt eius in quantum huiusmodi. Ratione potest haec sententia ita probari. Necesse est, conceptum formalem entis habere aliquod adaequatum obiectum; sed illud non est aggregatum ex variis naturis entium secundum aliquas determinatas rationes earum, quantumvis simplices: ergo

7. But as I mentioned in the preceding section, it does not seem to me that these distinctions serve to explain the matter. Rather, the more they are multiplied, the more does the matter seem to be obscured and confused. Setting aside, therefore, the distinct or particular concepts of substance and the other genera or members dividing being in general, here we are treating only of that objective concept which immediately and adequately corresponds to that formal concept which, we said in the preceding section, corresponds in the mind to this word "being" and to the thing$_{r}$ immediately signified by that word. For the other particular concepts taken by themselves are not concepts of being as being, but concepts of beings insofar as they are beings of this or that type.

First assertion.

There is a single objective character$_{r}$ of being.

8. First, then, I say that to the formal concept of being there corresponds a single objective, adequate, and immediate concept that does not expressly signify$_{d}$ substance, or accident, or God, or creature, but all of these in the manner of one thing, namely, insofar they are in some way similar to each other and agree in being$_{e}$. The authors who hold the second opinion agree with this conclusion, and Fonseca does not disagree with it, and St. Thomas very much favors it in the passages cited above, *On Truth*, q. 1, art. 1, and q. 21, art. 1, insofar as he says that the concept of being is the simplest and the first of all, and that it is determined to substance, quantity, etc., by a certain determination and expression of a being's particular type of mode,[66] where the discussion must be about the objective concept, since the formal concept is not determined or contracted. For this reason, in *ST* I, q. 5, art. 3, ad 1, St. Thomas more clearly says: "Substance, quantity, and quality contract being by applying being to some quiddity or nature."[67] For contraction cannot be understood without some unity and community of the objective concept. And Aristotle likewise favors this view, *Metaph.* IV, text 7, when he says that metaphysics considers being as being, under which other genera are contained.[68] Commenting on this passage,

St. Thomas.

66. Thomas Aquinas, *Sancti Thomae de Aquino opera omnia* (Leonina), t. 22, vol. 1, fasc. 2, pp. 4b–5a, and vol. 3, fasc. 1, pp. 592b–93a.

67. Thomas Aquinas, *Sancti Thomae Aquinatis opera omnia* (Leonina), t. 4, p. 59b.

68. Aristotle, *Metaph.* IV, ch. 3, 1005a19–b2.

oportet, ut ille conceptus sit unus secundum aliquam convenientiam & similitudinem entium inter se. Consequentia est evidens a sufficiente enumeratione, quia supponimus (quod est per se notum) illum conceptum obiectivum non esse unum unitate reali, id est, numerali seu entitativa: nam constat hunc conceptum esse communem multis rebus. Maior item assumpta evi⟨72b⟩dens est, quia ille conceptus formalis est actus intellectus; omnis autem actus intellectus, sicut & omnis actus, quatenus unus est, habere debet aliquod obiectum adaequatum a quo habeat unitatem. Minor vero probatur, quia, si obiectum illud adaequatum est ex aggregatione plurium naturarum entis, quaero, quae sint istae naturae, & quomodo in illo conceptu aggregentur; nullo enim modo id concipi, & intelligi potest. Quod patebit etiam, excludendo omnes modos quibus id assertum est, vel excogitari potest.

Ens non significat substantiam, & accidens immediate.

9. Primo enim, quod Soncinas ait conceptum illum constare ex substantia & accidente ut sic, est plane falsum: nam, vel in illo conceptu includuntur illa duo copulative; & hoc ipse non dicit, nec dicere potest: alias falso diceretur substantia esse ens, vel qualitas esse ens, quia nec substantia est substantia & accidens, neque qualitas, & sic de aliis. Aut includuntur illa duo disiunctive, ut ipse Soncinas dicit; & hoc, praeterquam quod est contra experientiam, ut statim dicam, ex illo sequitur univocatio entis, quam ipse vitare intendit: nam hoc disiunctum, *substantia vel accidens*, tam vere, simpliciter, & aeque primo convenit accidenti, sicut substantiae, quia sicut ad veritatem disiunctivae sufficit veritas unius partis; ita ut praedicatum disiunctum aeque primo ac simpliciter praedicetur, sufficit ut una pars eius aeque primo ac simpliciter subiecto conveniat: tam vere autem & tam proprie accidens est accidens, sicut substantia est substantia: ergo disiunctum illud tam vere ac proprie convenit accidenti ratione unius partis, sicut substantiae ratione alterius. Quod in omnibus similibus praedicatis videre licet: nam esse Deum vel creaturam, verbi gratia, tam vere ac proprie dicitur

St. Thomas says that first philosophy considers being in general and those things which belong to it insofar as it is such.[69] And this opinion can be proved by reason in the following way. It is necessary that the formal concept of being have some adequate object. But this object is not something aggregated from various natures of beings according to certain determinate concepts$_r$ of them, however simple. Therefore, that concept must be one according to some agreement and similarity among beings themselves. The consequence is evident by sufficient enumeration, for we suppose (something known$_n$ *per se*) that this objective concept is not one with a real unity, that is, with a numerical or entitative unity, since it is clear that this concept is common to many things$_r$. Likewise, the assumed major is evident, since that formal concept is an act of the intellect, and like every act, each intellective act, insofar as it is one, must have some adequate object from which it has unity. And the minor is proved because, if that adequate object results from the aggregation of several natures of being, I ask what these natures are, and how they are aggregated in that concept, for this can in no way be conceived and understood. This is also clear by ruling out all the ways in which it has been maintained or can be imagined.

"Being" does not signify substance and accident immediately.

9. For, in the first place, what Soncinas says—namely, that this concept is composed from substance and accident as such—is plainly false. For either these two are included in that concept copulatively—and this he himself does not say, nor can say, otherwise it would be false to say that a substance is a being or that a quality is a being, since a substance is not a substance and an accident, nor is a quality, and similarly in other cases. Or substance and accident are included [in the objective concept of being] disjunctively, as Soncinas himself says.[70] However, aside from the fact that it is contrary to experience, as I shall presently affirm, this view entails the univocation of being, which he himself aims to avoid. For this disjunctive predicate, *substance or accident*, agrees as truly, as unqualifiedly, and in just as primary a way with accident as it does with substance, since, just as the truth of one of its parts suffices for the truth of a disjunctive proposition, so also, in order for a disjunctive predicate

69. Thomas Aquinas, *In duodecim libros metaphysicorum Aristotelis expositio* (Taurini & Romae: Marietti, 1950), p. 164 (bk. IV, lect. 5, ns. 588–93).

70. See n. 54 above.

de homine, sicut de Deo, & sic de aliis. Vel denique includuntur illa duo simpliciter, id est, absque coniunctione, vel disiunctione, scilicet *substantia accidens*. Et hoc in primis est contra experientiam, quia id quod concipitur, mente percipitur, & hoc modo sub experientiam cadit; nos autem, audito nomine *entis*, & concipiendo praecise id quod hac voce significari intelligimus, non percipimus mente substantiam ut sic, neque accidens ut sic, ut quilibet in se se experiri potest.

10. Deinde ille conceptus formalis simplex est, & limitatus, ac re ipsa praecisus a propriis conceptibus formalibus substantiae, & acci⟨73a⟩dentis, ut talia sunt: ergo per illum non repraesentantur substantia, & accidens proprie & distincte, sicut repraesentantur per duos conceptus substantiae, & accidentis. Neque enim dici potest, quod ille unus conceptus entis eminentiori modo contineat totam [54a] illam formalem repraesentationem, quae est in duobus illis conceptibus simul sumptis: nam hic modus universalitatis in conceptu formali est alienus ab intellectu humano, de quo agimus, & vix reperitur in angelico: non est ergo ille conceptus universalis per eminentem repraesentationem plurium, ut plura sunt, sed per confusionem plurium ut aliquo modo unum sunt. Quod si per illum conceptum non repraesentantur substantia & accidens tam proprie ac distincte, sicut per duos proprios conceptus substantiae, & accidentis, non intelligitur medium, quomodo repraesentari possint secundum propria, sed tantum prout inter se sunt aliquo modo similia: ergo non constat conceptus ille ex substantia & accidente repraesentatis etiam dicto modo absolute & simpliciter.

to be predicated unqualifiedly and in an equally primary way, it suffices that one of its parts agree unqualifiedly and in an equally primary way with the subject. But an accident is as truly and properly an accident as a substance is a substance. Therefore, this disjunctive predicate agrees as truly and properly with accident by reason of its one part as it does with substance by reason of its other part. And one can see that the same goes for all similar predicates, since "is God or a creature," for example, is as truly and properly said of the human being as it is said of God, and similarly in other cases. Or finally, substance and accident are included [in the objective concept of being] without qualification, i.e., without conjunction or disjunction, namely, *substance accident*. But this, in the first place, is contrary to experience, since what is conceived is perceived by the mind, and in this way falls under experience. But, upon hearing the name "being" and conceiving precisely what we understand to be signified by this word, we do not mentally perceive substance as such or accident as such, as anyone can experience in herself.

10. Second, that formal concept is simple as well as marked off and really prescinded from the proper formal concepts of substance and accident insofar as they are such. Therefore, substance and accident are not represented by means of it particularly and distinctly, as they are represented by the two concepts of substance and accident. For it cannot be said that this single concept of being contains in a more eminent way the whole of that formal representation which is in those two concepts taken at the same time, since this mode of universality in a formal concept is foreign to the human intellect, of which we are treating, and is hardly found in an angelic intellect. Therefore, that concept is not universal by an eminent representation of several things insofar as they are several, but by a confusion of several things insofar as they are in some way one. And if, by means of that concept, substance and accident are not represented as particularly and distinctly as they are by means of the two proper concepts of substance and accident, one can understand no middle way in which they can be represented in terms of what is proper to them, but only insofar as they are in some way similar to each other. Therefore, that concept is not composed from substance and accident represented in the mentioned way, absolutely and without qualification.

11. Accedit praeterea quod iuxta huiusmodi conceptum vix intelligitur quid definite praedicetur de aliquo, cum dicitur esse ens: nam id, quod praedicatur, est conceptus obiectivus: si ergo ille conceptus est totum hoc substantia accidens, haec praedicatio, hoc est ens; aequivalet huic: hoc est substantia accidens; huiusmodi autem praedicatio non potest determinate fieri aut vere, vel falso, nisi utraque pars praedicati intelligatur copulative aut disiunctive praedicari, cum illae duae partes non coniungantur per modum substantivi & adiectivi, ut per modum unius praedicentur: quanvis, etiam si hoc modo fieret, sensus rediret copulativus, & fieret falsa propositio. Rursus accedit contra totam hanc sententiam, quia si in illo conceptu reperitur utrumque horum, substantia & accidens quocunque ex praedictis modis inquiro ulterius, quis conceptus substantiae ibi includatur: nam substantia vel ibi sumitur pro substantia creata, vel pro increata, vel pro aliquo conceptu obiectivo communi utrique. Primum & secundum dici non possunt; quia ens, de quo nunc loquimur, commune est enti creato, & increato, prout supra diximus esse obiectum huius scientiae: si vero dicatur tertium, consurgit inde argumentum ad hominem contra praedictos autores, tum quia substantia est quid analogum ad increatam, & creatam substantiam: ergo si, non obstante analogia, da⟨73b⟩tur unus conceptus obiectivus communis substantiae creatae & increatae, poterit etiam dari conceptus entis. Tum etiam quia magis distat substantia creata ab increata, quam accidens a substantia creata: oporteret ergo, consequenter loquendo, addere aliquid illi conceptui, dicendo constare ex determinata ratione substantiae creatae, & accidentis, quod tamen per se est incredibile, & efficacius impugnari potest argumentis factis. Et adhuc superest simile argumentum ex parte alterius membri, scilicet *accidens*: nam hoc etiam secundum praedictos autores analogum est, & saltem respectu aliquorum accidentium est fortasse verum, ut infra dicam: inquiram ergo similiter, an accidens intret conceptum entis, secundum aliquem conceptum communem, vel (ut ita dicam) secundum partem conceptus obiectivi communis omnibus accidentibus: & contra utrumque possunt applicari argumenta facta, ac denique potest concludi, hoc etiam membrum esse in plura alia dividendum.

11. It is added, moreover, that it is hardly understood what exactly is predicated of something in accordance with such a concept when it is said to be a being. For what is predicated is the objective concept. If, therefore, that concept is this whole, *substance accident*, then the predication, "this is a being," is equivalent to this one: "this is a substance accident." But such a predication cannot determinately be made, either truly or falsely, unless both parts of the predicate are understood to be predicated copulatively or disjunctively, since those two parts are not conjoined in the manner of a substantive and adjective, so as to be predicated as one thing—although, even if they were predicated in this way, the sense would be rendered copulative, and the proposition would be made false. Again, against this entire opinion, there is this additional argument: because, if each of these—substance and accident—is found in that concept, in whichever of the mentioned ways, I ask, further: which concept of substance is included there? For substance is there taken either as created substance, or as uncreated substance, or as some objective concept common to both. The first and the second cannot be said, since being, of which we are now speaking, is common to created and uncreated being, given that we said above that it is the object of this science.[71] But if the third is said, there arises therefrom an *ad hominem* argument against the mentioned authors, both because substance is something analogical in relation to uncreated and created substance, and therefore if, notwithstanding the analogy, there is a single objective concept common to created and uncreated substance, there will also be able to be a [single objective] concept of being; and also because created substance is further removed from uncreated substance than accident is from created substance. Therefore, for consistency's sake, it will be necessary to add something to that concept, saying that it is composed from the determinate nature$_r$ of created substance, [the determinate nature$_r$ of uncreated substance,[72]] and the determinate nature$_r$ of accident, which, however, is *per se* unbelievable and can more effectively be opposed by means of the arguments that have been

71. See *DM* 1.1.

72. The argument makes a lot more sense with this addition. Compare this argument, moreover, to the argument that Suárez goes on to make next, regarding accident, and note in particular the claim that "it can be concluded that this member also is to be divided into several."

Conceptus entis non includit genera omnia prima.

12. Propter hanc ergo fortasse causam dixerunt alii obiectum adaequatum illius conceptus formalis entis esse, vel includere genera omnia prima seu omnes entitates simplices, quae proxime dividunt ens. Sed contra hanc sententiam procedunt eodem modo priora argumenta. Primum, quia tales naturae nec copulative nec disiunctive, nec simpliciter, & absque ulla copula possunt in tali conceptu includi, ut patet applican[54b]do eodem modo discursum factum: habet enim eandem vim, ut facile cuivis consideranti patebit. Secundum, ab experientia, quia ex vi conceptionis entis non percipimus has omnes definitas naturas entis, ut tales sunt, & prout inter se distinguuntur: multoque difficilius esset, tot percipere naturas, quam substantiam & accidens tantum: multoque incredibilius est dari unum conceptum formalem in nobis, qui distincte repraesentet has omnes naturas, quam solam substantiam, & accidens: quod si conceptus formalis entis non ita distincte repraesentat has naturas ut tales sunt, & prout inter se distinguuntur, concluditur, solum repraesentare illas prout inter se se conveniunt, & aliquo modo similes sunt, quod est intentum. Sequela vero patet, quia, ut paulo antea declaravi, inter haec duo non potest in praesenti medium inveniri. Tertium, quia fere eadem ratione, qua dicitur conceptus hic obiectivus entis includere omnia prima genera, vel om⟨74a⟩nes entitates simplices, dicendus esset includere omnes entitates, quantumvis compositas, hominem, leonem &c. secundum proprias rationes suas: quod nullus hactenus dixit. Sequela patet, quia, si ens includit in conceptu suo omnia genera, vel naturas simplices; vel est quia ratio entis ut sic secundum rem non praescindit ab ipsis, vel est, quia illae nihil addunt supra ens, quod non sit ens: vel est, quia ratio entis secundum rationem intelligitur immediate determinari, seu contrahi ad illas natu-

made. And there still remains a like argument with respect to the other member, namely, *accident*. For this also, according to the mentioned authors, is analogical, and at least with respect to some accidents this is perhaps true, as I shall say below.[73] I will therefore likewise inquire whether accident enters into the concept of being according to some common concept or (so to speak) according to a part of the objective concept that is common to all accidents. And against each option one can apply the arguments that have been made, and in the end it can be concluded that this member also must be divided into several others.

The concept of being does not include all the primary genera.

12. Perhaps for this reason, then, other people have said that the adequate object of this formal concept of being is or includes all the primary genera or all the simple entities that immediately divide being. But against this opinion the earlier arguments succeed in the same way. First, because such natures can be included in such a concept neither copulatively, nor disjunctively, nor unqualifiedly and without any bond, as is clear if one applies the argument that was made in the same way. For it has the same force, as will readily be evident to anyone who examines it. Second, from experience, since by virtue of the conception of being we do not perceive all these definite natures of being insofar as they are such and insofar as they are distinguished from each other. Indeed, to perceive so many natures would be much more difficult than to perceive substance and accident alone. In fact, that there is a single formal concept in us that distinctly represents all these natures is much harder to believe than it is to believe that there is a single formal concept in us that represents only substance and accident. But if the formal concept of being does not thus distinctly represent these natures insofar as they are such and insofar as they are distinguished from each other, it follows that it only represents them insofar as they agree among themselves and are in some way similar, as I claim. The consequence is clear, since, as I explained a little earlier, between these two options there can be no intermediate in the present case. Third, because for almost the same reason that this objective concept of being is said to include all the primary genera, or all simple entities, it would have to be said to include all entities, however composite—for instance,

73. See *DM* 39.3.

ras. At vero prima & secunda harum rationum eodem modo procedunt in quacunque entitate, etiam in speciebus infimis, nam secundum rem, non magis praescindit ratio entis a ratione hominis vel equi &c. quam a ratione substantiae & accidentis, neque etiam homo addit supra ens aliquid quod non sit ens, magis quam substantia, vel quantitas &c. Tertia vero ratio non affertur consequenter, quia, si ens ut sic non dicit unam obiectivam rationem seu conceptum: nihil est in ente ut sic, quantum ad rem conceptam, quod proprie dividi, determinari, aut contrahi possit, neque immediate, neque mediate: ergo illa ratio nihil obstat, quominus omnes entitates quaecunque illae sint, includantur in conceptu entis si aliquae dicuntur determinate includi, nec de quibusdam poterit sufficiens ratio assignari magis quam de aliis.

Conceptus entis non includit substantiam explicite, & alia implicite.

13. Propterea tandem aliter dici potest, in obiecto adaequato conceptus formalis entis non includi plures naturas entis determinatas ac distinctas secundum propria, neque omnes sub una aliqua ratione[16] communi; sed unam tantum determinate & expresse, alias vero implicite, & confuse, v. g. naturam substantiae ut sic determinate & expresse, naturas vero accidentium implicite. Sed hic etiam modus non minus efficaciter impugnari potest, quam praecedentes. Primo, quia supra ostendi, per conceptum formalem explicite & determinate repraesentantem substantiam, ut substantia est, nullo modo repraesentari accidentia, neque implicite, neque confuse, si proprie loquamur, ut late declaravi sect. praeced. Secundo hic etiam urgeri potest argumentum

16. Reading "ratione" here with C_1, C_2, G_2, M_1, M_2, M_3, M_4, P_1, P_2, S, V_1, V_2, V_3, and V_4. The following omit "ratione": V_5 and Vivès.

the human being, the lion, etc.—according to their proper natures$_r$, which is something that no one has hitherto claimed. The consequence is clear, since if being includes in its concept all the genera or simple natures, this is because the nature$_r$ of being as such does not in reality prescind from them, or it is because they add nothing to being that is not a being, or else it is because, according to reason, the nature$_r$ of being is understood to be immediately determined or contracted to those natures. But the first and second of these reasons apply in the same way in the case of any entity, even in the case of a lowest species, for in reality the nature$_r$ of being no more prescinds from the nature$_r$ of the human being or from the nature$_r$ of the horse, etc., than it does from the nature$_r$ of substance and the nature$_r$ of accident; nor does human being, any more than substance or quantity, etc., add anything to being that is not a being. The third reason, moreover, is not consistently adduced, since, if being as such does not signify$_d$ a single objective character$_r$ or concept, there is nothing in the case of being as such, as far as the thing$_r$ conceived is concerned, that could properly be divided, determined, or contracted, either immediately or mediately. Therefore, that reason in no way prevents all entities, whichever they may be, from being included in the concept of being if some are said to be included determinately, and no sufficient reason will be able to be assigned in the case of some rather than others.

13. Finally, for these reasons one might take a different tack and claim that neither several determinate natures of being, distinguished in terms of what is proper to them, nor all natures under some one common nature$_r$, are included in the adequate object of the formal concept of being, but only one nature determinately and expressly, and others implicitly and confusedly—for example, the nature of substance as such determinately and expressly, but the natures of accidents implicitly. But this approach, too, can be opposed no less effectively than the preceding ones. First, because I have proved above that, by means of a formal concept that explicitly and determinately represents substance insofar as it is substance, accidents can in no way be represented, either implicitly or confusedly, if we are speaking properly, as I have

The concept of being does not include substance explicitly & other things implicitly.

sumptum ab experientia, ex Scoto,[17] nam experimur de aliqua re nos concipere quod sit ens, & dubitare, an sit substantia, vel accidens, ut v. g. de quantitate, evidenter scimus esse realitatem, an vero sit substantia vel ac⟨74b⟩cidens, vel dubitamus, vel in opinione versatur: ergo in illo conceptu entis non includitur substantia, ut substantia, id est, expresse, & secundum propriam rationem. Tertio, quia alias idem esset conceptus obiectivus entis, & conceptus obiectivus [55a] substantiae; quia conceptus obiectivus substantiae nihil aliud est, quam ratio substantiae determinate & secundum proprium modum ab intellectu conceptae: sed eodem modo dicitur concipi ratio substantiae per conceptum entis. Rursus si in ratione substantiae sic concepta includuntur confuse vel implicite conceptus accidentium, sive significetur nomine entis, sive nomine substantiae, includentur eodem modo, quia ratio concepta est eadem, & modus concipiendi illam est idem, scilicet expresse, ac determinate: conceptus ergo obiectivus substantiae & entis erit idem: consequens autem est plane falsum, & contra communem modum concipiendi: nam haec praedicatio: substantia est substantia, est identica: haec autem minime: substantia est ens: non ergo differunt tantum in nominibus, sed etiam in rationibus obiectivis, quae praedicantur. Item alias perinde esset distribuere omnem substantiam, & omne ens. Item tam falsa esset haec propositio accidens est ens, sicut haec, accidens est substantia: quae omnia sunt plane falsa.

A priori probatio conclusionis.

14. Ultimo ex re ipsa, & quasi a priori probatur nostra sententia contra omnes praedictas, quia omnia entia realia vere habent aliquam similitudinem & convenientiam in ratione essendi: ergo possunt concipi & repraesentari sub ea praecisa ratione, qua inter se conveniunt: ergo possunt sub ea ratione unum conceptum obiectivum constituere: ergo ille est conceptus obiectivus entis. Antecedens per se notum videtur

17. Reading "Scoto" here with S, V_1, and V_2. The following read "Soto" instead: C_1, C_2, G_2, M_1, M_2, M_3, M_4, P_1, P_2, V_3, V_4, V_5, and Vivès.

explained at length in the preceding section.[74] Second, here also an argument taken from experience can be urged, borrowed from Scotus,[75] for we experience that we both conceive of some thing$_{r}$ that it is a being and doubt whether it is a substance or accident. For instance, regarding quantity, we evidently know that it is a reality, but regarding the question of whether it is a substance or accident, we either hesitate or have recourse to opinion. Therefore, substance as substance, i.e., expressly and according to its proper nature$_{r}$, is not included in that concept of being. Third, because otherwise the objective concept of being and the objective concept of substance would be the same, for the objective concept of substance is nothing other than the nature$_{r}$ of substance conceived by the intellect determinately and according to its proper mode. But the nature$_{r}$ of substance is said to be conceived in the same way by means of the concept of being. Again, if concepts of accidents are included confusedly or implicitly in the nature$_{r}$ of substance so conceived, they will be included in the same manner whether it is signified by the name "being" or by the name "substance," for the conceived nature$_{r}$ is the same, and the manner of conceiving it is the same, namely, expressly and determinately. Therefore, the objective concept of substance and the objective concept of being will be the same. But this consequent is plainly false and contrary to the common manner of conceiving, for this predication, "a substance is a substance," is identical, but this one, "a substance is a being," is not at all so. Therefore, they do not differ merely in respect of names, but also in respect of the objective characters$_{r}$ that are predicated. Again: otherwise, to distribute every substance and to distribute every being would come to the same thing. Again: this proposition, "an accident is a being," would be as false as this one, "an accident is a substance." All these claims are plainly false.

An a priori *proof of the conclusion.*

14. Finally, our opinion is proved against all the mentioned ones by appeal to the thing$_{r}$ itself and, as it were, *a priori*: because all real beings truly have some likeness and agreement in the character$_{r}$ of being$_{e}$. Therefore, they can be conceived and represented under that prescinded character$_{r}$ in which they agree with each other. Therefore, they can

74. See *DM* 2.1.7–8.

75. See John Duns Scotus, *Ord.* I, d. 3, p. 1, qq. 1–2, ns. 27–34, in: John Duns Scotus, *Opera omnia*, vol. 3 (Vaticana), pp. 18–21.

ex terminis: nam, sicut ens & non ens sunt primo diversa & opposita, propter quod dicitur esse primum principium omnium, *quodlibet esse vel non esse*, ita quodlibet ens habet aliquam convenientiam & similitudinem cum quolibet ente: maiorem enim convenientiam invenit intellectus inter substantiam, & accidens, quam inter substantiam & non ens seu nihil: creatura etiam participat aliquo modo esse Dei, & ideo dicitur saltem esse vestigium eius propter aliquam convenientiam, & similitudinem in essendo: qua ratione ex esse creaturae investigamus esse Dei, & similiter ex esse accidentis, esse substantiae. Denique hac ratione tribuimus ⟨75a⟩ illis proprietates aliquas seu attributa communia, ut habere bonitatem aliquam, vel perfectionem, posse agere, vel se communicare, & similia: est ergo in re ipsa aliqua convenientia & similitudo inter entia omnia realia. Prima consequentia etiam est per se satis clara, tum quia omnia entia sub illa ratione & convenientia sunt cognoscibilia: tum etiam quia hac ratione aliae res, quae habent inter se convenientiam aliquam, sub ea concipiuntur unite & coniunctim magis autem vel minus pro ratione maioris, vel minoris convenientiae: tum denique quia in re est fundamentum sufficiens ad hunc modum concipiendi, & in intellectu non deest virtus & efficacia ad huiusmodi conceptionis modum, nam est summe abstractivus, & praecisivus rationum omnium. Et hinc etiam facilis est secunda consequentia, quia, ut diximus, unitas conceptus obiectivi non consistit in unitate reali, & numerali, sed in unitate formali, seu fundamentali, quae nihil aliud est, quam praedicta convenientia & similitudo. Ultima vero consequentia evidens est praesuppositis aliis, quia, si talis conceptus obiectivus est possibilis ille est transcendens, simplicissimus, & hoc modo primus omnium, quae sunt attributa conceptus entis. Item illa convenientia fundatur in actu essendi, qui est veluti formale in conceptu entis, unde etiam sumitur argumentum, quod sicut conceptus obiectivus ipsius esse seu existentiae unus est, ita etiam conceptus entis. Tandem omnia
D. Thom. fundantur in eo quod supra ex D. Thom. adduximus, quod analogia entis non est [55b] in aliqua forma, quae intrinsece tantum sit in uno analogato, & extrinsece in aliis, sed in esse seu entitate quae intrinsece participatur ab omnibus: in illa ergo ratione habent omnia realem convenientiam, & consequenter unitatem obiectivam in ratione entis.

constitute one objective concept under that $character_r$. Therefore, this is the objective concept of being. The antecedent seems to be $known_n$ *per se* on the basis of the terms, for just as being and non-being are primarily diverse and opposed—for which reason "any given thing either is or is not" is said to be the first of all principles—so also does any given being have some agreement or similarity with any given being. For the intellect finds a greater agreement between substance and accident than between substance and non-being or nothing. A creature also participates in some way in the $being_e$ of God and is therefore said at least to be an image of him on account of some agreement or similarity in $being_e$—for which reason we investigate the $being_e$ of God by appeal to the $being_e$ of the creature, and similarly, by appeal to the $being_e$ of an accident we investigate the $being_e$ of a substance. Finally, it is for this reason that we attribute to them some common properties or attributes, for instance, having some goodness or perfection, being able to act or communicate themselves, and the like. There is, therefore, in reality some agreement or likeness among all real beings. The first consequence also is clear enough *per se*, because all beings are cognizable under that $character_r$ and agreement. And also because, for this reason, other $things_r$ that have some agreement among themselves are conceived under that agreement in a united and common fashion, more or less so in accordance with a $basis_r$ of greater or lesser agreement. And also, finally, because in reality there is a sufficient foundation for this manner of conceiving, and in the intellect power and efficacy are not lacking for such a mode of conception, since the intellect is in the highest degree abstractive and precisive of all $natures_r$. And hence also the second consequence is easy, since, as we have said, the unity of the objective concept does not consist in a real and numerical unity, but in a formal or fundamental unity, which is nothing other than the mentioned agreement and likeness. The final consequence is evident when the others are presupposed, since, if such an objective concept is possible, it is transcendent, the simplest, and in this way the first of them all, and these are attributes of the concept of being. Again, that agreement is founded on the act of $being_e$, which is, as it were, something formal in the concept of being, and on this also is based the argument that, just as the objective concept of $being_e$ or existence is one, so also is the

Posterior assertio.

Conceptus entis obiectivus praecisus est ab omni ratione particulari.

15. Dico secundo. Hic conceptus obiectivus est secundum rationem praecisus ab omnibus particularibus, seu membris dividentibus ens, etiam si sint maxime simplices entitates. Haec conclusio videtur mihi necessario consequens ex praecedente: quia cum omnia entia determinata aliquo modo dividentia ens sint inter se distincta, & plura obiective, non possunt intelligi convenire in unum obiectivum conceptum nisi saltem secundum rationem fiat praecisio, & ⟨75b⟩ abstractio a propriis rationibus in quibus distinguuntur. Sed, quia tota difficultas in hac abstractione & praecisione consistit, prius declaranda est, & postea conclusio per se & ex propriis probanda.

16. Est ergo advertendum, abstractionem seu praecisionem intellectus non requirere distinctionem rerum, seu praecisionem alicuius rationis, vel modi, quae ex natura rei antecedat in re ipsa praecisionem intellectus, sed in re simplicissima posse fieri huiusmodi praecisionem variis modis, scilicet, vel per modum formae a subiecto, vel e contrario per modum subiecti a forma: vel per modum formae a forma, ut in Deo praescindimus Deum ut sic a suo actu voluntatis, & actum voluntatis a Deo, & actum voluntatis ab actu intellectus: & similiter praescindimus subsistentiam Dei a natura Dei tanquam modum eius, non quod intellectus affirmet esse modum, sed quod instar modi ex parte sua illam concipiat. Sic igitur abstrahit & praescindit intellectus aliquid ab aliquo tanquam commune a particulari, non ob distinctionem vel praecisionem, quae in re antecedat, sed ob imperfectum, confusum, seu inadaequatum modum concipiendi suum; ratione cuius in obiecto, quod considerat, non comprehendit totum, quod est in illo, prout a parte rei existit, sed solum secundum aliquam convenientiam vel similitu-

concept of being. Finally, all of this is founded on what we adduced above by appeal to St. Thomas, that the analogy of being is not based on some form that is intrinsically in one analogate alone and extrinsically in the rest, but on being$_e$ or entity, in which all of them participate intrinsically. Therefore, all things have a real agreement in that nature$_r$ and consequently an objective unity in the nature$_r$ of being.

St. Thomas.

Second assertion.

The objective concept of being is prescinded from every particular nature$_r$.

15. I say, second: this objective concept is rationally prescinded from all particulars or members that divide being, even though they are entities that are simple in the highest degree. This conclusion seems to me to follow necessarily from the preceding one, for since all determinate beings that in some way divide being are distinct from each other and objectively several, they cannot be understood to agree in a single objective concept unless precision and abstraction is made, according to reason at least, from the proper natures$_r$ in terms of which they are distinguished. But, since the entire difficulty consists in this abstraction and precision, it must first be explained, and then the conclusion will have to be proved *per se* and by appeal to things proper [to the case of being].

16. It must, therefore, be observed that an abstraction or precision of the intellect does not require a distinction of things$_r$, or a precision of some nature$_r$ or mode, that *ex natura rei* really precedes the precision of the intellect. Rather, in the case of a most simple thing$_r$, a precision of this type can be made in various ways, namely, in the manner of a form from a subject, or contrariwise, in the manner of a subject from a form, or in the manner of a form from a form, just as, in the case of God, we prescind God as such from his act of will, and an act of will from God, and an act of his will from an act of his intellect. And similarly, we prescind the subsistence of God from the nature of God as a mode of his, not because the intellect affirms that it is a mode, but because for its part the intellect conceives God's subsistence in the manner of a mode. It is in this way, then, that the intellect abstracts and prescinds something from something as common from particular—not on account of a distinction or precision that in reality precedes [the operation of the intellect], but on account of the intellect's imperfect,

dinem quam plures res inter se habent, quae per modum unius sub ea ratione considerantur. Quo fit, ut ad conceptum obiectivum praecisum secundum rationem ab aliis rebus seu conceptibus, non sit necessaria praecisio rerum secundum se, sed sufficiat denominatio quaedam a conceptu formali repraesentante illum obiectivum, quia scilicet per illum non repraesentatur obiectum illud secundum id totum quod est in re, sed solum secundum talem rationem convenientiae, ut patet in conceptu obiectivo hominis ut sic, qui secundum rationem praecisus dicitur a Petro, Paulo, & aliis singularibus, a quibus in re non differt. Illa autem praecisio secundum rationem est denominatio a conceptu formali: quia nimirum homo, ut obiicitur tali conceptui, non est repraesentatus secundum omnem modum quo in re existit, sed secundum convenientiam quam plures homines habent, qui per modum unius sub ea ratione concipiuntur.

Ratio conclusionis.

17. Sic ergo explicata hac praecisione rationis in conceptu obiectivo, non est difficile ostendere reperiri in con⟨76a⟩ceptu obiectivo entis, quia per conceptum formalem entis, neque Deus, neque substantia creata, neque accidens repraesentantur, secundum modum quo in re sunt; neque prout inter se differunt: sed solum prout aliquo modo inter se conveniunt ac similia sunt: ergo id quod immediate & adaequate obiicitur huic conceptui formali, est secundum rationem prae[56a]cisum a proprio conceptu obiectivo substantiae, vel accidentis. Antecedens probatum est praecedente conclusione adiunctis etiam quae dicta sunt superiori sectione: consequentia vero patet, quia praecisio secundum rationem in nullo alio consistit, ut explicatum est. Et confirmatur primo, nam conceptus obiectivus entis secundum rationem non est conceptus obiectivus substantiae, aut accidentis, aut alicuius alterius determinati generis: neque etiam est aggregatum ex omnibus illis: ergo est aliquid unum secundum rationem praecisum ab illis. Maior & minor probatae sunt in superioribus; consequentia patet, quia haec praecisio

confused, or inadequate mode of conceiving. By virtue of this, in the case of an object that it considers, the intellect does not grasp all that is in the object as it exists *a parte rei*, but rather [grasps the object] only in accordance with some agreement or likeness that several things$_r$ have among themselves, which things$_r$ are considered in the manner of one thing under that character$_r$. From this it results that, for an objective concept which is rationally prescinded from other things$_r$ or concepts, a precision of things$_r$ in themselves is not necessary. Rather, a certain denomination from the formal concept which represents that objective concept is sufficient—since, namely, by means of that concept that object is not represented in accordance with all that there is in reality, but only in accordance with such a type$_r$ of agreement, as is clear in the case of the objective concept of the human being as such, which is said to be rationally prescinded from Peter, Paul and other singulars, from whom it does not differ in reality.[76] But that rational precision is a denomination from the formal concept, since, without doubt, the human being, as the object of such a concept, is not represented in accordance with every mode in which she exists in reality, but in accordance with the agreement that obtains among several human beings who are conceived in the manner of one thing under that character$_r$.

Argument for the conclusion.

17. Having thus explained this precision of reason in the case of an objective concept, it is not difficult to prove that it is found in the case of the objective concept of being, since, by means of the formal concept of being, neither God, nor created substance, nor accident is represented in accordance with the mode in which it exists$_e$ in reality, nor are these represented insofar as they differ from each other, but only insofar as they agree with each other in some way and are similar. Therefore, that which immediately and adequately serves as the object of this formal concept is rationally prescinded from the proper objective concepts of substance and accident. The antecedent is proved by means of the preceding conclusion, together with the things that were said in the previous section. And the consequence is clear, since a rational precision consists in nothing else, as has been explained. And it is confirmed, in the first place, because the objective concept of being, according to reason, is not the

76. Cf. *DM* 5.2.9.

secundum rationem solum consistit in distinctione rationis in ordine ad conceptus formales. Confirmatur secundo, nam propter hanc praecisionem haec non est identica: *substantia est ens*: neque haec, *accidens est ens*: & tamen utraque est vera, quia in eis intelligitur praedicari aliquid commune utrique, & secundum rationem ab utroque distinctum. Et hac etiam ratione, ut supra argumentabamur, fieri potest, ut post conceptionem alicuius sub ratione entis, dubitetur an sit substantia vel accidens, quod sine distinctione saltem rationis neque intelligi potest. Confirmatur tertio quia non alia ratione datur conceptus obiectivus substantiae secundum rationem praecisus ab omnibus substantiis: & accidentis ab accidentibus, nisi propter convenientiam quam habent, & secundum quam praecise concipi possunt: ergo idem dicendum est de conceptu entis.

Evasio refellitur.

18. Fortasse aliquis respondebit non esse convenientiam realem inter omnia entia in ratione entis, sicut est inter omnes substantias in ratione substantiae, vel inter accidentia in ratione accidentis. Sed, vel est sensus inter entia ut sic nullam esse realem convenientiam, vel non esse tantam quanta est inter alia. Primum est plane falsum, neque intelligi potest nisi ab his, qui existimant accidens v. g. non dici ens nisi extrinseca denominatione, sicut medicina dicitur sana, ut interdum videtur insinuare ⟨76b⟩ Caiet. opusc. de analo. nom. c. 2. sed non est verisimile, eum ita sensisse, ut dicetur latius infra tractando de analogia entis, & expresse idem Caiet. 1. p. q. 13. art. 5. docet ens, licet analogice dicatur de Deo & creaturis, intrinsece de illis dici: & per se quidem notum videtur non posse aliquid esse reale ens per denominationem extrinsecam: nam haec est propria ratio vel fundamentum entium rationis, ut postea dicetur: necesse est ergo, ut quod est ens reale, sit tale realiter ac formaliter per suam intrinsecam entitatem, quae est idem cum ipso, & inseparabilis ab ipso, etiam si reliqua omnia ab eo praescindi, vel

objective concept of substance, or accident, or any other determinate genus. Nor also is it something aggregated from all of these. Therefore, it is some one thing rationally prescinded from them. The major and minor were proved above. The consequence is clear, since this rational precision consists only in a distinction of reason in relation to formal concepts. It is confirmed, in the second place, because on account of this precision the proposition, "a substance is a being," is not identical, nor is this one, "an accident is a being," and nevertheless both are true, since in them something is understood to be predicated that is common to both substance and accident and also rationally distinct from both substance and accident. And for this reason also, as we argued above,[77] it can happen that, after conceiving something under the character$_r$ of being, we doubt whether it is a substance or an accident, which is something that cannot be understood without a distinction, at least a rational one. It is confirmed, in the third place, because there is an objective concept of substance that is rationally prescinded from all substances, as well as an objective concept of accident that is rationally prescinded from all accidents, for no reason other than the agreement they have, and in accordance with which they can be precisely conceived. Therefore, the same must be said of the concept of being.

An evasion is refuted.

18. Someone will perhaps reply that there is not a real agreement between all beings in the nature$_r$ of being, as there is among all substances in the nature$_r$ of substance, or as there is among accidents in the nature$_r$ of accident. But the view is either that there is no real agreement among beings as such, or that there is not as much as there is among other things. The first is plainly false, nor can it be understood except by those who judge that an accident, for example, is not called a being except by extrinsic denomination, in the way medicine is called healthy, as Cajetan seems at times to suggest in the short work *On the Analogy of Names*, ch. 2.[78] But it is not likely that he thought this, as will be said more fully below when treating of the analogy of being. And the same Cajetan, in *ST* I, q. 13, art. 5, expressly teaches that being, although

77. *DM* 2.2.13.

78. Cajetan, *Scripta Philosophica: De Nominum Analogia, De Conceptu Entis*, pp. 13–14 (n. 10). Cf. Cajetan, *Scripta Philosophica: De Nominum Analogia, De Conceptu Entis*, pp. 14–15 (n. 11).

separari intelligantur: & ita etiam accidentia, licet entitas substantiae ab eis separetur, intelliguntur intrinsece retinere suam entitatem, qua sunt entia realia, & ideo supra cum D. Tho. dicebamus, analogiam entis non excludere, quin formalis ratio significata per ens intrinsece in omnibus analogatis reperiatur. Hinc autem necessario sequitur, ut illa habeant inter se aliquam realem convenientiam secundum suam intrinsecam rationem entis, ut supra etiam probatum est: Quod autem haec convenientia fortasse non sit tanta, quanta est inter substantias, vel accidentia inter se in propriis rationibus, ad rem praesentem non refert, nam ad summum concludit, unitatem conceptus entis non esse tantam, non vero quod non sit aliqua & sufficiens ad praecisionem conceptus obiectivi secundum rationem: Sicut etiam non est tanta convenientia inter substantias ut sic, quanta est inter homines: & nihilominus utraque sufficit ad uni[56b]tatem & praecisionem conceptus obiectivi.

19. Aliter potest responderi, & assignari differentia, quia ratio entis est intima omnibus, & ideo non videtur posse praescindi, etiam secundum rationem, ab aliquibus, aliae vero rationes non sunt tam intimae rebus. Sed haec etiam differentia nulla est, si cum proportione sumatur, nam etiam rationes[18] substantiae & accidentis communissime sumptae intime sunt in omnibus substantiis, & accidentibus, sub quacunque ratione praescindantur, & considerentur. Hoc ergo nihil impedit ad praecisionem conceptus obiectivi, maxime cum ostensum sit, hanc praecisionem non fundari semper in aliqua distinctione rei, sed solum

18. Reading "rationes substantiae & accidentis" here in accordance with Charles Berton's emendation in the Vivès edition. See Francisco Suárez, *Opera Omnia*, vol. 27, p. 363b. The following read "ratio entis substantiae & accidentis" instead: C_1, C_2, G_2, M_1, M_2, M_3, M_4, P_1, P_2, S, V_1, V_2, V_3, and V_5. (Scan of V_4 is missing the relevant portion.)

said analogically of God and creatures, is said of them intrinsically.[79] And indeed, it seems to be known$_{n}$ *per se* that something cannot be a real being by extrinsic denomination, for this is the proper nature$_{r}$ or foundation of beings of reason, as will be said hereafter.[80] It is therefore necessary that what is a real being is such really and formally through its intrinsic entity, which is the same as itself and inseparable from itself, even if everything else is understood to be prescinded or separated from it. And thus accidents, too, even if a substance's entity is separated from them, are understood intrinsically to retain their entity, by virtue of which they are real beings. And therefore, earlier, we said with St. Thomas that the analogy of being does not prevent its being the case that the formal character$_{r}$ signified by "being" is found intrinsically in all of its analogates.[81] From this it necessarily follows that they have some real agreement with each other in accordance with their intrinsic character$_{r}$ of being, as was also proved above. And that this agreement is perhaps not as great as that which obtains among substances, or among accidents, in respect of their proper natures$_{r}$ is not relevant to the matter at hand. For at most this proves that the unity of the concept of being is not as great, but it does not prove that there is not some agreement that is sufficient for the rational precision of an objective concept. It is likewise the case that there is not as much agreement among substances as such as there is among human beings, and yet each of these agreements suffices for the unity and precision of an objective concept.

19. One can respond in another way by positing a difference, namely, that the nature$_{r}$ of being is inmost in all things and therefore seems not to admit of being prescinded from some things even rationally, whereas other natures$_{r}$ are not so deeply in things$_{r}$. But this difference also comes to nothing, if it is taken proportionately, for the natures$_{r}$ of substance and accident as well, taken in the most common way, are inmost in all substances and accidents, under whatever conception$_{r}$ they are prescinded and considered. This, therefore, in no way prevents the precision of an objective concept, especially since it has been shown that this precision is not always founded on some real distinction, but

79. Thomas Aquinas, *Sancti Thomae Aquinatis opera omnia* (Leonina), t. 4, p. 149b.
80. See *DM* 54.1.4–7.
81. See *DM* 2.1.14, above.

in tali concipiendi modo, quo res sub una habitudine, & non sub alia consideretur.[19]

20. Contra hanc vero doctrinam multa obiici possunt, quae ⟨77a⟩ partim attingunt analogiam entis, partim distinctionem, vel inclusionem eius in omnibus rebus vel modis determinantibus ipsum, de quibus in sequentibus dicendum est. Nunc solum illud obiicitur, quia ex dictis sequitur praedicamenta non esse primo diversa, quia in aliqua ratione communi conveniunt. Respondetur praedicamenta non dici primo diversa, quia in nullo conveniant, cum constet plures convenientias vel similitudines inter varia praedicamenta intercedere, nam praedicamenta accidentium praeter rationem[20] entis conveniunt in ratione accidentis, quaedam etiam conveniunt in ratione accidentis absoluti, & distinguuntur a respectivis, &c. Dicuntur ergo primo diversa, quia in nullo genere conveniunt, ut Porphyrius significavit in capite de specie. Item, quia non propriis differentiis differunt, sed se ipsis, ut ex dicendis sectione 6.[21] constabit.

Altera evasio refutatur.

Corollaria ex superiori doctrina.

Modus intrinsecus substantiae vel accidentis non includitur in conceptu entis.

21. Ex his infero primo in hoc conceptu entis obiectivo, & sic praeciso non includi actu modos intrinsecos substantiae vel aliorum membrorum, quae dividunt ens. Patet, quia vel includerentur, ut constituentes illum conceptum entis, vel ut dividentes. Non primum, quia impossibile est unum ut unum modis seu differentiis oppositis constitui. Neque etiam secundum, quia iam ille conceptus actu esset divisus in duos, & ita ille conceptus non esset unus, cuius oppositum probatum est. Et confirmo, nam interrogo, quid sit actu includere illos modos: aut enim est, quod in re ipsa communis ille conceptus entis actu includat,

19. Reading "consideretur" here with S, V_1, and V_2. The following read "consideratur" instead: C_1, C_2, G_2, M_1, M_2, M_{33}, M_4, P_1, P_2, V_3, V_5, and Vivès. (Scan of V_{44} is missing the relevant portion.)

20. Reading "rationem" here with C_1, C_2, G_2, M_1, M_2, M_3, M_4, P_1, P_2, S, V_1, V_2, and V_3. Vivès and V_5 have "rationes" here. (Scan of V_4 is missing the relevant portion.)

21. Reading "6" here with C_1, C_2, G_2, M_1, M_2, M_3, M_4, P_1, P_2, S, V_1, V_2, V_3, and V_5. Vivès reads "5" instead. (Scan of V_4 is missing the relevant portion.)

only on that manner of conceiving by which a thing$_r$ is considered under one relation but not under another.

20. But against this doctrine many things can be objected, things which partly touch on the analogy of being, and partly on being's distinction from, or inclusion in, all things$_r$ or modes that determine it, about which it will be necessary to speak in what follows.[82] For now, only this is objected: from the things that have been said it follows that the categories are not primarily diverse, since they agree in some common nature$_r$. I reply that the categories are not called primarily diverse because they agree in nothing, since it is clear that several agreements or similarities obtain among various categories, for the accidental categories agree not only in the nature$_r$ of being, but also in the nature$_r$ of accident, and some of them also agree in the nature$_r$ of absolute accident and are distinguished from relative accidents, etc. Therefore, they are called primarily diverse because they agree in no genus, as Porphyry indicates in the chapter on species.[83] Also, because they do not differ by means of proper differences, but by themselves, as will be clear from the things to be said in section 6.

Another evasion is refuted.

Corollaries of the preceding doctrine.

21. From these things I infer, first, that the intrinsic modes of substance and of the other members that divide being are not actually included in this objective and thus prescinded concept of being. This is clear, since they would be included either as things which constitute that concept of being or as things that divide it. Not the first, since it is impossible for one thing, insofar as it is one, to be constituted by opposed modes or differences. Nor also the second, since that concept would already be actually divided into two concepts, and so that concept would not be one, the opposite of which has been proved. And I confirm this, for I ask what actually including those modes means: for either it means that in reality this common concept of being, in those things$_r$ in which it exists, actually includes those modes, or it means that those

The intrinsic mode of substance or accident is not included in the concept of being.

82. See *DM* 2.5 and 2.6.

83. Adolfus Busse, ed., *Commentaria in Aristotelem Graeca*, vol. 4, part 1 (Berolini: Typis et Impensis Georgii Reimer, 1887), p. 4, ll. 16–17; p. 5. ll. 9–12 and ll. 17–18; p. 6, ll. 5–12.

in rebus illis, in quibus existit, illos modos: aut est, quod in mente seu in conceptu illo obiectivo, ut praecise terminante talem conceptum formalem, includantur actu illi modi oppositi. Primum horum est verum, sed non est ad rem, quia hic conceptus obiectivus consideratur, ut praecisus, & adaequatus conceptui formali entis ut sic: & non secundum totam realitatem, quam in re habet in omnibus inferioribus suis: hoc enim modo conceptus entis nec praecisus esse potest, neque unus, cum includat actu totum id, quod ad distinctionem omnium generum, & conceptuum necessarium est: nec proprie ac vere dici potest conceptus entis ut sic, sed sunt potius plures conceptus omnium entium secundum totas realitates eorum, [57a] a quibus con⟨77b⟩ceptus praecisus entis re ipsa non distinguitur. Confirmatur, nam hoc modo, etiam conceptus hominis dici potest actu includere omnia individua, quia conceptus obiectivus hominis prout in re ipsa existit, realiter includit ipsa individua, & proprios modos eorum, nec magis distinguitur in re homo a suis individuis, quam distinguitur[22] ens a substantia, accidente, & aliis generibus, ut inferius constabit, valde autem improprie propter hanc causam dicetur conceptus obiectivus hominis actu includere omnia individua, seu principia individuantia eorum. Loquendo autem de conceptu entis praeciso in alio sensu, qui magis est ad rem, falsum est, includere actu modos oppositos inferiorum generum, quia ut sic solum includit id quod repraesentatur per conceptum formalem eius: per illum autem conceptum formalem non repraesentantur hi modi expresse ac distincte secundum proprias rationes eorum, quia intellectus ut sic concipiens, nihil horum percipit, ut ex dictis, & ex ipsa etiam experientia notum est, & ex aliis similibus: non enim alia ratione homo dicitur non includere actu individua, sed potentia tantum, nisi quia ut repraesentatur per conceptum praecisum hominis, non consideratur in illo aliqua individualis ratio, sed solum ratio hominis.

Ens non significat immediate substantiam, vel accidens.

22. Secundo infertur hanc vocem, *ens*, non significare immediate substantiam vel accidens, aut alia genera seu entitates simplices se-

22. Reading "distinguitur" with V_1 and V_2. S reads "distinguatur" instead. The following read "dividitur" instead: C_1, C_2, G_2, M_1, M_2, M_3, M_4, P_1, P_2, V_3, V_5, and Vivès. (Scan of V_4 is missing the relevant portion.)

opposed modes are actually included in the mind or in this objective concept insofar as it precisely terminates such a formal concept. The first of these is true, but is not relevant, since this objective concept is being considered as prescinded and adequate to the formal concept of being as such, and not in accordance with that whole reality which it really has in all of its inferiors. For in the latter way the concept of being cannot be prescinded or one, since it actually includes all that is necessary for the distinction of all genera and concepts, nor can it properly and truly be called the concept of being as such, but there are, rather, multiple concepts of all beings in accordance with their entire realities, from which the prescinded concept of being is not really distinguished. And this is confirmed, for the concept of the human being as well can in this way be said actually to include all individuals, since the objective concept of the human being, as it exists in reality, really includes the same individuals and their proper modes, nor is human being more distinguished in reality from its individuals than being is distinguished from substance, accident, and the other genera, as will become clear below.[84] But the objective concept of the human being will very improperly be said actually to include, for this reason, all individuals or their individuating principles. However, speaking of the prescinded concept of being in the other way, which is more relevant to the matter at hand, it is false that it actually includes the opposed modes of the lower genera, since, as such, it only includes what is represented by its formal concept. But these modes are not represented by that formal concept expressly and distinctly according to their proper natures$_r$, since the intellect, insofar as it conceives in this way, perceives nothing of them, as is known$_n$ from the things that have been said, from experience itself, and from other similar cases. For human being is not said to include individuals actually, but only potentially, for no other reason than because, insofar as it is represented by the prescinded concept of the human being, no individual nature$_r$ is considered in it, but only the nature$_r$ of the human being.

"Being" does not signify substance or accident immediately.

22. Second, it is inferred that this word "being" does not immediately signify substance, or accident, or other genera or simple entities according to their proper natures$_r$, but the objective concept of being

84. See *DM* 5.2.8–9.

cundum proprias rationes earum, sed conceptum obiectivum entis ut sic, & ratione illius genera seu entitates, in quibus in re ipsa existit. Ita sentiunt omnes autores citati, tam hic, quam in conclusione sectionis praecedentis praesertim Scot. in 1.[23] d. 3. q. 1. & 3. citantur etiam Avicen. 1. suae Metaph. c. 4. Algazel. c. 6. & sumitur ex D. Tho. cit. locis, & de ente & essentia c. 1. ubi Caie. in re idem sentit quanvis ab Scoto differat, & constituat in hoc differentiam inter ens & alia nomina significantia determinata genera, vel species: sed re vera nulla intercedit, quae ad rem praesentem multum spectet, praeter eam, quae tractanda est sect. seq. Unde potius hoc declaratur, & probatur primo exemplo hominis (& idem est de similibus) significat enim immediate hominem, & mediate Petrum, in quo a parte rei ratio hominis reperitur: ergo similiter ens, &c. Probatur conseq.[24] ex paritate rationis, quia utrobique nomen est ⟨78a⟩ commune, & utrobique conceptus obiectivus est secundum rationem praecisus ab inferioribus, & nomen non significat illa, nisi ob aliquam convenientiam, quam inter se habent.

23. Secundo declaratur a priori, quia, sicut voces exprimunt conceptus formales mentis, ita etiam immediate significant obiecta quae per huiusmodi conceptus immediate repraesentantur: nam in tantum deserviunt ad exprimendos conceptus, in quantum illud ipsum, quod conceptus naturaliter repraesentant voces ex impositione significant, & ideo vox interdum in communi imponitur: quia conceptus, quem exprimit, communis etiam est: ergo illud ipsum, quod est immediatum obiectum formalis conceptus, est immediatum significatum vocis adaequatae illi conceptui: huiusmodi autem est haec vox, *ens*, respectu conceptus formalis entis.

23. Reading "Scot. in 1." here in accordance with Charles Berton's emendation in the Vivès edition. See Francisco Suárez, *Opera Omnia*, vol. 27, p. 363b. All earlier editions read "sect. 1." instead.

24. Reading "conseq." here with the older editions. Vivès reads "consequens" here.

as such and, by reason of this, the genera or entities in which it really exists. This is the view of all the authors cited both here and in the conclusion of the preceding section, especially Scotus, *Sent.* I, d. 3, q. 1 and q. 3.[85] Cited also are Avicenna, in book I, ch. 4, of his *Metaphysics*,[86] and Al-Ghazali, ch. 6,[87] and it is taken from St. Thomas, in the places cited,[88] and in *On Being and Essence*, ch. 1,[89] where Cajetan really believes the same, although he differs from Scotus and on this founds a difference between "being" and other names that signify determinate genera or species.[90] But really there is no difference that has much to do with the present matter, aside from that which is to be discussed in later sections. For this reason it is, rather, made clear and proved, in the first place, by the example of "human being" (and the same is true in similar cases), for it immediately signifies human being and mediately Peter, in whom *a parte rei* the nature$_r$ of the human being is found. Therefore, similarly in the case of "being," etc. The consequence is proved by parity of reasoning, since in both cases the name is common, and in both cases the objective concept is rationally prescinded from inferiors, and the name does not signify them except on account of some agreement that they have among themselves.

23. Second, it is made clear *a priori*, since, just as words express formal concepts of the mind, so also do they immediately signify the objects immediately represented by such concepts. For words serve to express concepts to the extent that they signify, by imposition, the same

85. See *DM* 2.2.5 above.

86. In the 1508 Venice edition of various philosophical works by Avicenna, book (or treatise) I, ch. 4, of his *Metaphysics* coincides with part of what the modern edition labels treatise I, ch. 3. See Avicenna, *Avicenne perhypatetici philosophi: Ac medicorum facile primi opera in lucem redacta* (Venetiis: Heredes Octaviani Scoti, 1508), fols. 71va–72ra, and Avicenna, *Liber de philosophia prima, sive scientia divina I–IV*, pp. 23–27. However, in neither edition does the text labeled book I, ch. 4, offer anything like a discussion of the immediate significate of the word "being." Suárez seems rather to have book I, ch. 2, in mind. See Avicenna, *Avicenne perhypatetici philosophi: Ac medicorum facile primi opera in lucem redacta*, fol. 70vb, and Avicenna, *Liber de philosophia prima, sive scientia divina I–IV*, pp. 12–13.

87. Al-Ghazali, *Algazel's Metaphysics* (Toronto: Institute of Mediaeval Studies, 1933), pp. 24–26.

88. See ns. 66, 67, and 69 above.

89. Thomas Aquinas, *Sancti Thomae de Aquina opera omnia*, t. 43 (Roma: Editori di San Tommaso, 1976), p. 369b.

90. Cajetan, *In De Ente et Essentia D. Thomae Aquinatis Commentaria*, pp. 23–29 (ns. 11–14).

24. Tertio, hoc amplius declaratur, quia haec vox, *ens*, ita significat plura, ut ex unica & prima impositione illa omnia comprehendat: ergo signum est non significare illa immediate, sed medio aliquo con[57b] ceptu obiectivo communi omnibus illis. Antecedens declaratur ex differentia inter analogiam huius vocis, & aliarum, quae per solam proportionalitatem, vel extrinsecam habitudinem ad unum analoga sunt: nam in caeteris semper vox ex primaeva impositione significat unum tantum, postea vero per Metaphoram aliquam translata est ad significandum aliud: unde fit ut immediate significet utrumque, quasi duplici impositione & significatione. In quo cum aequivocis conveniunt, solumque differunt, quod in aequivocis utraque impositio est aeque prima, & [una[25]] non manat ab altera, sicut in praedictis analogis. Exempla sunt, *risus* ex prima impositione solum significat quandam hominis actionem, postea vero translata est haec vox ad significandam agri amoenitatem: similiter *sanum* ex prima impositione significat solum sanitatem in animali existentem, deinde vero translatum est ad significanda alia quae habent habitudinem ad sanitatem animalis. Et ratio est, tum quia haec multiplex significatio & impositio non est orta[26] ex uno conceptu, sed ex multis, tum etiam, quia non fundatur in reali convenientia rerum significatarum, sed solum in extrinseca habitudine, vel proportione. At vero nomen, *ens*, ex propria & primaeva impositione habet significationem communem omnibus entibus, ut patet, tum ex communi usu, & apprehensione talis vocis, tum ex formali, vel quasi formali significato ⟨78b⟩ eius, quod est esse, quod de se commune est, & intrinsecum omnibus realibus entibus: tum denique, quia illa impositio orta est ex unico conceptu formali entis ut sic. Atque

25. In his notes on the Vivès edition, Charles Berton plausibly suggests inserting "una" here. See Francisco Suárez, *Opera Omnia*, vol. 27, p. 368a.

26. Reading "orta" with C_1, C_2, G_2, M_1, M_2, M_3, M_4, P_1, P_2, V_3, V_4, V_5, and Vivès. The following read "certa" instead: S, V_1, and V_2.

thing that concepts naturally represent. And thus a word is sometimes imposed in a general way, since the concept that it expresses is also common. Therefore, that very thing which is the immediate object of the formal concept is the immediate significate of the word adequate to that concept, and of this sort is the word "being" in relation to the formal concept of being.

24. Third, this is further made clear because this word "being" signifies various things in such a way that it embraces all of them by virtue of a single and primary imposition. This is, therefore, a sign that it does not signify them immediately, but through the mediation of some objective concept common to them all. The antecedent is made clear by the difference between the analogy of this word and that of other words which are analogical only by proportionality or by extrinsic relation to some one thing. For in cases of the latter sort, the word always signifies only one thing by virtue of its original imposition but is thereafter transferred by means of some metaphor to signify something else, from which it results that the word immediately signifies both things by a kind of twofold imposition and signification. (In this respect the latter analogicals agree with equivocals, and they differ only because in the case of equivocals each imposition is equally primary, and [one] does not arise from the other, as it does in the case of these analogicals.) Examples are: "laughter," which, by virtue of its primary imposition, only signifies a certain action of the human being, but later this word was transferred to signify the loveliness of a field. Similarly, "healthy thing," by virtue of its primary imposition, signifies only health existing in an animal, but later it was transferred to signify other things that have some relation to the health of an animal. And the reason [for this twofold imposition] is: because this manifold signification and imposition did not arise from a single concept, but from many, and also because it is not founded on a real agreement among the things$_r$ signified, but only on an extrinsic relation or proportion. But the name "being," by virtue of its proper and original imposition, has a signification common to all beings, as is clear from the common use and understanding of this word, from its formal, or quasi-formal, significate, which is being$_e$ (which of itself is common and intrinsic to all real beings), and finally, from the fact that that imposition arose from a single formal concept

hinc probata etiam relinquitur prima consequentia, quia una vox non potest ex vi unius impositionis significare plura ut plura, sed ut sunt aliquo modo unum, & ideo de ratione vocis communis est, ut, saltem secundum rationem, & in ordine ad conceptus, quos voces exprimunt, non significet immediate plura ut talia sunt. Quod in praesente ostendi potest, nam ens non significat immediate substantiam solam, alias accidens non esset intrinsece ens, neque etiam significat simul substantiam, ut substantiam, atque[27] accidens ut accidens, ut declarari facile potest, discurrendo per illa tria membra supra posita, quia scilicet nec disiunctive, nec copulative, nec simpliciter, potest illa immediate significare, ut facile patebit applicando argumenta supra facta. Haec enim tria, *conceptus formalis, obiectivus,* & *vox*, proportionem inter se servant, & ideo ab uno ad aliud saepe argumentamur, non quidem vitiosum circulum committendo, sed de unoquoque sumendo, quod nobis notius, aut ab aliis facilius concessum videtur.

25. Quarto argumentor, quia propter hanc immediatam significationem conceptus seu rationis communis entis potest propriissime ens distribui dicendo, omne ens est bonum, & dividi, verbi gratia, in substantiam & accidens, non enim sola vox ibi dividitur, sed quod voce significatur. Propterea etiam optime fit comparatio, dicendo hoc esse perfectius ens, quam illud, quam etiam facit Aristotel. 6. Metaphysic. capit. 1. Ac denique optime utimur hac voce tanquam extremo, vel medio syllogismi, nam vocis unitas non deserviret ad ratiocinandum, nisi ratione unius significati proximi, & immediati. Atque [58a] hoc modo est optima illa communis ratio, quod ens in quantum ens, est obiectum intellectus, vel scientiae Metaphysicae: unde necesse est, ut sit aliquid unum immediate illa voce significatum: haec enim ratio in tantum efficax esse potest, in quantum illud non est utcunque obiectum sed etiam est subiectum, de quo fiunt demonstrationes, & medium ad demonstrandum aliqua de inferioribus. Ultimo accedit experientia saepe tacta, quia audito nomine entis aliquid concipimus, & non substantiam,

27. Reading "atque" here in accordance with Charles Berton's suggestion. See Francisco Suárez, *Opera Omnia*, vol. 27, p. 368a. All earlier editions read "neque" here.

of being as such. And hence the first consequence is also proved, since a single word, by virtue of a single imposition, cannot signify several things insofar as they are several, but only several things insofar as they are in some way one, and therefore it pertains to the nature$_r$ of a common word that, at least according to reason and in relation to the concepts that words express, it does not immediately signify several things insofar as they are such. And this can be shown in the present case, for "being" does not immediately signify substance alone, otherwise an accident would not intrinsically be a being, nor also does it signify at the same time substance as substance and accident as accident, as can easily be shown by considering the three possibilities mentioned earlier: for it can immediately signify these neither disjunctively, nor copulatively, nor unqualifiedly, as is easily seen by applying the arguments made earlier.[91] For these three things—the formal concept, the objective concept, and the word—observe a proportion among themselves, and therefore we often argue from one to another, not indeed reasoning in a vicious circle, but taking from each what is better known$_n$ to us, or assuming what seems more readily conceded by others.

25. I argue, fourth: because, on account of this immediate signification of the common concept or nature$_r$ of being, being can most properly be distributed by saying "every being is good," and it can be divided, for example, into substance and accident, since not only is the word there divided, but also what is signified by the word. For this reason also a comparison is rightly made by saying that this being is more perfect than that one, which Aristotle also does at *Metaph.* VI, ch. 1.[92] And moreover, we correctly use this word as an extreme or middle term in a syllogism, for the unity of a word does not serve for reasoning unless it has a single proximate and immediate significate. And thus the following common argument is best: because being as being is the object of the intellect or the object of the science of metaphysics. Therefore, it is necessary that there be some one thing immediately signified by that word, for this nature$_r$ can serve such a function to the extent that it is, not an object in any way whatsoever, but also a subject about which demonstrations are made, and also a middle term

91. See *DM* 2.2.9–11.

92. Aristotle, *Metaph.* VI, ch. 1, 1026a10–32.

neque accidens. Dici enim non potest (ut aliqui significant) tunc nos sistere in conceptu vocis, quia id est contra experien⟨79a⟩tiam: alium enim conceptum format, qui scit vocis *ens* significationem, quam qui ignorat: hic enim concipit vocem, & ibi sistit, vel dubitat, quid ea voce significetur: ille vero praeter vocem concipit rem significatam, & de significatione nullo modo dubitat, & tamen non concipit substantiam, neque accidens: habet ergo haec vox aliud immediatius significatum.

26. Sed obiicit Soncinas nonnullas rationes quas sequenti sectione afferemus, solum enim probant, ens non significare aliquod medium ex natura rei distinctum a substantia, & accidentibus, non vero quod ratione distingui non possit per confusum mentis conceptum. Obiicit deinde Aristot. 10. Metaphysicae, tex. 8. dicentem, ens significare decem praedicamenta, quod Averroes exponit de prima significatione & sine medio, quem ibi sequitur Alex. Alens. Obiicit secundo Arist. 6. Metap. tex. 4. dicentem, si non dantur entia abstracta a materia, Philosophiam naturalem esse primam Philosophiam, id est, Metaphysicam scientiam ab illa distingui minime posse, quae consequentia non esset bona, si ens ut ens significaret aliquid commune substantiae, & accidenti, nam illud esse posset obiectum Metaphysicae, etiam si non essent immaterialia entia. Tertio obiicere possumus Aristotelem 1. Physic. tex. 25. ubi significat, ens non significare aliquid unum, quod possit esse medium syllogismi, ea enim de causa reiicit illam ratiocinationem Parmenidis. Quicquid est praeter ens, est non ens, sed non ens est nihil: ergo quicquid est praeter ens, est nihil.

for demonstrating certain things regarding its inferiors. Finally, there is also the experience often mentioned, that, when we hear the name "being," we conceive something, but not substance, nor accident. For it cannot be said (as some allege) that in this case we stop at the concept of the word, since that is contrary to experience, for the person who knows the signification of the word "being" forms a concept that is other than the one formed by someone ignorant of its signification. For the latter conceives the word and stops there, or is uncertain about what is signified by that word, but the former conceives the thing$_r$ signified in addition to the name, and regarding the signification she in no way entertains doubts, and yet she does not conceive substance or accident. This word, therefore, has another, more immediate significate.

26. But against this Soncinas offers some arguments that we shall relate in the following section,[93] for they only prove that "being" does not signify some intermediate that is distinct *ex natura rei* from substance and accidents, but not that being cannot be rationally distinguished by means of a confused concept of the mind. He further objects[94] that Aristotle, in *Metaph.* X, text 8, says that "being" signifies the ten categories,[95] which Averroes expounds as having to do with its primary and unmediated signification,[96] and Alexander of Hales there follows Averroes in this.[97] He objects, in the second place,[98] that in *Metaph.* VI, text 4,[99] Aristotle says that if there are no beings abstracted from matter, then natural philosophy is first philosophy, that is, that metaphysical science cannot be distinguished at all from natural philosophy, and this consequence, he says, would not be a good one if being as being signified something common to substance and accident, for this could be the object of metaphysics even if there were no immaterial beings.

93. See *DM* 2.3.10.

94. Paul Soncinas, *Quaestiones Metaphysicales acutissimae*, p. 4a.

95. Aristotle, *Metaph.* X, ch. 2, 1054a13–19.

96. Averroes, *Aristotelis opera cum Averrois Commentariis*, vol. 8 (Venetiis: apud Junctas, 1562), fol. 257G–H.

97. [Ps.-]Alexander of Hales [Alexander Bonini], *In Duodecim Aristotelis Metaphysicae Libros Dilucidissima Expositio* (Venetiis: apud Simonem Galignanum de Karera, 1572), fol. 284rb–va.

98. Paul Soncinas, *Quaestiones Metaphysicales acutissimae*, p. 4a.

99. Aristotle, *Metaph.* VI, ch. 1, 1026a27–29.

27. Quarto obiici potest Aristoteles 7. Metaph. c. 4. tex. 15. dicens, ipsum ens dici de omnibus generibus seu praedicamentis, non tamen similiter, id est non secundum eandem rationem & conceptum. Quinto citatur idem Aristoteles 8. Metaphys. c. 6. tex. 16. dicens, *ipsum ens hoc quidem*, id est, per se & ut tale est, *statim esse substantiam, quale, quantum, &c.* & ideo non poni in definitione, quasi dicat, ens immediate descendere ad prima genera, quibus locis Averroes, Alexander, & D. Th. ita exponunt & sentiunt. Sexto affertur Aris. 1. Prior. c. 28. ubi significat, prima genera talia esse, ut de ipsis nihil dicatur, ut Alexander & Philoponus videntur exponere.

Solutio. 28. Ad primum testimonium respondetur Arist. nihil ibi dicere de significatione immediata, sed solum de ge⟨79b⟩nerali, & aequali praedicatione entis, & unius: nam in omnibus praedicamentis aeque reperiuntur, & inde concludit inter se idem esse. Ad cuius rationis efficaciam necesse non est, ut in hac significatione tollatur omne medium rationis. Unde D. Tho. ibi ait, ens significare naturas decem generum secundum quod sunt actu, vel potentia, in quo satis indicat, non significare illas immediate secundum rationes proprias, sed secundum aliquam communem. Expositio itaque Averrois necessaria nobis non est, quan[58b]quam ipse satis declaret, se solum excludere medium quod sit genus, quodque dicat naturam definitam & proprie contrahibilem, de quo postea dicemus. Ad secundum respondent aliqui, argumentum Aristotelis bonum esse, non tamen fundari in eo, quod ens significare non possit conceptum communem substantiae & accidenti: sed in hoc, quod si nulla esset res abstrahens secundum esse a materia, ratio entis ut sic non abstraheret a materia magis, quam ratio corporis vel entis naturalis, & ideo consideratio entis ut sic non transcenderet limites Philosophiae naturalis, quia tunc materialis substantia esset primum ens, eadem autem est scientia primi entis, & entis communis, ut in

Third, we can object that Aristotle, in *Phys.* I, text 25,[100] indicates that "being" does not signify some one thing that can be the middle term of a syllogism, for this is why he rejects the following argument of Parmenides: Whatever is apart from being is not-being. But not-being is nothing. Therefore, whatever is apart from being is nothing.

27. Fourth, it can be objected that Aristotle, in *Metaph.* VII, ch. 4, text 15,[101] says that being itself is said of all genera or categories, but not in a like manner, that is, not in accordance with the same nature$_r$ and concept. Fifth, the same Aristotle is cited as saying, in *Metaph.* VIII, ch. 6, text 16, that "this being itself indeed," that is, *per se* and insofar as it is such, "is immediately substance, quality, quantity," etc., and is therefore not put in a definition,[102] as if to say that being immediately descends to the primary genera, which is how Averroes, Alexander, and St. Thomas explain and understand these passages.[103] Sixth, Aristotle's *Prior An.* I, ch. 28, is brought forth, where he indicates that the primary genera are such that nothing is said of them,[104] as Alexander and Philoponus seem to explain.[105]

Reply.

28. To the first testimony, I reply that Aristotle says nothing there about immediate signification, but only speaks of the general and equal predication of being and one. For they are found equally in all the categories, and thus he concludes that they are the same as each other. For the effectiveness of this argument it is not necessary that every intermediate nature$_r$ be excluded from this signification. For this reason, St. Thomas says in connection with this passage that "being" signifies the natures of the ten genera according as they exist$_e$ actually or potentially,[106] and in this way he makes it sufficiently clear that it does not

100. Aristotle, *Phys.* I, ch. 3, 186a22–32.

101. Aristotle, *Metaph.* VII, ch. 4, 1030a27–b4.

102. Aristotle, *Metaph.* VIII, ch. 6, 1045a36–b3.

103. Averroes, *Aristotelis opera cum Averrois Commentariis*, vol. 8, fols. 224K–225A, [Ps.-]Alexander of Hales [Alexander Bonini], *In Duodecim Aristotelis Metaphysicae Libros Dilucidissima Expositio*, fol. 258va–vb, Thomas Aquinas, *In duodecim libros metaphysicorum Aristotelis expositio*, pp. 420b–21a (bk. VIII, lect. 5, n. 1763).

104. Aristotle, *Pr. An.* I, ch. 27, 43a29–30.

105. Philoponus, *In libros Priorum resolutivorum Aristotelis* (Venetiis: apud Hieronymum Scotum, 1555), fol. 46rb–46va, and Alexander of Aphrodisias, *Super Priora resolutoria Aristotelis subtilissima Explanatio* (Venetiis: apud Hieronymum Scotum, 1560), col. 262.

106. Thomas Aquinas, *In duodecim libros metaphysicorum Aristotelis expositio*, p. 472b (bk. X, lect. 3, n. 1982).

principio lib. 4. dixerat, & D. Tho. & Scotus in dicto loco lib. 6. animadvertunt.

29. Haec vero communis responsio maiori eget examine. Dubitari enim in primis potest, an, licet nullae essent immateriales substantiae, danda esset scientia Metaphysicae a Physica & Mathematica distincta. Nam videtur ita esse asserendum, nam tunc daretur ratio entis abstrahens a substantia materiali, & a quantitate, aliisque accidentibus. Darentur etiam proprietates communes, ut *verum, unum, idem, diversum, totum, pars,* &c. de quibus nec Physica, nec Mathematica tractant nunc, neque etiam tunc tractarent, cum sint communiora, & excedentia propria obiecta. Ergo necessaria esset tertia scientia utraque superior, quae proinde esset Metaphysica. Unde potest secundo dubitari, an illa scientia esset prior tunc, quam naturalis philosophia, videtur enim ita dicendum, quia esset de obiecto abstractiori & priori.

signify them immediately in accordance with their proper natures$_{r}$, but in accordance with some common nature$_{r}$. And so the exposition of Averroes is not forced upon us, although he himself makes it sufficiently clear that he is only excluding an intermediate that both is a genus and signifies$_{d}$ a nature that is definite and properly contractible.[107] Of this we shall speak later. To the second some reply that Aristotle's argument is good, but that it is not founded on the claim that being cannot signify a concept common to substance and accident, but on the claim that if there were no thing$_{r}$ that abstracts from matter with respect to existence$_{e}$, then the nature$_{r}$ of being as such would not abstract from matter more than the nature$_{r}$ of body or natural being does, and therefore the consideration of being as such would not transcend the limits of natural philosophy, since then material substance would be the first being, and the science of the first being and that of being in general are the same, as he says at the beginning of book IV,[108] and St. Thomas[109] and Scotus[110] take note of this in the mentioned passage from book VI.

29. But this common reply requires further examination. For, in the first place, one might wonder whether there would need to be a science of metaphysics distinct from physics and mathematics even if there were no immaterial substances. For it seems that this must be asserted, since then there would be a nature$_{r}$ of being that abstracts from material substance, quantity, and the other accidents. There would also be common properties, such as, *true*, *one*, *same*, *diverse*, *whole*, *part*, etc., with which neither physics nor mathematics deals as things are, nor in that case would they deal with them, since these properties are more common and surpass their proper objects. A third science superior to these two would therefore be necessary, a science that would therefore be metaphysics. For this reason, one might wonder, in the second place,

107. Averroes, *Aristotelis opera cum Averrois Commentariis*, vol. 8, fol. 257G–H.

108. At *Metaph.* IV, ch. 1, 1003a26–32, Aristotle asserts that the consideration of first principles and highest causes belongs to the science of being in general. Of course, God is the absolutely first principle and highest cause.

109. Thomas Aquinas, *In duodecim libros metaphysicorum Aristotelis expositio*, p. 298b (bk. VI, lect. 1, n. 1170).

110. This reference seems to be to a commentary on Aristotle's *Metaphysics* that was once attributed to Scotus, but is now commonly attributed to Antonius Andreas (ca. 1280–ca. 1320/5). The commentary appears under the title *In XII Libros Metaphysicorum Aristotelis Expositio*, in vols. 5 and 6 of the Vivès edition of Scotus's works. See John Duns Scotus, *Opera omnia*, vol. 6 (Parisiis: apud Ludovicum Vivès, 1892), p. 136.

30. Mihi quidem probabile est, etiam data illa hypothesi, adhuc relinqui locum Metaphysicae scientiae: nunc enim una tantum pars eius est, quae de substantiis spiritualibus disputat: quoad reliquas ergo partes manere tunc posset, disputareque de ente, ⟨80a⟩ aliisque transcendentibus, & de decem praedicamentis, & de principiis ac causis universalibus. Hoc tamen posito, nihilominus iuxta mentem Aristotelis citato loco, naturalis philosophia esset prima scientia seu philosophia, saltem dignitate & praestantia, quoniam ageret de nobilissimo obiecto, scilicet de substantia ut sic, & de omni substantia: & consequenter etiam ageret de primis causis rerum & principiis, non quidem secundum abstractionem mentis, sed secundum rem.

31. Unde tandem dicitur probabilius videri, in eo casu non fore necessariam scientiam Metaphysicae specialem, & a naturali Philosophia distinctam. Ratio est, quia tunc Philosophia ageret de omni substantia & consequenter de omnibus accidentibus, etiam de quantitate prout est proprietas substantiae, & quoad entitatem & essentiam eius, & quatenus distinguitur, tam ab ipsa substantia, quam ab aliis omnibus proprietatibus eius, quia tota haec consideratio quantitatis non abstraheret a materia sensibili, nec excederet latitudinem obiecti Philosophiae. Atque eadem ratione ad eandem Philosophiam spectaret omnium praedicamentorum divisio & consideratio, quia nihil in eis esset re ipsa non fundatum in substantia sensibili: nec enim latius se extenderent praedicamenta accidentium, quam praedicamentum substantiae. Rursus omnium essentiarum, omniumque causarum realium consideratio ad Philosophiam spectaret, propter eandem causam. Ac denique pari ratione eadem ageret de praedicatis communibus substantiae & accidentibus, nec propter illa sola oporteret spe[59a]cialem scientiam constituere, quia non abstraherent a materia sensibili, & conceptus entis non esset alius a conceptu entis materialis. Neque obstaret, quod ratio entis & similes, communes essent rebus Mathematicis & Physicis: quia illa communitas solum esset secundum convenientiam realem, non secundum aliquam peculiarem abstractionem pertinentem ad con-

whether that science would in this case be prior to natural philosophy, for it seems that this must be affirmed, since it would deal with an object that is prior and more abstract.

30. To me indeed it is plausible that, even on this hypothesis, a place for the science of metaphysics still remains, for as things are there is only one part of it that treats of spiritual substances. With respect to the other parts, therefore, it could remain on this hypothesis and deal with being and the other transcendentals, the ten categories, and universal principles and causes. But granting this, nevertheless, according to Aristotle's thinking in the cited passage, natural philosophy would be the first science or philosophy, at least as regards worth and preeminence, since it would deal with the most noble object, namely, substance as such, and with every substance, and consequently it would also deal with the first causes and principles of things$_r$, not indeed according to an abstraction of the mind, but really.

31. For this reason, in the end I say that it seems more plausible that in this case a special science of metaphysics distinct from natural philosophy would not be necessary. The reason is that in this case philosophy would deal with every substance, and consequently with all accidents, and also with quantity insofar as it is a property of substance, both as regards its entity and essence, and insofar as it is distinguished from substance itself and from all of its other properties, since this entire consideration of quantity would not abstract from sensible matter, nor would it surpass the scope of philosophy's object. And for the same reason the division and consideration of all the categories would pertain to the same philosophy, since nothing in them would really not be founded on sensible substance, since the accidental categories would not extend further than the category of substance. Again, the consideration of all essences, and of all real causes, would pertain to philosophy, for the same reason. And finally, for a like reason, philosophy would deal with predicates common to substance and accidents, nor would it be necessary to constitute a special science merely for their sake, since they would not abstract from sensible matter, and the concept of being would not be other than the concept of material being. Nor would it be a problem that the nature$_r$ of being and similar ones would be common to mathematical and physical things$_r$, since that community would only

stituendum obiectum scientiae. Sicut etiam nunc quantitas continua & discreta conveniunt in communi ratione quantitatis, & tamen non datur una Mathematica communis, quia Physica sufficienter tractat de illa convenientia & ratione communi, in qua non reperitur specialis abstractio constituens peculiare obiectum scibile: ita ergo esset in eo casu.

32. Ad tertium testimonium, omissa Soti, & aliorum expositione, dicentium illam pro⟨80b⟩positionem esse falsam: *Quicquid est praeter ens, est non ens*, quia ens simpliciter dictum accipitur pro substantia: hoc enim in rigore falsum est, ut infra ostendam: & praeterea servata proportione praedicati & subiecti, adhuc esset verum dicere, quidquid est praeter ens, esse non ens. Hac (inquam) omissa expositione, respondetur Aristotelem non negare ens posse esse medium syllogismi, neque hac de causa reiicere rationem Parmenidis, sed quia & sumebat ens esse[28] unum proprie & in rigore, cum solum sit analogum: tum etiam quia voce unius aequivoce utebatur: sic enim ex praemissis supra positis concludebat, id quod est, seu ens, esse unum: ergo quidquid est praeter unum est nihil, ut ita conficeret, omnia unum esse, quae est manifesta aequivocatio, nam ipse intendebat omnia esse unum in re ipsa, ens autem si praecise sumatur, & quasi immobiliter, non est hoc modo unum, sed ratione tantum: si autem sumatur distributive & pro singulis entibus, sic quidem unumquodque ens unum est, non tamen omnia sunt unum.

33. Ad quartum negatur illa expositio, cum enim ait Aristoteles, ens existere in omnibus, sed non similiter, non recte exponitur, id est, non uno conceptu, sed non eodem modo, quia de substantia simpliciter, de aliis vero secundum quid dicitur, ut D. Tho. exponit. Quintum solum probat ens non esse tale medium quod proprie contrahatur ad inferiora per aliquid quod non sit ens, sed per simplicem determinationem,

28. Reading "ens esse" with C, S, V_1, and V_2. The following have "esse ens": C_1, C_2, G_2, M_1, M_2, M_3, M_4, P_1, P_2, V_3, V_5, and Vivès. (Scan of V_4 is missing the relevant portion.)

be in accordance with a real agreement, not in accordance with some special abstraction pertaining to the constitution of a science's object. Moreover, the situation in this case would be similar to that which exists now regarding quantity, for although continuous and discrete quantity agree in the common nature$_r$ of quantity, still, there is not a single common mathematics, since physics sufficiently treats of that agreement and common nature$_r$, in which one does not find a special abstraction constituting a particular knowable object.

32. To the third testimony, setting aside the exposition of Soto and others,[111] who say that the proposition "whatever is apart from being is not-being" is false, because being spoken of without qualification is taken for substance (for this, strictly speaking, is false, as I will show below, and what's more, even with the proportion of predicate and subject preserved, it would still be true to say that whatever is apart from being is not-being)—setting this exposition aside (I say), I reply that Aristotle does not deny that being can be the middle term of a syllogism, nor does he reject the argument of Parmenides for this reason, but rather because Parmenides also took being to be one properly and strictly, when in fact it is only analogical, and also because Parmenides used the word "one" equivocally, for thus does he conclude from the premises set forth above that that which is, or being, is one, and that whatever is other than the one is therefore nothing, so that in this way he makes all things one—which is a manifest equivocation, for he himself meant that all things are one in reality, whereas, if being is taken precisely, and as it were immovably, it is not one in this way, but according to reason only. And if it is taken distributively and for singular beings, then in this way, to be sure, each being is one, but it is not the case that all beings are one thing.

33. With respect to the fourth testimony, I deny the exposition. For when Aristotle says that being exists in all things, but not similarly, this is not rightly glossed as "not in accordance with a single concept," but rather as "not in the same way." For being is said of substance without qualification, but it is said of the other categories in a qualified way, as

111. See Domingo de Soto, *Super octo libros Physicorum Aristotelis Commentaria* (Salmanticae: ex Officina Ildefonsi à Terranova & Neyla, 1582), fol. 10v.

qua unumquodque genus se ipso est ens, & tale ens, quod verissimum est, ut latius videbimus, sect. 5. & 6. non tamen excludit medium conceptum ex confuso modo concipiendi nostro. Ad sextum respondeo in primis, Aristotelem nullam ibi mentionem facere decem primorum generum: sed absolute ait, quaedam esse quae de aliis praedicantur, de ipsis autem nihil, quod nos possumus exponere de transcendentibus, de quibus nihil ut superius praedicatur: sic enim restringenda videtur illa propositio, nam ut aequale nihil est de quo non possit aliquid praedicari, nam ipsa transcendentia de se invicem praedicantur proprie, & non omnino identice. Unde si quis velit de decem generibus illud membrum exponere, necesse est ut aliter illud restringat ad praedicata superiora, quae sint genera, vel species, nam absolute quomodo potest esse verum, cum evidenter constet multa de primis generibus praedicari? Imo ipse Aristoteles 2. Posterior. cap. 14. si⟨81a⟩gnificat, praedicata superiora, seu universaliora quaedam contineri intra genus, quaedam vero de aliis dici etiam extra genus, quod expositores omnes dictum esse intelligunt propter ens, & similia.

Conceptus entis etiam ut comparatur ad inferiora, est praecisus ab illis.

34. Ultimo sequitur ex dictis, ens non solum dice[59b]re conceptum unum & praecisum, prout absolute abstractum consideratur, sed etiam prout comparatur ad inferiora ut de eis praedicetur, vel existens in eis consideretur. Probatur, quia post quamcunque notitiam abstractivam conceptus communis a particularibus, potest intellectus facere comparativam: ergo illud ipsum, quod abstractum est in ente, potest ad inferiora comparare, non est enim maior repugnantia in hoc[29] conceptu entis, quam in aliis communibus: sed potius est eadem ratio, scilicet quia totus ille conceptus est in ipsis inferioribus, sive ab eis re distin-

29. Reading "hoc" here with S, M_1, P_1, P_2, V_1, and V_2. The following omit "hoc": C_1, C_2, G_2, M_2, M_3, M_4, V_3, V_5, and Vivès. (Relevant portion of the scan of V_4 is illegible.)

St. Thomas explains.[112] The fifth testimony only proves that being is not an intermediate of the sort that is properly contracted to inferiors by something that is not a being, but [is rather an intermediate of the sort that is contracted to inferiors] by a simple determination, by means of which each genus is by itself both a being and a being of a particular sort. And this is most true, as we shall see more fully in sections 5 and 6, but it does not preclude an intermediate conceived in conformity with our confused way of conceiving. To the sixth testimony I reply, in the first place, that Aristotle makes no mention there of the ten primary genera. Rather, he simply says that there are certain things that are predicated of other things, while of themselves nothing is predicated. And this we can expound as having to do with the transcendentals, of which nothing is predicated as something superior. For that proposition, it seems, should be restricted in this way, for there is nothing of which something equally universal cannot be predicated, since the transcendentals themselves are properly predicated of each other, and not altogether identically. For this reason, if someone wishes to expound that text in such a way that it concerns the ten genera, it is necessary that she restrict it in another way, to higher predicates that are genera or species. For how can this claim be true without qualification when it is utterly evident that many things are predicated of the primary genera? In fact, Aristotle himself, in *Post. An.* II, ch. 14, indicates that certain superior or more universal predicates are contained within a genus, while others are said also of other things outside the genus,[113] and this all expositors understand as having been said on account of being and the like.

The concept of being, even as compared to inferiors, is prescinded from them.

34. Finally, it follows from the things that have been said that "being" signifies$_d$ a concept that is one and prescinded, not only insofar as it is considered abstracted absolutely, but also insofar as it is compared to inferiors, in order that it might be predicated of them or considered existent in them. This is proved because after any knowledge$_n$ abstractive of a common concept from particulars, the intellect can produce comparative knowledge$_n$. Therefore, it can compare the very thing that is abstracted in the case of being to its inferiors. For there is no greater

112. See Thomas Aquinas, *In duodecim libros metaphysicorum Aristotelis expositio*, pp. 331b–332a (bk. VII, lect. 4, ns. 1335–38).

113. Aristotle, *Post. An.* II, ch. 13, 96a24–32.

guatur, sive ratione tantum, hoc enim nihil refert: imo quo minor fuerit inter illa distinctio in re, eo verius unum attribuetur alteri: sic enim, quanvis sapientiam Dei praescindamus, & ratione a Deo distinguamus, illam ad Deum comparantes, vere ac proprie dicimus sapientiam esse in Deo. Ad hunc ergo modum ratio entis praecise concepta recte ad substantiam & accidens comparatur, & in eis esse dicitur, & hoc modo fiunt hae praedicationes, *substantia est ens, & accidens est ens.* Unde confirmatur, quia omnis haec comparatio, vel compositio fit ex simplicibus conceptibus: ergo, postquam intellectus concepit praecise ens, potest simul concipere substantiam, vel accidens secundum proprios conceptus, quia hi conceptus simplices non habent inter se repugnantiam, ut per se constat: ergo similiter potest tunc intellectus ens ad substantiam comparare tanquam in illa existens, & similiter ad accidens: ergo conceptus entis, etiam ut comparatus ad conceptum substantiae, & accidentis, est secundum rationem praecisus ab illis.

35. Dices, Ergo conceptus entis, etiam ut inclusus in inferioribus, est praecisus ab illis, quod repugnat supra dictis: quia inclusus in inferioribus, nihil aliud est, quam ipsa, quia nihil in ipsis est, quod non sit ens: sequela vero patet, quia ens non potest comparari ad inferiora, vel praedicari de illis, nisi ut est in illis: ergo, si ut dicit praecisum conceptum, comparatur ad inferiora, etiam ut est in illis erit praeci⟨81b⟩sus. Respondetur esse aequivocationem [argumentando[30]] a modo concipiendi nostro ad rem ipsam, & e contrario. In rigore ergo negatur sequela, quia licet conceptus entis, qui a nobis praescinditur secundum rationem, sit in inferioribus, tamen ut est praecisus, formaliter loquendo, non est in inferioribus, id est, non habet in illis eum statum, seu modum essendi,

30. In his notes on the Vivès edition, Charles Berton plausibly suggests inserting "argumentando" here, referring the reader to *DM* 2.3.12, where one finds (in all editions save S—see n. 38 on the Latin text below) the words "esse magnam aequivocationem argumentando a ratione obiectiva ut praecisa ab intellectu, ad illam prout est in re." See Francisco Suárez, *Opera Omnia*, vol. 27, p. 368b.

impossibility in the case of this concept of being than there is in the case of other common concepts. Rather, there is the same basis$_r$—namely, because that entire concept is in the inferiors themselves, whether it be distinguished from them really or only rationally, for this makes no difference. In fact, the smaller the distinction between them is in reality, the more truly is the one attributed to the other. For, likewise, even if we prescind the wisdom of God and rationally distinguish it from God, when we compare it to God, we truly and properly say that wisdom is in God. Therefore, the nature$_r$ of being, precisely conceived in this way, is correctly compared to substance and accident and is said to be in them, and it is in this way that those predications, "a substance is a being" and "an accident is a being," are made. And this is confirmed for the following reason: because this entire comparison or composition is made from simple concepts. Therefore, after the intellect has conceived being precisely, it can at the same time conceive substance or accident according to their proper concepts, since these simple concepts are not incompatible with each other, as is clear *per se*. Therefore, in like fashion, the intellect can then compare being to substance as something existing in substance, and likewise to accident. Therefore, the concept of being, even insofar as it is compared to the concepts of substance and accident, is rationally prescinded from them.

35. You will say: therefore, the concept of being, even as included in its inferiors, is prescinded from them, which is incompatible with the things said above, for when included in its inferiors, it is not other than them, since there is nothing in them that is not a being. The consequence is clear, since being cannot be compared to its inferiors or predicated of them except insofar as it is in them. Therefore, if it is compared to its inferiors insofar as it signifies$_d$ a prescinded concept, it will also be prescinded insofar as it is in them. I reply that there is an equivocation [in arguing] from our mode of conceiving to the thing$_r$ itself, and conversely. Therefore, the consequence is denied, strictly speaking, since, although the concept of being, which is rationally prescinded by us, is in its inferiors, nevertheless, formally speaking, insofar as it is prescinded, it is not in its inferiors, that is, it does not have in them that state or mode of being$_e$ which it has by extrinsic denomination from the precision of the intellect. And when this concept, even as prescind-

quem habet per denominationem extrinsecam ex praecisione intellectus. Quando autem dicitur hic conceptus, etiam ut praecisus, comparari ad inferiora, eisque attribui, non est sensus, quod secundum eam praecisionem seu denominationem attribuatur inferioribus, sed solum quod ratio illa sic concepta ad inferiores comparata in omnibus illis inclusa inveniatur. Quocirca si non fiat illa reduplicatio de ratione entis ut praecisa, sed simpliciter sit sermo de ratione entis praecise concepta, verum est rationem illam esse in inferioribus, & in eis omnino, & intime includi, & nihilominus ratione praescindi, quanvis in re non sit praecisa.

36. Sed statim urget difficultas, quia iuxta haec nihil videtur deesse conceptui entis ad rationem proprii universalis, nam erit unum in multis, & de multis. Sed haec difficultas pendet ex duabus rationibus dubitandi in principio sectionis positis. Una est de [60a] univocatione entis, quia si ens non est univocum, illa ratio sufficit, ut non sit proprie universale: quomodo autem ex dictis non sequatur esse univocum, & quid illi ad univocationem desit, infra in proprio loco est tractandum, agendo de divisionibus entis: nunc solum assero, omnia quae diximus de unitate conceptus entis, longe clariora & certiora videri, quam quod ens sit analogum, & ideo non recte propter defendendam analogiam negari unitatem conceptus, sed si alterum negandum esset, potius analogia, quae incerta est, quam unitas conceptus, quae certis rationibus videtur demonstrari, esset neganda. Re tamen vera neutram negari necesse est, quia ad univocationem non sufficit, quod conceptus in se sit aliquo modo unus, sed necesse est, ut aequali habitudine & ordine respiciat multa, quod non habet conceptus entis, ut latius citato loco exponemus. Alia difficultas erat de modo, quo ens descendit, vel trahitur ad inferiora secundum rationem, de qua re paulo inferius propriam faciemus sectionem, quia & obscuram habet difficultatem, & ex aliis prius dicendis pendet. ⟨82a⟩

ed, is said to be compared to its inferiors and attributed to them, the sense is not that it is attributed to its inferiors in accordance with that precision or denomination, but only that that nature$_r$, so conceived and compared to its inferiors, is found included in them all. For this reason, if one does not make that reduplication regarding the nature$_r$ of being as prescinded, but the discussion is simply about the nature$_r$ of being conceived precisely, it is true that that nature$_r$ is in its inferiors and is included in them wholly and intimately, and that, nevertheless, it is rationally prescinded, although it is not prescinded in reality.

36. But a difficulty immediately presents itself, since, according to what has been said, the nature$_r$ of being seems to be lacking in nothing that pertains to the nature$_r$ of a proper universal, for it will be one in many and one [predicable] of many. But this difficulty depends on the two reasons for doubt set forth at the beginning of the section. The one concerns the univocity of being, since if being is not univocal, that is reason enough for it not to be properly universal. But I shall explain below, in its proper place, when dealing with the divisions of being, how it does not follow from what has been said that being is univocal, and what element, necessary for univocity, is lacking to it.[114] For now, I only affirm that all the things we have said regarding the unity of the concept of being seem far clearer and more certain than the claim that being is analogical, and therefore, that the unity of the concept of being is not rightly denied for the sake of defending the analogy of being. Indeed, if one of these must be denied, one should deny analogy (which is uncertain), rather than the unity of the concept (which seems to be demonstrated by sure arguments). But really it is necessary to deny neither, since for univocity it is not enough that the concept in itself be one in some way. Rather, it is [also] necessary that it be related to many things by an equal relation and ordering, which is something that is lacking in the case of the concept of being, as we shall explain more fully in the mentioned place. The other difficulty had to do with the way being descends or is contracted to its inferiors according to reason, to which matter we shall devote a section a little bit later,[115] since it both involves a hidden difficulty and depends on other things that must be said beforehand.

114. See *DM* 28.3 and 32.2.
115. See below, *DM* 2.6.

Sectio III.

Utrum ratio seu conceptus entis in re ipsa & ante intellectum sit aliquo modo praecisus ab inferioribus.

Explicatio quaestionis.

1. Haec quaestio videri potest communis omnibus gradibus seu conceptibus superioribus respectu inferiorum, de quibus agendum est disp. 5. sec. 2.[31] & disp. 6. sect. 2. Sed hic habet difficultatem specialem propter transcendentiam entis, & necessaria est ad explicandam hanc rationem entis,[32] & ideo breviter expedienda hic est: supponendo, praeter distinctionem realem perfectam, quae intercedit inter entitates mutuo separabiles, posse in rebus ante intellectum aliam minorem inveniri, qualis esse solet inter rem, & modum rei, ut infra latius dicturi sumus. Hic ergo ut certum supponimus rationem entis non distingui realiter priori modo ab inferioribus, in quibus existit, quod per se notum est in omni communi praedicato, & a fortiori patebit ex dicendis, *Disp. 7.* inquirimus autem, an esse tale vel tale ens, addat aliquem modum ex natura rei, & ante intellectum, distinctum ab ipso ente, ita ut ens, &[33] tale ens, v. g. substantia, ex natura rei in ratione sua formali distinguantur, quatenus substantia addit aliquem modum, quem non dicit ens.

31. Reading "2" here with S, V_1, and V_2. The following read "1": C_1, C_2, G_2, M_1, M_2, M_3, M_4, P_1, P_2, V_3, V_4, V_5, and Vivès.

32. Reading "& necessaria est ad explicandam hanc rationem entis," here with S, V_1, and V_2. These words are omitted in: C_1, C_2, G_2, M_1, M_2, M_3, M_4, P_1, P_2, V_3, V_4, V_5, and Vivès.

33. Reading "&" here with P_1, P_2, S, V_1, and V_2. The following read "vel" instead: C_1, C_2, G_2, M_1, M_2, M_3, M_4, V_3, V_4, V_5, and Vivès.

Section 3

Whether the Nature$_R$ or Concept of Being Is in Some Way Prescinded from Inferiors Really and Antecedently to the Intellect's Operation.

Explanation of the question.

1. This question can seem common to all superior grades or concepts in relation to their inferiors, which issue is to be dealt with in Disputation V, sec. 2, and Disputation VI, sec. 2.[116] But here there is a special difficulty on account of being's transcendence, and [a resolution of this difficulty] is necessary for explaining the nature$_r$ of being, and therefore it must briefly be dispatched here by assuming that, in addition to the perfect real distinction, which obtains between entities that are mutually separable, there can be found in reality, before any operation of the intellect, another lesser distinction of the sort that normally obtains between a thing$_r$ and a mode of that thing$_r$, as we shall say below at greater length.[117] Here, therefore, we assume as certain that the nature$_r$ of being is not really distinguished in the first way from the inferiors in which it exists, which is something known$_n$ *per se* in the case of every common predicate and will *a fortiori* be clear from the

116. I think Suárez means to refer not to *DM* 6.2 ("Whether the universal unity of a nature, distinct from its formal unity, exists actually in things prior to the mind's operation"), but to *DM* 6.9 ("How the unity of the genus and the unity of the difference are in reality distinguished both from each other and from specific unity"). In the first edition of the *Metaphysical Disputations*, the running header in this section of *DM* 2 reads "On the distinction between the concept of being and its inferiors" (*De distinc. conceptus entis ab inferioribus*).

117. See *DM* 7.1.

Argumenta partis affirmantis.

Primum. 2. Videtur ex dictis sequi ita esse affirmandum. Primo, quia ratio entis eadem est in re, quae mente concipitur, sed in mente concepta non includit modum substantiae, vel accidentis: ergo neque in re ipsa: sed rationes substantiae vel accidentis includunt suos modos: ergo ratio entis in re est distincta ab illis. Maior (caetera enim omnia nota sunt) probatur, quia non dicimus rationem entis eodem modo esse in re, quo concipitur, quantum ad modum scilicet, quem habet ex praecisione concipientis, sed dicimus rationem illam conceptam esse eandem, quae est in re, & hoc videtur per se notum, quia intellectus in hoc conceptu non fingit rem, vel rationem conceptam: ergo eandem concipit, quae est in re.

Secundum. 3. Secundo, quae in re sunt separabilia, in re sunt [60b] aliquo modo distincta, quia includunt haec duo negationes eiusdem rationis seu aequivalentes, maxime in rebus ⟨82b⟩ finitis: sed ratio entis est in re separabilis a ratione substantiae, nam salvatur in accidente, & e contrario est separabilis a ratione accidentis, quia salvatur in sola substantia: ergo est aliquo modo in re distincta ab illis. Dices, rationem entis quae est in substantia, non esse separabilem ab illa, neque quae in accidente, ab illo, & ideo non esse necessariam distinctionem ex natura rei inter illa. Sed contra, nam ad distinctionem ex natura rei sufficit praedictus separationis modus, scilicet, quod alicubi possit una ratio reperiri sine alia: quia, si in re sint omnino idem, non videtur intelligibile, praesertim in rebus finitis, quod non se semper comitentur, quia quae in re omnino idem sunt, ubique sunt idem: sed in accidenti,

things that are to be said. But we are inquiring whether to be a being of this or that sort adds some mode that is distinct *ex natura rei* and prior *Disp. VII.* to [the operation of] the intellect from being itself, so that being and being of a particular sort (substance, for example) are distinguished *ex natura rei* in respect of their formal character$_r$, insofar as substance adds some mode that being does not signify$_d$.

Arguments for the affirmative.

First argument.

2. It seems to follow from what has been said that this must be affirmed. First, because the nature$_r$ of being in reality is the same as that which is conceived in the mind. But as conceived in the mind it does not include the mode of substance or accident. Therefore, neither does it include it in reality. But the natures$_r$ of substance and accident include their modes. Therefore, the nature$_r$ of being is in reality distinct from them. The major (for all the other claims are known$_n$) is proved because we do not say that the nature$_r$ of being exists$_e$ in reality in the same way it is conceived, namely, as far as the mode that it has from the conceiver's precision is concerned. Rather, we say that that conceived nature$_r$ is the same as that which exists$_e$ in reality, and this seems known$_n$ *per se*, since in the case of this concept the intellect does not feign the thing$_r$ or conceived nature$_r$. Therefore, it conceives the same thing that exists$_e$ in reality.

Second argument.

3. Second, things that are in reality separable are in reality distinct in some way, since these two things[118] involve negations of the same kind$_r$ or equivalent ones, especially in the case of finite things$_r$. But the nature$_r$ of being is in reality separable from the nature$_r$ of substance, since it is found in an accident, and, conversely, it is separable from the nature$_r$ of accident, since it is found in a substance taken on its own. Therefore, it is in some way really distinct from them. You will say that the nature$_r$ of being which is in substance is not separable from it, and that the nature$_r$ of being which is in accident is not separable from it, and that therefore a distinction *ex natura rei* between them is not necessary. But to the contrary, since, for a distinction *ex natura rei*, the

118. I.e., being separable in reality and being distinct in reality.

verbi gratia, ratio entis, & ratio substantiae non sunt idem: ergo neque secundum se & absolute idem sunt.

Tertium. 4. Quod in hunc modum tertio declaratur, quia substantia a parte rei non ex eo est substantia, ex quo est ens (& idem est de accidente) ergo est aliqua distinctio ex natura rei inter conceptum obiectivum entis, & substantiae, etiam prout in re sunt in ipsamet substantia. Antecedens patet, quia substantia ex eodem est ens, ex quo accidens, nam in ratione entis unum sunt: ergo substantia non est substantia ex eo quod ens, alioqui quidquid ea ratione constitueretur in ratione entis, constitueretur etiam in ratione substantiae. Prima vero consequentia probatur, quia distinctio ex natura rei optime colligitur ex effectibus formalibus seu constitutis[34] distinctis: cum ergo aliud quid constituatur per rationem substantiae, quam per rationem entis ut sic, necesse est, ut in re habeant aliquam distinctionem.

Quartum. 5. Quarto censeri solet difficile argumentum, quia impossibile videtur, ut eadem res secundum idem conveniat cum alia, & ab ea differat, sed substantia a parte rei, & ante omnem intellectum convenit seu est similis accidenti in ratione entis, differt autem seu est dissimilis in ratione substantiae: ergo haec duo distinguuntur ex natura rei aliquo modo in ipsamet substantia, alioqui secundum idem omnino esset similis, & dissimilis accidenti. Quod esse impossibile probatur, quia haec duo includunt contradictionem, nam convenientia & similitudo dicit aliquam rationem unitatis, similitudo enim fundatur in unitate, ut Aristoteles dixit 5. Metaphysicae: dissimilitudo autem dicit potius rationem multitudinis. Et confirmatur, & explicatur con⟨83a⟩tradictio:

34. Reading “constitutis” with C_1, C_2, G_2, M_1, M_2, M_3, M_4, P_1, S, V_1, V_2, V_3, V_4, and V_5. The following read “constitutivis” instead: P_2 and Vivès.

mentioned mode of separation suffices, namely, that somewhere the one nature$_r$ is found without the other. For if in reality they are altogether the same, it does not seem intelligible—especially in the case of finite things$_r$—that they should not always accompany each other, since things that are in reality altogether the same are everywhere the same. But in an accident, for example, the nature$_r$ of being and the nature$_r$ of substance are not the same. Therefore, neither is it the case that in themselves and absolutely they are the same.

Third argument.

4. Third, this is made clear in the following way: because *a parte rei* what makes a substance a substance is not what makes it a being (and the same goes for an accident). Therefore, there is some distinction *ex natura rei* between the objective concept of being and the objective concept of substance, even insofar as they are really in a substance itself. The antecedent is clear, since what makes a substance a being is the same as what makes an accident a being, for they are one in the nature$_r$ of being. Therefore, what makes a substance a substance is not what makes it a being, otherwise whatever was constituted by this nature$_r$ in the nature$_r$ of being would be constituted also in the nature$_r$ of substance. And the first consequence is proved, since a distinction *ex natura rei* is best inferred from distinct formal or constituted effects. Since, therefore, there is something constituted by the nature$_r$ of substance that is other than something constituted by the nature$_r$ of being as such, they necessarily have some distinction in reality.

Fourth argument.

5. Fourth, the following argument is normally thought formidable: because it seems impossible that the same thing$_r$ should both agree with another thing$_r$ and differ from it in the same respect. But substance *a parte rei* and before every operation of the intellect agrees with, or is similar to, accident in respect of the nature$_r$ of being, but it differs from, or is dissimilar to, accident in respect of the nature$_r$ of substance. Therefore, the nature$_r$ of substance and the nature$_r$ of being are somehow distinguished *ex natura rei* in a substance itself, for otherwise it would be both like and unlike an accident in altogether the same respect. That this is impossible is proved because these two are contradictory, for agreement and similarity signify$_d$ some kind$_r$ of unity, since similarity is founded on unity, as Aristotle says in *Metaph.* V,[119] whereas dissimilari-

119. Aristotle, *Metaph.* V, ch. 9, 1018a15–19.

quia, si in substantia ratio substantiae & entis est omnino eadem: ergo quicquid est de essentia substantiae, est de essentia entis, & e contrario: alioqui differrent essentialiter, nam quocunque addito, vel ablato mutatur essentia: si autem differunt essentialiter: ergo in re ipsa habent distinctionem aliquam, nam essentialis ratio in re ipsa consistit. Si autem, quicquid est de essentia substantiae, est de essentia entis, sequitur & rationem substantiae reperiri in accidente, cum quo convenit in ratione entis, & non reperiri, quia re vera accidens non est substantia, sed dissimile illi. Sequitur etiam, substantiam esse similem accidenti in ratione entis, quia hoc supponitur, & non esse similem, quia ratio entis in substantia non est eiusdem modi cum ratione entis in accidenti. Et consequenter etiam sequitur rationem entis af[61a]fimari de accidente propter convenientiam cum substantia, & negari posse propter disconvenientiam, quam in eadem ratione habere dicitur. Denique convenientia, & disconvenientia dicunt relationes essentialiter diversas: ergo requirunt in re fundamenta & rationes fundandi seu terminandi essentialiter diversas.

6. Propter haec & similia argumenta opinantur aliqui ens dicere conceptum obiectivum ex natura rei distinctum ac praecisum ab omnibus inferioribus, & a conceptibus quantumvis simplicibus sub eo contentis, ut sunt *substantia, accidens*, & similia, & haec censetur communiter opinio Scoti in 1. d. 3. q. 1. & 3. & d. 8. q. 2. & in 2. d. 3. q. 1. & eam sequuntur Scotistae, qui a fortiori idem sentiunt de omnibus praedicatis universalibus, de quibus latius inferius.

ty signifies$_d$ instead a kind$_r$ of multiplicity. And the contradiction is confirmed and explained, for if in a substance the nature$_r$ of substance and the nature$_r$ of being are altogether the same, then whatever pertains to the essence of substance pertains to the essence of being, and conversely; otherwise, they would differ essentially, for an essence is changed whenever anything is added or taken away. But if they differ essentially, then in reality they have some distinction, for the essential character$_r$ consists in the thing$_r$ itself. But if whatever pertains to the essence of substance pertains to the essence of being, it follows that the nature$_r$ of substance is both found in an accident, with which it agrees in the nature$_r$ of being, and also not found there, since really an accident is not a substance but dissimilar to it. It also follows that substance is similar to accident in the nature$_r$ of being (since this is assumed) and is also not similar, since the nature$_r$ of being in substance is not of the same mode as the nature$_r$ of being in accident. And consequently it also follows that the nature$_r$ of being is affirmed of accident on account of an agreement with substance, and that it can be denied on account of a disagreement which it is said to have in the same nature$_r$. Finally, agreement and disagreement signify$_d$ essentially diverse relations. Therefore, they require in reality foundations and kinds$_r$ of founding or terminating that are essentially diverse.

6. Because of these and similar arguments, some hold that being signifies$_d$ an objective concept that is distinct and prescinded *ex natura rei* from all inferiors and from all concepts contained under it, however simple, as for instance *substance, accident* and the like. And this is commonly judged to be the opinion of Scotus, *Sent.* I, d. 3, q. 1 and q. 3,[120] and d. 8, q. 2,[121] and *Sent.* II, d. 3, q. 1.[122] And this opinion is followed by the Scotists, who *a fortiori* believe the same of all universal predicates, about which we shall speak more fully below.[123]

120. John Duns Scotus, *Opera omnia*, vol. 3 (Vaticana), pp. 18–38 (ns. 26–55), pp. 94–103 (ns. 152–66).

121. Suárez would here seem to have *Ord.* I, d. 8, p. 1, q. 3, in mind, and in particular, Scotus's discussion of intrinsic modes at ns. 100–107 and 136–50. See John Duns Scotus, *Opera omnia*, vol. 4 (Vaticana), pp. 199–202 and 221–27.

122. John Duns Scotus, *Opera omnia*, vol. 7 (Vaticana), pp. 391–410 (ns. 1–42).

123. See *DM* 6.9.

Vera sententia.

7. Nihilominus dicendum est, conceptum entis obiectivum prout in re ipsa existit, non esse aliquid ex natura rei distinctum ac praecisum ab inferioribus, in quibus existit. Haec est opinio communis totius Scholae D. Tho. quam in primis necessario docent omnes, qui negant conceptum obiectivum entis esse ratione praecisum, ut Soncinas, Caie. Ferrar. & specialiter id declaravit Caiet. in dicto opusc. de ente & essentia, c. 1. q. 2. & idem tenet Fonseca loco citato, quanvis de distinctione inter praedicata essentialia superiora, & inferiora aliter sentire videatur, 2. Metaph. c. 2. tex. 11. & alibi, de quo infra suo loco. ⟨83b⟩ Idem etiam a fortiori tenent omnes qui negant genus ex natura rei distingui ab speciebus, vel speciem ab individuis, ut Greg. in 1. d. 8, q. 2. & 3. Capreol. q. 4. ar. 3. ad argu. contra 2. conc. Soncin. 7. Metaph. q. 36. Soto in Logic. q. 3. art. 2. Eandem opinionem specialiter tenet Capreol. in 1. d. 2. q. 1. ad arg. Scoti cont. ultimam concl. Et est aperta sententia D. Tho. 1. cont. Gent. c. 26. rat. 4. imo & Scotus 10. Metap. tex. 3. hanc videtur tenere sententiam, constituit enim differentiam inter ens & unum: nam ens (inquit) praedicat eandem naturam realiter & formaliter de generibus, de quibus quidditative praedicatur: unum vero, licet praedicet eandem naturam realiter, non tamen formaliter: quia unum dicit passionem, non essentiam. Quanvis fortasse in alio sensu ibi Scotus locutus est: scilicet ens dicere essentiam omnium generum, non tamen totam: unum vero omnino esse extra essentiam. Sumiturque haec sententia ex Arist. 8. Metap. c. ult. tex. 16. ubi dicit, ipsum ens se ipso absque aliquo addito determinari ad substantiam, quantitatem, qualitatem, & ideo non poni in definitionibus, quia non dicit determinatam naturam contrahibilem per aliquam differentiam. Et ita exposuerunt Commentator, D. Tho. & Alex. Alens. ibi. Scotus vero exponit, quod Arist. excludat differentias realiter distinctas, non vero formaliter. Sed hoc, & est aperte contra mentem Aristot. & ab ipso etiam Scoto non dicitur consequenter, quia etiam inferiora genera non distinguuntur realiter a suis differentiis, sed ad summum formaliter, iuxta eiusdem Scoti doctrinam: ergo hanc etiam distinctionem, & compositionem excludit Aris. in determinatione entis ad sua inferiora.

Vide Anton. Trombeta. 7. Metap. q. 16. Anton. And. q. 7.

The true opinion.

7. Nevertheless, it must be said that the objective concept of being, as it exists in reality, is not something *ex natura rei* distinct and prescinded from the inferiors in which it exists. This is the common opinion of the entire school of St. Thomas, and this opinion, in the first place, is necessarily taught by all those who deny that the objective concept of being is rationally prescinded—for instance, Soncinas, Cajetan, and Ferrara.[124] And Cajetan makes this especially clear in the mentioned short work, *On Being and Essence*, ch. 1, q. 2.[125] And Fonseca maintains the same thing in the cited passage,[126] although he seems to think otherwise regarding the distinction between superior and inferior essential predicates in *Metaph.* II, ch. 2, text 11,[128] and elsewhere, about which we shall speak below in its proper place.[129] And *a fortiori* all those who deny that a genus is distinguished *ex natura rei* from its species, or a species from its individuals, also think the same, for instance, Gregory of Rimini, *Sent.* I, d. 8, q. 2 and q. 3,[130] Capreolus, q. 4, art. 3, in reply to the arguments against the second conclusion,[131]

See Antonio Trombetta, 7. Metaph., q. 16. Antonius Andreas, q. 7.[127]

124. See *DM* 2.2.4 above.

125. Cajetan, *In De Ente et Essentia D. Thomae Aquinatis Commentaria*, pp. 23–29 (ns. 11–14).

126. Pedro da Fonseca, *Commentaria in Libros Metaphysicorum Aristotelis Stagiritae*, vol. 1, cols. 716–18.

127. Antonio Trombetta's question-commentary on Aristotle's *Metaphysics* devotes only nine questions to book VII. Suárez, however, may have in mind *Metaph.* VII, q. 4, "Whether the predicates pertaining to the what-it-is are prescinded by an operation of the intellect" ("*Utrum praedicata pertinentia ad quod quid est sint praecise per opus intellectus*"). See Antonio Trombetta, *Antonii trombette Patavini minoriste theologi Opus in Metaphysicam Aristotelis* (Venetiis, 1504), fols. 56va–57va. In Antonius Andreas's questions on Aristotle's *Metaph.* VII, q. 7 reads: "Whether the what-it-is is the same as that of which it is the what-it-is" ("*Utrum quod quid est sit idem cum eo cuius est quod quid est*"). See Antonius Andreas, *Questiones Antonii Andree super xii libros metaphysice* (Venetiis: Heredes Octaviani Scoti, 1523), fols. 33vb–34va. This seems not to be relevant to the topic under discussion here. Suárez, however, may have in mind Andreas's *Metaph.* VII, q. 14, "It is asked whether the concept of the genus is other than the concept of the species" ("*Queritur utrum conceptus generis sit alius a conceptu speciei*"). See Antonius Andreas, *Questiones Antonii Andree super xii libros metaphysice*, fols. 38vb–39va.

128. Pedro da Fonseca, *Commentaria in Libros Metaphysicorum Aristotelis Stagiritae*, vol. 1, cols. 431–34.

129. See *DM* 6.9.6.

130. Gregory of Rimini, *Lectura super Primum et Secundum Sententiarum*, t. 2 (Berlin & New York: Walter de Gruyter), pp. 75–141.

131. Capreolus's *Sent.* I, d. 8, q. 4, contains only two articles. Suárez, I think, means

Soncinas, *Metaph.* VII, q. 36,[132] and Soto in his *Logic*, q. 3, art. 2.[133] Capreolus expressly maintains the same opinion, *Sent.* I, d. 2, q. 1, in response to Scotus's argument against the final conclusion.[134] And it is the manifest opinion of St. Thomas, *Summa Contra Gentiles* I, ch. 26, argument 4.[135] In fact, Scotus as well seems to hold this opinion in *Metaph.* X, text 3, since he establishes a difference between being and one: for being (he says) predicates the same nature really and formally of the genera of which it is quidditatively predicated, whereas one, although it predicates the same nature really, yet does not predicate it formally, since one signifies$_{d}$ a passion, not the essence.[136] But perhaps what Scotus says there has another meaning, namely, that being signifies$_{d}$ the essence of all genera, yet not the whole essence, whereas one is altogether outside the essence. And this opinion is taken from Aristotle, *Metaph.* VIII, final chapter, text 16, where he says that being itself by itself and without anything added is determined to substance, quantity, quality, and is therefore not put in definitions, since it does not signify$_{d}$ a determinate nature contractible by some difference.[137] And thus do the Commentator,[138] St. Thomas,[139] and Alexander of Hales[140] expound the passage, whereas Scotus[141] interprets Aristotle as excluding really distinct differences, but not formally distinct ones. But this is manifestly contrary to Aristotle's thought and is also not affirmed consistently by Scotus himself, since inferior genera too are

to refer to Capreolus, *Sent.* I, d. 8, q. 2, art. 2, reply to the arguments against the first conclusion. See Capreolus, *Defensiones Theologiae Divi Thomae Aquinatis*, vol. 1, pp. 340b–58b, and especially p. 346a ("ad septimum principale") and p. 354b ("ad quintam probationem").

132. Paul Soncinas, *Quaestiones Metaphysicales acutissimae*, pp. 153b–55a.

133. Domingo de Soto, *In Dialecticam Aristotelis Commentarii*, fols. 14va–15ra.

134. John Capreolus, *Defensiones Theologiae Divi Thomae Aquinatis*, vol. 1, pp. 141a–44a.

135. Thomas Aquinas, *Sancti Thomae Aquinatis opera omnia*, t. 13 (Leonina), pp. 81b–82a.

136. *Metaph.* X, text 3, is our *Metaph.* X, ch. 1, 1052b24–53a8. At no point in this text does Aristotle compare being and one. Suárez has in mind *Metaph.* X, ch. 2, 1054a13–19, which is text 8. See John Duns Scotus, *Opera omnia*, vol. 6 (Vivès), pp. 380b–81a, and n. 110 above.

137. Aristotle, *Metaph.* VIII, ch. 6, 1045a36–b7.

138. Averroes, *Aristotelis opera cum Averrois Commentariis*, vol. 8, fol. 224L–25A.

139. Thomas Aquinas, *In duodecim libros metaphysicorum Aristotelis expositio*, pp. 420b–21a (bk. VIII, lect. 5, n. 1763).

140. [Ps.-]Alexander of Hales [Alexander Bonini], *In Duodecim Aristotelis Metaphysicae Libros Dilucidissima Expositio*, fol. 258va–b.

141. See John Duns Scotus, *Opera omnia*, vol. 6 (Vivès), p. 306b, and n. 110 above.

Prima ratio. 8. Ratione probatur primo. Si ens, & substantia ex natura rei distinguuntur, vel se habent ut totum & pars, seu includens & inclusum, vel ut omnino condistincta. Hoc posterius nemo dicit, neque apprehendi potest, alias substantia praecise & forma[61b]liter sumpta, ut condistincta ab ente non includeret ens, quod est impossibile, cum de conceptu essentiali substantiae sit esse ens simpliciter. Quod vero nec primum dici possit, probatur, nam, si ens & substantia illo modo distinguuntur, resolvi potest substantia in duos conceptus ex natura rei distinctos, ⟨84a⟩ ergo in qualibet singulari substantia datur illa distinctio ex natura rei, quae antecedit intellectum, & debet esse in rebus ipsis singularibus, illi ergo duo conceptus, non tantum prout a nobis apprehenduntur, sed etiam in re ipsa distinguentur. Hoc autem esse impossibile ex parte utriusque conceptus ostendi potest, primo ex parte conceptus ipsius entis, nam si in re ipsa praescindit, & distinguitur a modo contrahente ipsum ad esse substantiae, quaero, quale ens est illud, quod manere intelligitur praeciso illo modo? Aut enim est ens commune, & ab omni singularitate abstractum, aut determinatum ad singulare ens. Primum est evidenter falsum, tum quia alias in re ipsa esset res universalis, & universaliter, quod repugnat, quia illud ens est a parte rei existens, & productum: ergo est intrinsece determinatum ac singulare, tum etiam quia est incommunicabile alteri, praeter quam huic substantiae, si in individuo loquamur. Secundum ergo necessario dicendum est, & tunc interrogo, an in ente sic praeciso a modo substantiae sit aliqua distinctio ex natura rei inter communem rationem entis, & tale ens, vel non: nam si est distinctio, redit idem argumentum, oportebit enim resolvere illum conceptum in duos, & sic procedere in infinitum, si vero non est distinctio: ergo, ut communis ratio entis determinetur ad tale ens, non oportet inter ea distinctionem ex natura rei fingere: ergo neque ut determinetur ens ad substantiam: est enim eadem ratio, & omnia argumenta in principio facta applicari possunt ad illum conceptum entis, qui dicitur esse praecisus a substantia prout in ea realiter existit, & in illo necessario solvenda sunt, & ita nullum manebit fundamentum ad

not really distinguished from their differences, but are at most formally distinguished, according to the teaching of Scotus himself. Therefore, Aristotle also excludes this distinction and composition in the determination of being to its inferiors.

First argument.

8. This is first proved by reason. If being and substance are distinguished *ex natura rei*, they are related either as whole and part, i.e., as including and included, or as altogether condistinguished. Nobody takes the latter view, nor can it be grasped, otherwise substance, taken precisely and formally as condistinguished from being, would not include being, which is impossible, since to be a being without qualification pertains to the essential concept of substance. But that the first cannot be said either is proved because, if being and substance are distinguished in that way, substance can be resolved into two concepts that are distinct *ex natura rei*, and therefore, in any given singular substance there is that distinction *ex natura rei* and prior to any operation of the understanding, and it must be in singular things$_{r}$ themselves. Therefore, those two concepts will be distinguished not only insofar as they are grasped by us, but also in reality. But that this is impossible can be proved with respect to both concepts, first with respect to the concept of being. For if it really prescinds and is distinguished from the mode that contracts it to the being$_{e}$ of substance, I ask: what sort of being is that which is understood to remain when that mode is prescinded? For either it is being in general abstracted from every singularity, or it is determined to singular being. The first is obviously false, both because otherwise there would be in reality a universal thing$_{r}$ and in a universal way, which is contradictory, since that being is existent *a parte rei* and produced, and therefore intrinsically determined and singular; and also because it is incommunicable to anything other than this substance, if we are speaking of it in the individual. The second, therefore, must necessarily be said, and then I ask whether in a being thus prescinded from the mode of substance there is some distinction *ex natura rei* between the common nature$_{r}$ of being and this being, or not. For if there is a distinction, the same argument arises, for it will be necessary to resolve that concept into two concepts and continue in the same way to infinity. But if there is no distinction, then, in order that the common nature$_{r}$ of being might be determined to this being,

talem distinctionem fingendam. Praeterquam quod vix potest mente concipi entitas realis & singularis, & tamen quod in sua intrinseca, & essentiali ratione formalissime non includat rationem substantiae aut accidentis.

9. Deinde idem ostendi potest ex parte alterius conceptus, seu modi contractivi entis: nam inquiro, an in illo intrinsece includatur ens, nec ne, si non includitur, nihil est, nihil ergo addit substantia supra ens, neque illud potest efficere distinctionem inter ens, & substantiam: imo nec potest determinare seu contrahere ens, aut constituere substantiam, quomodo enim id quod est nihil, haec omnia praestabit? Si autem includitur, ergo & modus ille includit totum conceptum substantiae, & de illo redit quaestio, an distinguatur ex ⟨84b⟩ natura rei ab ente, vel non: nam si non distinguitur, idem dici poterit de substantia: si vero distinguitur, oportebit illum resolvere in alios duos conceptus ex natura rei distinctos, & sic in infinitum procedere. Posset huic argumento responderi, negando bimembrem partitionem in principio positam, scilicet ens distingui a substantia tanquam partem a parte, vel tanquam partem a toto: sed ut simplicem conceptum communem a simplici conceptu particulari, ita ut communis in particulari includatur, quanvis non e contrario. Sed, quanvis haec responsio [62a] verum fortasse sumat, ut inferius latius exponemus tamen ex[35] ea manifeste sequitur non posse esse distinctionem ex natura rei inter conceptum entis prout existentem realiter in suis inferioribus, & illa. Nam si conceptus inferior, v. g. substantiae, est simplex, ita ut non possit resolvi in duos conceptus inter se ex natura rei distinctos, quomodo potest intelligi, quod in eo sit distinctio ex natura rei inter ipsum & aliquid in illo inclusum?[36] Igitur hoc ipsum satis declarat hunc distinctionis

35. Reading "ex" with C_1, C_2, G_2, M_1, M_2, M_3, P_1, P_2, S, V_1, V_2, V_3, and V_4. The following read "ab": M_4, V_5, and Vivès.

36. Reading a question mark here with C_1, C_2, G_2, M_1, M_2, M_3, M_4, P_1, P_2, V_1, V_2, V_3, V_4, V_5, and Vivès. S omits the question mark.

it is not necessary to imagine a distinction *ex natura rei* between them. Therefore, it is not necessary in order to determine being to substance, either, for the rationale$_r$ is the same, and all the arguments made at the beginning[142] can be applied to that concept of being which is said to be prescinded from substance as it really exists in substance, and they must necessarily be refuted in its case, and thus no foundation for supposing such a distinction will remain. But in addition to this, the mind can hardly conceive a real and singular entity which does not include, in the most formal way, the nature$_r$ of substance or the nature$_r$ of accident in its intrinsic and essential character$_r$.

9. Further, the same thing can be shown in the case of the other concept, that is, the mode contractive of being. For I ask whether being is intrinsically included in it or not. If it is not included, then the mode is nothing, and therefore substance adds nothing to being, nor can it bring about a distinction between being and substance. In fact, neither can it determine or contract being, or constitute a substance, for how will that which is nothing accomplish all these things? But if being is included in it, then that mode too includes the whole concept of substance,[143] and regarding that concept the question arises again whether it is distinguished *ex natura rei* from being or not. For if it is not distinguished, the same will be able to be said about substance. But if it *is* distinguished, one will have to resolve it into two other concepts that are distinct *ex natura rei* and continue in this way to infinity. To this argument one could reply by denying the division into two members posited at the beginning—namely, that being is distinguished from substance either as part from part, or as part from whole—maintaining instead that being is distinguished from substance as a simple common concept is distinguished from a simple particular concept, in such a way that the common concept is included in the particular concept, but not conversely. However, although this reply perhaps grasps the truth, as we shall explain more fully below, nevertheless, it clearly follows from it that there cannot be a distinction *ex natura rei* between the concept of being, as really existent in its inferiors, and those inferiors. For if the inferior concept—for example, the concept of substance—is

142. Suárez is referring to the arguments in *DM* 2.3.2–5.
143. Cf. *DM* 2.6.3–4.

modum non esse in rebus ipsis actualiter, sed solum ut in fundamento, per rationis autem praecisionem consummari.

Secunda ratio. 10. Secundo, conceptus entis non solum a creaturis, sed etiam a Deo praescinditur: sed in Deo non distinguitur ex natura rei conceptus entis ut sic a conceptu talis entis, scilicet increati, vel infiniti: ergo neque in caeteris entibus. Maior constat ex dictis, & minor etiam est certa, tum ex summa Dei simplicitate, nam si in eo esset aliqua distinctio ex natura rei, non esset summe simplex, tum etiam, quia alias daretur in rebus aliqua ratio realis ex natura rei distincta ab omnibus aliis, ex se & natura sua prior Deo ut Deus est, scilicet illa ratio entis, quae in Deo esset distincta a ratione Dei: hoc autem est impossibile, quia Deus ut Deus essentialiter est primum ens, & duratione, & perfectione, & natura. Denique, quia illamet ratio entis, quae in Deo est, essentialiter habet divinas proprietates, ut esse independentem, & increatam: unde etiam secundum illam rationem entis prout est in re, infinite distat Deus a creaturis. Quibus argumentis Soncinas li. 4. Metap. q. 2. contendit probare, ens non dicere conceptum obiectivum praecisum, sed probant de praecisione secundum rem, non tamen de praecisione secundum rationem. Prima vero consequentia argumenti probatur, quia ⟨85a⟩ licet conceptus inferiores enti in creaturis non sint aeque simplices conceptui Dei, & ideo videri possit dispar eorum ratio, tamen in praesenti est eadem, tum quia, si rationes in principio factae ostenderent distinctionem ex natura rei inter ens & inferiora, eandem omnino ostenderent in Deo, nam eodem modo applicari possunt, ut in solutionibus patebit, tum etiam, quia respectu entis ut sic, etiam inferiores conceptus creaturarum sunt simplices, & in eis non potest intelligi aliqua realitas prior natura, quam sit propria uniuscuiusque entitas secundum determinatam rationem eius. Quomodo enim concipi potest, ut in substantia sit realiter seu ex natura rei prior aliqua entitas sub ratione entis, quam sub ratione substantiae?

simple, so that it cannot be resolved into two concepts that are distinct *ex natura rei* from each other, how can it be understood that in it there is a distinction *ex natura rei* between itself and something included in it? Therefore, this makes it sufficiently clear that this sort of distinction is not in things$_{r}$ themselves actually, but only as in a foundation, and that it is accomplished by a precision of reason.

Second argument.

10. Second, the concept of being is prescinded not only from creatures, but also from God. But in God the concept of being as such is not distinguished *ex natura rei* from the concept of a particular being, namely, from the concept of the uncreated or infinite being. Therefore, neither is it so distinguished in other beings. The major is clear from the things that have been said. And the minor is also certain, because of the supreme simplicity of God, for if there were some distinction *ex natura rei* in God, he would not be supremely simple. And also because otherwise there would be in things$_{r}$ some real essence$_{r}$, distinct *ex natura rei* from all others, that is of itself and by its nature prior to God insofar as he is God, namely, the nature$_{r}$ of being, which in God would be distinct from the nature$_{r}$ of God. But this is impossible, since God, as God, is essentially the first being in duration, perfection, and nature. And finally, because that very nature$_{r}$ of being which exists$_{e}$ in God essentially has divine properties, for instance, the property of being$_{e}$ independent and uncreated. Therefore, God is infinitely distant from creatures even in respect of that nature$_{r}$ of being as it exists$_{e}$ in reality. By means of these arguments, Soncinas, *Metaph.* IV, q. 2,[144] endeavors to prove that being does not signify$_{d}$ a prescinded objective concept, but these arguments are probative as regards a real precision, but not as regards a rational precision. The first consequence of the argument is proved because, although in creatures concepts inferior to being are not equally simple as the concept of God, and therefore their nature$_{r}$ might seem different, nevertheless, as far as the present issue is concerned, it is the same, both because, if the arguments made in the beginning proved a distinction *ex natura rei* between being and its inferiors, they would prove altogether the same distinction in God, for they can be applied in the same way, as will be clear in the solutions;

144. Paul Soncinas, *Quaestiones Metaphysicales acutissimae*, p. 4a–b.

Tertia ratio. 11. Ultimo argumentor, quia sola distinctio conceptuum nostrorum, quibus aliquid concipimus per modum communis & particularis, non indicat sufficienter distinctionem ex natura rei in re concepta: ergo neque illam indicat in conceptu entis respectu inferiorum: ergo nulla est talis distinctio. Haec secunda consequentia patet, quia nullum aliud excogitari potest indicium aut vestigium talis distinctionis, quae non solum sine sufficiente, verum etiam sine cogente ratione asserenda non est: quia & in universum loquendo distinctiones non sunt multiplicandae sine causa, & praesertim ac specialiter haec, quae vix mente concipi potest. Prima vero consequentia patet, quia non est maior ratio de conceptu communi & particulari in ente, quam in reliquis, imo in ente propter transcendentiam suam est minor distinctionis ratio. Primum vero antecedens patet in primis in rebus divinis tantum, nam conceptus personae divinae communis est tribus di[62b]vinis personis, quae in ea communi ratione conveniunt & in propriis distinguuntur, & tamen in unaquaque earum ratio personae, & ratio talis personae non distinguuntur ex natura rei, sed ratione tantum. Deinde patet etiam in rationibus communibus Deo, & creaturis, ut fere iam explicatum est in ratione entis prout in Deo existit. Et declarari etiam potest in ratione sapientiae, v. g. in qua conveniunt aliquo modo sapientia creata, & increata, & tamen neque in increata sapientia distinguuntur ex natura rei communis ratio sapientiae, & propria talis sapientiae, propter summam simplicitatem, & perfectionem eius: neque etiam in sapientia creata possunt illae duae rationes ex natura ⟨85b⟩ rei distingui, quia, quantumvis praescindas rationem sapientiae, si illam consideres in re existentem in sapientia creata, intelliges illam intrinsece creatam, & consequenter in re ipsa indistinctam, & minime praecisam ex natura rei ab illo modo, quo determinatur ad esse sapientiae creatae, alioqui oporteret intelligere in sapientia creata rationem aliquam realem sapientiae, quae non solum secundum rationem, sed etiam secundum rem

and also because, in relation to being as such, the inferior concepts of creatures are also simple, and some reality, prior by nature to the proper entity of each in accordance with its determinate nature$_r$, cannot be understood in them. For how can it be conceived that in a substance some entity under the notion$_r$ of being is really or *ex natura rei* prior to [one] under the notion$_r$ of substance?

Third argument.

11. Finally, I argue: because a mere distinction between our concepts, by means of which concepts we conceive something in a common way and in a particular way, does not suffice to establish a distinction *ex natura rei* in the thing$_r$ conceived. Therefore, neither does it establish a distinction *ex natura rei* in the case of the concept of being in relation to its inferiors. Therefore, there is no such distinction. This second consequence is clear, since no other sign or mark of such a distinction can be imagined, and such a distinction is not to be asserted, not only without a sufficient reason, but also without a compelling reason, since, generally speaking, distinctions are not to be multiplied without cause, and especially and particularly this one, which can hardly be conceived by the mind. And the first consequence is clear, for when it comes to common and particular concepts there is not a greater basis$_r$ in the case of being than there is in other cases.[145] In fact, the ground of distinction is less in the case of being, on account of its transcendence. And the first antecedent is clear, to begin with, in the case of things$_r$ pertaining to God alone, for the concept of a divine person is common to the three divine persons, who agree in that common character$_r$ and are distinguished in respect of their proper characters$_r$, and yet in each of them the character$_r$ of person and the character$_r$ of a particular person are not distinguished *ex natura rei*, but only rationally. Next, it is clear also in the case of natures$_r$ common to God and creatures, as has already been fully explained in the case of the nature$_r$ of being as it exists in God. And it can also be made clear in connection with the nature$_r$ of wisdom, for example, in which created and uncreated wisdom in some way agree: nonetheless, in uncreated wisdom the common nature$_r$ of wisdom and the proper nature$_r$ of that particular wisdom

145. In other words, the distinction between a common and a particular concept is no more indicative of a distinction *ex natura rei* in the case of being and its inferiors than it is in the case of (say) animal and its inferiors.

abstraheret a ratione creatae, & increatae, quod & absurdissimum est, & mente concipi non potest, quia quidquid est entitatis in sapientia creata, est factum, & pendens.[37] Tandem idem ostendi potest rationibus communibus solis rebus creatis, quod late praestabimus infra, de universalibus disputantes: nunc breviter declaratur, quia possunt ex subtilitate & modo concipiendi humani intellectus hi conceptus superiores & inferiores infinitis modis variari & multiplicari: signum ergo est id non semper fundari in distinctione, quae sit in rebus, sed in modo concipiendi nostro, supposito aliquo fundamento similitudinis, convenientiae, aut eminentiae ipsarum rerum: alioqui oporteret fingere in unaquaque re infinitos modos ex natura rei distinctos, quibus in se plene constituatur, & ab aliis plene distinguatur. Quod uno vel alio exemplo declaratur, nam sensus communis, v. g. habet vim percipiendi obiecta omnium sensuum externorum: potest ergo abstrahi communis conceptus visui, & interiori sensui, scilicet sensus perceptivi coloris, & alius communis auditui & sensui communi, scilicet sensus perceptivi soni, & sic de reliquis. Quis autem dicat in sensu communi ex natura rei distingui vim percipiendi colorem, vel sonum inter se, aut vim sentiendi in communi distingui in eo sensu a propria vi & modo, quo attingit sua obiecta, & non potius esse ibi unam simplicem virtutem, quae attingit omnia illa obiecta, quam intellectus inadaequate concipiens comparat cum aliis rebus, & sic abstrahit conceptus communes non re, sed ratione distinctos? Idem est in luce solis, quatenus & virtutem habet illuminandi in qua convenit cum splendore ignis, & calefaciendi, in qua convenit cum calore, & exiccandi, in qua convenit cum siccitate, & ab his omnibus potest intellectus varios conceptus abstrahere, quos omnes in luce ex natura rei existimare distinctos, frivolum est & sine fundamento. ⟨86a⟩

37. Reading "pendens" with C_1, C_2, G_2, M_1, M_2, M_3, M_4, P_1, S, V_1, V_2, V_3, V_4, and V_5. The following read "dependens": P_2 and Vivès.

are not distinguished *ex natura rei*, given uncreated wisdom's supreme simplicity and perfection. Nor also in created wisdom can those two natures$_r$[146] be distinguished *ex natura rei*, since, however much you prescind the nature$_r$ of wisdom, if you consider it existing in reality in created wisdom, you will understand it to be intrinsically created, and consequently indistinct in reality and in no way prescinded *ex natura rei* from that mode by which it is determined to the being$_e$ of created wisdom. Otherwise, it would be necessary to understand in created wisdom some real nature$_r$ of wisdom that would abstract, not only rationally, but also in reality, from the nature$_r$ of created wisdom and the nature$_r$ of uncreated wisdom, which is most absurd and cannot be conceived by the mind, since whatever there is of entity in created wisdom is made and dependent. Finally, the same can be shown in the case of natures$_r$ common only to created things$_r$, which we shall do at length below while treating of universals.[147] For now, this is briefly made clear, since, thanks to the human intellect's subtlety and mode of conceiving, these superior and inferior concepts can be varied and multiplied in infinitely many ways. This, then, is a sign that it is not always founded on a distinction that is in things$_r$, but on our mode of conceiving, granted some foundation of similarity, agreement, or eminence in things$_r$ themselves. Otherwise, it would be necessary to imagine in each thing$_r$ infinite modes that are distinct *ex natura rei*, by which it is fully constituted in itself and fully distinguished from other things. This is made clear by one example or another, since the common sense, for example, has the power to perceive the objects of all the external senses. A concept common to sight and inner sense—namely, of sense perceptive of color—as well as another concept common to hearing and the common sense—namely, of sense perceptive of sound—can therefore be abstracted, and so on regarding the others. But who would say that in the common sense the power of perceiving color and the power of perceiving sound are distinguished from each other *ex natura rei*, or that in this sense the power of sensing in general is distinguished from a special power and the way it reaches its own objects—and not, rather, that in the common sense there is one simple power which reaches all

146. Sc. the common nature$_r$ of wisdom and the particular nature$_r$ of created wisdom.
147. See *DM* 6.9.

Argumentorum solutiones.

12. Ad argumenta ergo in principio posita respondetur, primum in genere, in illis omnibus esse magnam aequivocationem argumentando a ratione obiectiva ut praecisa ab intellectu, ad illam[38] prout est in re, & attribuendo rebus ipsis, quod solum per denominationem extrinsecam convenit rationibus conceptis ac prae[63a]cisis, ut sunt sub tali consideratione ac praecisione intellectus. Et hoc est maxime considerandum in his omnibus argumentationibus, quae solum in modo loquendi, & concipiendi fundantur. Nos enim, sicut concipimus, ita loquimur: unde sicut conceptus nostri, etiam si veri, & non falsi sint, non tamen semper sunt adaequati rebus ipsis, ita etiam voces sunt commensuratae conceptibus nostris, & ideo cavendum est, ne modum concipiendi nostrum transferamus ad res ipsas, & propter diversum loquendi modum existimemus, esse distinctionem in rebus, ubi vere non est.

Ad primum respondetur.[39]

13. Ad primum ergo respondetur, negando primam consequentiam, nam ratio entis dicitur esse eadem in re, quae est in mente, quia re vera omnia entia habent in re eam similitudinem & convenientiam, sub qua intellectus illa concipit, cum concipit ens, & quia hic modus concipiendi ens est inadaequatus respectu entium, prout sunt in re, ideo dicitur

38. Reading "ad illam" with C_1, C_2, G_2, M_1, M_2, M_3, M_4, P_1, P_2, V_1, V_2, V_3, V_4, V_5, and Vivès. S reads simply "&" in place of "ad illam."

39. Reading "*Ad primum respondetur.*" here next to para. 13, with C_1, C_2, G_2, M_1, M_2, M_3, M_4, P_1, P_2, S, V_1, V_2, V_3, and V_4. The following place these words next to, or at the start of, para. 12: V_5 and Vivès.

those objects, but that the intellect, conceiving this power inadequately, compares it with other things$_{r}$, and so abstracts common concepts that are distinct, not in reality, but rationally? The same goes for the sun's light,[148] insofar it has the power to illuminate (in which respect it agrees with the brightness of fire), the power to warm (in which respect it agrees with heat), and the power to dry out (in which respect it agrees with dryness): from all of these the intellect can abstract various concepts, but to judge that in this light they are distinct *ex natura rei* is frivolous and without foundation.

Refutations of the arguments.

12. To the arguments set forth at the beginning, then, I respond, first in a general way, that in all of them there is a great equivocation in arguing from an objective character$_{r}$, insofar as it is prescinded by the intellect, to the same character$_{r}$, insofar as it is in reality, and in attributing to things$_{r}$ themselves that which agrees with conceived and prescinded characters$_{r}$ only through extrinsic denomination, insofar as they are under such a consideration and precision of the intellect. And this is especially to be observed regarding all these arguments, which are founded only on a manner of speaking and conceiving. For as we conceive, so do we speak. Therefore, just as our concepts, even if they are true and not false, are nonetheless not always adequate to things$_{r}$ themselves, so also are our words commensurate with our concepts. And therefore we must beware not to transfer our manner of conceiving to things$_{r}$ themselves and judge, on account of a diverse manner of speaking, that there is a distinction in things$_{r}$ when there truly is not.

Reply to the first argument.

13. To the first argument, then, I respond by denying the first consequence, for the nature$_{r}$ of being is said to be the same in reality as it is in the mind because really all beings have in reality that likeness and agreement under which the intellect conceives them when it conceives being. And since this way of conceiving being is inadequate in comparison with beings as they are in reality, the nature$_{r}$ of being thus

148. The word rendered "light" here and later in this paragraph is "*lux*," which is often used specifically to refer to a light source, as opposed to *lumen*, which is commonly used to refer to emitted light.

ratio entis sic concepta non includere determinatos modos entium, in qua locutione iam non est sermo de ratione entis absolute, & ut in se est, sed ut est sub denominatione intellectus: unde perinde est, ac si diceretur, per illum conceptum non considerari ens sub expressis rationibus inferiorum entium, sed solum communi, & inadaequato conceptu, & ideo non recte infertur, quod etiam in re ipsa ratio entis prout est in singulis entibus non includat proprias rationes seu modos eorum: posset etiam distingui maior propositio assumpta, scilicet, rationem entis eandem esse in re, quae mente concipitur: est enim eadem realiter, non tamen ratione, & hoc satis est, ut in re possit includere proprias rationes inferiorum entium, quanvis ut concepta praecise illas non includat: sicut sapientia Divina eadem est in re, quae mente concipitur, quanvis ut mente concepta, non intelligatur includere iustitiam, quam in re ipsa essentialiter includit, quia, quod ut concepta non includat, solum est quod non expresse & di⟨86b⟩stincte consideratur ut includens illam, conceptu illo praecisivo, non negativo.

Ad secundum.

14. Ad secundum recte ibi responsum est, rationem entis in substantia non esse separabilem a substantia, & similiter in accidente, & hinc potius colligi identitatem, & indistinctionem ex natura rei, quia quae ita se habent in re, ut nec realiter distinguantur, nec unum ab alio separari possit, neque e converso, non est cur in re ipsa distinguantur, nisi aliunde sit aliquod sufficiens principium distinctionis, quod in praesente nullum invenitur. Unde ad replicam respondetur, rationem entis, quae in substantia reperitur, non reperiri eandem secundum rem in accidente, neque e converso, sed solum eandem secundum rationem, id est, secundum quandam convenientiam, & similitudinem, quam potest ratio per modum unius praecise concipere, & ad hoc satis est, quod huiusmodi ratio, quae hoc modo ut communis concipitur, secundum rationem distincta sit a propriis rationibus substantiae, & accidentis. Quod enim est proprium rei infinitae, solum est, ut eadem numero res sit communicabilis multis rebus realiter distinctis, per identitatem perfectam cum omnibus, & singulis earum, quanvis earum

conceived is said not to include determinate modes of beings, in which pronouncement the discussion no longer concerns the nature$_r$ of being absolutely and as it is in itself, but the nature$_r$ of being as it is under a denomination of the intellect. For this reason, it amounts to the same as saying that, through this concept, a being is not considered under the expressed natures$_r$ of inferior beings, but only by means of a common and inadequate concept, and therefore it is not rightly inferred that in reality as well the nature$_r$ of being, as it exists$_e$ in all beings one by one, does not include their proper natures$_r$ or modes. The assumed major proposition—namely, that the nature$_r$ of being is the same in reality as the nature$_r$ conceived by the mind—could also be distinguished: for it is really the same, but not according to reason, and this is enough for it to be able to include in reality the proper natures$_r$ of inferior beings, even though as precisely conceived it does not include them. In the same way, the divine wisdom is the same in reality as that which is conceived by the mind, although as conceived by the mind it is not understood to include justice, which in reality it essentially includes, since its not including justice insofar as it is conceived is merely its not being expressly and distinctly considered—by means of that precisive (not negative) concept—as including justice.[149]

Reply to the second argument.

14. To the second argument, it was there rightly replied that the nature$_r$ of being in substance is not separable from substance, and similarly in the case of accident, and that identity and indistinction *ex natura rei* are for this reason inferred instead. For when things are so related in reality that they are not really distinguished, nor is either capable of being separated from the other, there is no reason why they should be

149. See Johannes Micraelius, *Lexicon Philosophicum Terminorum Philosophis Usitatorum* (Jenae: impensis Jeremiae Mamphrasii, 1653), cols. 6–7: "Abstraction, *ἀφαίρεσις*, is either *real*, i.e., *πραγματώδης*, as when something is really separated from another, or *intellectual*, i.e., *mental, & νοητική*, and this is accomplished with the aid of the intellect, and for this reason it is called a *precision of the mind*, or *a precisive abstraction*, by which I apprehend one of several conjoined things, the other not being apprehended, [and this is] also called *a definitive abstraction or abstraction of simplicity*. If one thing is denied of another, the abstraction is called *negative or divisive*." ("*Abstractio ἀφαίρεσις* est vel *realis* seu *πραγματώδης*, cum aliquid reipsa ab alio separatur; vel *intellectualis seu mentalis, & νοητική*, quae ope intellectus perficitur, & ob id dicitur *praecisio mentis*, seu *abstractio praecisiva*, qua ex quibusdam conjunctis unum apprehendo, non apprehenso altero: item *abstractio simplicitatis seu definitiva*. Si unum de altero negatur, dicitur abstractio, *negativa seu divisiva*.") See *DM* 2.4.11, below.

quaelibet incommunicabilis sit. Quod vero eadem res, quae in se est realiter simplex, id est non composita ex gradibus ex natura rei distinctis, sit realiter incommunicabilis alteri, cum [63b] qua habet aliquam similitudinem, & convenientiam, ratione cuius concipiatur in eis aliqua ratio communis utrique, hoc non excedit perfectionem rei finitae, imo in qualibet re quantumvis imperfecta aliquid huiusmodi reperiri potest.

Ad tertium.

15. Ad tertium respondetur primo, substantiam in re ipsa ex eodem esse ens, ex quo est substantia, & e converso, nimirum per suam intrinsecam naturam, & entitatem, quam in re habet, & idem est, servata proportione in accidente. Quocirca in eodem sensu non ex eodem substantia est ens, ex quo accidens, neque e converso, nam accidens est ens per entitatem accidentalem, & in ordine ad substantiam, substantia vero est ens per entitatem substantialem, & in se absolutam ab ordine seu habitudine ad subiectum, neque hoc modo (in eodem sensu loquendo) accidens & substantia sunt unum in ratione entis prout in re ipsa constituuntur. Secundo dicitur, si non loquamur secundum rem, sed secundum rationem praescindentem, sic substantiam non ex eodem esse substan⟨87a⟩tiam, ex quo est ens, ex eodem (inquam) secundum rationem: ex hoc vero sensu solum potest concludi, rationem entis, & substantiae distingui ratione in ipsa substantia, & rationem similiter entis & accidentis in accidente. Atque eodem modo substantia & accidens solum dici possunt ex eodem constitui in ratione entis eo modo, quo in illo conceptu unum sunt, scilicet secundum rationem. Unde

distinguished in reality unless there is, forthcoming from elsewhere, some sufficient principle of distinction—which is in no way found in the present case. For this reason, to the rejoinder I reply that the nature$_{r}$ of being which is found in substance is not really the same as that found in accident, nor conversely, but it is only the same according to reason, that is, according to a certain agreement and similarity that reason can conceive precisely in the manner of one thing. And for this it suffices that a nature$_{r}$ of this sort, which is in this way conceived as common, be rationally distinguished from the proper natures$_{r}$ of substance and accident. For what is proper to an infinite thing$_{r}$ is only that numerically the same thing$_{r}$ is communicable to many really distinct things$_{r}$, through a perfect identity with all and each of them, although each of these is incommunicable. But that the same thing$_{r}$ which is in itself really simple (i.e., not composed from grades that are distinct *ex natura rei*) should be really incommunicable to another thing with which it has some similarity and agreement, by reason of which agreement some nature$_{r}$ common to both is conceived in them—this does not exceed the perfection of a finite thing$_{r}$. In fact, in any given thing$_{r}$, however imperfect, something of this sort can be found.

Reply to the third argument.

15. To the third argument I reply, first, that in reality that by virtue of which a substance is a being is the same as that by virtue of which it is a substance, and conversely—to be sure, its own intrinsic nature and the entity that it has in reality. And the same goes, proportionately, for an accident. Therefore, [speaking] in the same sense, a substance is not a being by virtue of the same thing by virtue of which an accident is a being, nor conversely, for an accident is a being through accidental entity and in relation to substance, whereas a substance is a being through substantial entity and in itself, independently of any order or relation to a subject. And it is not in this way (speaking in the same sense) that an accident and a substance, as they are constituted in reality, are one in the nature$_{r}$ of being. Second, I say, if we are not speaking according to reality, but according to prescinding reason, in this way that by virtue of which a substance is a substance is not the same as that by virtue of which it is a being—not the same, I say, *according to reason*. But from this sense it can only be concluded that the nature$_{r}$ of being and the nature$_{r}$ of substance are rationally distinguished in a substance, and sim-

solum potest concludi, rationem illam communem utrique per intellectus praecisionem distingui a propriis earum.

16. Ad quartum. Quibusdam videtur impossibile, ut idem secundum rem absque ulla distinctione ex natura rei, quam in se habeat, possit esse principium seu fundamentum convenientiae, & distinctionis ab alio propter argumentum factum. Alii vero putant hoc quidem repugnare in convenientia univoca, non vero in analoga, quod nobis satis esset. Ego vero existimo, etiam in convenientia univoca id non repugnare, ut patet exemplis, tum in divinis, tum in creatis. Nam Pater & Filius univoce conveniunt in ratione personae: quis enim negabit ibi aliquam unitatem, & convenientiam, aut affirmabit illam esse analogam, cum in ratione personae tam perfecta sit una sicut alia? & tamen in singulis personis nulla fingi potest ex natura rei distinctio inter distinctionis & convenientiae fundamentum. Eadem enim paternitas in se simplicissima in sua entitate relativa, distinguitur realiter a filiatione, & convenit cum illa in communi ratione relationis seu personalitatis: estque similis quasi generice, & dissimilis quasi specifice, quanvis in ea hi gradus seu conceptus ex natura rei non distinguantur. In creaturis, quantitas, & qualitas (ut est probabile) univoce conveniunt in ratione accidentis, & tamen in unaquaque earum ratio accidentis non distinguitur ex natura rei a propria, ut infra latius dicetur: & idem existimo esse de omnibus speciebus respectu suorum individuorum, ut suo loco dicetur. Ratio vero est, quia, si distinctio & convenientia sint diversorum ordinum, non repugnat in eodem fundari, sic enim una non involvit negationem alterius, imo quodammodo illam requirit. Ita vero est in praesenti: nam distinctio est realis, convenientia autem secundum rationem tantum, & ideo non repugnat, ut duo simplicia quae secundum rem sunt realiter primo diversa, secundum ratio⟨87b⟩nem habeant unitatem fundatam [64a] in reali similitudine, vel convenientia, quam inter se habent. Ea enim, quae in re diversa sunt, in eo ipso in quo distinguuntur, possunt esse similia: quin potius similitudo intrinsece postulat distinctionem secundum rem cum aliqua unitate ratio-

Quomodo possit eadem entitas per eandem simplicissimam rationem convenire, & differre.

ilarly for the nature$_r$ of being and the nature$_r$ of accident in an accident. And it is only in this way that substance and accident can be said to be constituted in the nature$_r$ of being by the same thing, in the same way they are one in that concept—namely, according to reason. Therefore, it can only be concluded that the nature$_r$ common to both is distinguished from their proper natures$_r$ by means of a precision of the intellect.

16. To the fourth argument: to some it seems impossible, because of the argument proposed, that really the same thing, without any distinction *ex natura rei* that it has within itself, could be the principle or foundation of both agreement with, and distinction from, another thing. But others think that this is indeed impossible in the case of univocal agreement, but not in the case of analogical agreement, which would be enough for us. However, I believe that it is not impossible even in the case of univocal agreement, as is clear from examples, both in divine and created things. For the Father and the Son agree univocally in the character$_r$ of person, since who will deny some unity and agreement here, or affirm that it is analogical, given that one is as perfect as the other in the character$_r$ of person? And yet, in the individual persons no distinction *ex natura rei* can be imagined between the foundation of distinction and the foundation of agreement. For the same paternity, in itself most simple, is in its relative entity really distinguished from filiation, and also agrees with it in the common character$_r$ of relation or personality. And it is similar generically, as it were, and dissimilar specifically, as it were, even though in it these grades or concepts are not distinguished *ex natura rei*. In the case of creatures, quantity and quality (as is probable) agree univocally in the nature$_r$ of accident, and yet in each of these the nature$_r$ of accident is not distinguished *ex natura rei* from its proper nature$_r$, as will be said more fully below.[150] And I judge the same to be true regarding all species in relation to their individuals, as will be said in its place.[151] And the reason is: because if the distinction and the agreement belong to diverse orders, it is not impossible for them to be founded on the same thing, for in this way one does not involve the negation of the other, but in fact requires it in some way. And so it is in the present case, for

In what way the same entity can agree with, and differ from, another by means of the same most simple nature$_r$.

150. See *DM* 39.3.
151. See *DM* 5.2.9.

nis, seu formali, aut fundamentali, nam idem proprie non est sibi ipsi simile. Quod si haec convenientia vel similitudo sit imperfecta, qualis est in analogia entis, & similibus, facilius intelligitur quomodo possint res inter se, quantumvis primo diversae, habere nihilominus aliquam imperfectam convenientiam: non enim dicuntur primo diversae, quia nullo modo inter se similes sint: hoc enim in nullis rebus, vel rationibus realibus reperiri necesse est, sed quia se ipsis primo distinguuntur: cum qua distinctione stat praedicta imperfecta convenientia. Cuius rei exemplum est in Deo, in quo nulla distinctio graduum ex natura rei excogitari potest: unde illa simplicissima natura per se ipsam est prorsus distincta a natura creata, & tamen simul est principium alicuius convenientiae analogae & secundum quid cum eadem: haec ergo duo non repugnant.

17. Ad ultimam confirmationem responsio patet ex dictis. Iam enim dictum est rationem substantiae & entis in substantia esse quidem eandem omnino secundum rem, differre tamen ratione, & priori consideratione habere in substantia eandem rationem essentialem, ratione tamen diversam, & idem est de ratione entis, & accidentis prout in accidente reperiuntur, e contrario vero accidens & substantia inter se comparata dicuntur habere in ratione entis essentialem rationem eandem secundum rationem tantum, non secundum rem, & ideo in omnibus illationibus in ea confirmatione factis committitur aequivocatio, non distinguendo diversas rationes & modos convenientiae, & distinctionis.

the distinction is real, but the agreement is according to reason only, and therefore it is not impossible for two simple things, which in reality are really and primarily diverse, to have, according to reason, some unity founded on a real similarity or agreement that they have with respect to each other. For those things which are in reality diverse can be similar in that very respect in which they are distinguished. In fact, similarity intrinsically requires a real distinction together with some unity of reason, i.e., some formal or fundamental unity, for the same thing is not properly similar to itself. But if this agreement or similarity is imperfect, as it is in the case of the analogy of being and the like, it is more easily understood in what way things$_r$, however primarily diverse, can nonetheless have some imperfect agreement with each other. For they are not called primarily diverse because they are in no way similar to each other (for, necessarily, this is so in the case of no things$_r$ or real natures$_r$), but because they are distinguished primarily by themselves, and the mentioned imperfect agreement is compatible with this distinction. An example of this is to be found in God, in whom no distinction *ex natura rei* of grades can be imagined. For this reason, that most simple nature is *per se* utterly distinct from a created nature, and yet it is at the same time the principle of a certain analogical and qualified agreement with the created nature. Therefore, these two things are not incompatible.

17. The reply to the final confirmation is clear from the things that have been said. For it has already been said that, in a substance, the nature$_r$ of substance and the nature$_r$ of being are indeed altogether the same in reality, but differ according to reason, and that, from the former point of view, they have the same essential character$_r$ in a substance, but a diverse one according to reason. And the same goes for the nature$_r$ of being and the nature$_r$ of accident as they are found in an accident. But, to the contrary, an accident and a substance compared to each other are said to have the same essential character$_r$ in respect of the nature$_r$ of being according to reason only, and not in reality. And therefore, an equivocation is at work in all the inferences made in that confirmation, by virtue of a failure to distinguish between diverse kinds$_r$ and modes of agreement and distinction.

Sectio IIII.

In quo consistat ratio entis inquantum ens, & quomodo inferioribus entibus conveniat.

1. Cum dictum sit, ens dicere unum conceptum obiectivum, oportet in quo eius formalis seu essentialis ratio consistat, breviter declarare, saltem per descriptionem aliquam, aut terminorum explicationem, nam, cum illa ratio sit abstractissima, & simplicissima, proprie ⟨88a⟩ definiri non potest. Fuit ergo opinio Avicennae, quam referunt Commen. & D. Thom. 4. Metaph. commen. 3. & lib. 10. Metaph. comm. 8. ens significare accidens quoddam commune rebus omnibus existentibus, nimirum ipsum esse, quod rebus accidere dixit, cum eis possit conferri, & auferri. Quae opinio fundata est in significatione vocis, *ens*: derivatur enim a verbo, *sum*, estque participium eius: verbum autem, *sum*, absolute dictum significat actum essendi, seu existendi: esse enim & existere idem sunt, ut ex communi usu & significatione horum verborum constat: significat ergo adaequate *ens*, id quod est, [64b] unde apud Aristot. lib. 1. Physic. tex. 17. & saepe alibi loco *entis* ponitur, *id quod est*, id est, quod habet actum essendi, seu existendi, ut idem sit ens, quod existens: dicit ergo ens de formali esse seu existentiam, quae est extra rerum quidditatem.

Quid entis nomine intelligat Avicenna.

Section 4

In What the Nature$_R$ of Being as Being Consists, And How It agrees with Inferior Beings.

What Avicenna understands by the name "being."

1. Since it has been said that "being" signifies$_d$ a single objective concept, we must briefly make clear in what its formal or essential character$_r$ consists, at least by means of some description or explanation of terms, for since that nature$_r$ is the simplest and most abstract, it cannot properly be defined. It was, then, the opinion of Avicenna (to which opinion the Commentator and St. Thomas refer in *Metaph.* IV, comment 3, and *Metaph.* X, comment 8[152]) that "being" signifies a certain accident common to all existing things$_r$—namely, the very being$_e$ that, he said, accrues accidentally to things$_r$, since it can be given to them and taken away from them. This opinion is founded on the signification of the word "being," for it is derived from the verb "to be" and is its participle. But the verb "to be," spoken absolutely, signifies the act of being$_e$ or the act of existing, for to be and to exist are the same, as is clear from the common use and signification of these words. Therefore, "being" adequately signifies that which is. For this reason, in Aristotle, *Phys.* I, text 17,[153] and frequently elsewhere, "that which is"—i.e., what

152. See Averroes, *Aristotelis opera cum Averrois Commentariis*, vol. 8, fol. 67B and fol. 257E–G, and Thomas Aquinas, *In duodecim libros metaphysicorum Aristotelis expositio*, p. 155b (bk. IV, lect. 2, ns. 556 and 558) and pp. 471b–72b (bk. X, lect. 3, ns. 1981–82).

153. *Phys.* I, text 17, is 185b9–16 (from "εἰ μὲν τοίνυν" to "καὶ αὐτὰ αὑτοῖς"). The Greek words "τὸ ὄν"—which in some contexts are rendered "that which is" (*id quod est*), or something to that effect—do not appear in this text. However, in some Latin translations "εἰ μὲν τοίνυν συνεχές, πολλὰ τὸ ἕν" (185b9–10) is rendered in such a way that "id quod est" is

2. Hanc opinionem attingens Soto, tacito nomine Avicennae, cap. 4. Antepraed. quaest. 1. in fine, prius dicit ens semper esse participium verbi, *sum*, sicut existens verbi, *existo*, & de formali significare esse, de materiali vero quod habet esse, postea vero declarat, ens non solum significare, quod actu est, sicut existens, sed quod est actu, vel potentia: quia de homine non existente, vere dicitur esse ens, sicut esse animal vel substantiam; & nihilominus concludit, *ens* non dici quidditative de rebus, praesertim creatis, quia dicit habitudinem ad esse, quod est extra essentiam creaturae. Et in hoc constituit differentiam inter, *ens*, &, *res*, quod *res* quidditative praedicatur, quia significat quidditatem veram, & ratam absolute, & sine ordine ad esse, *ens* autem non praedicatur quidditative, quia non significat absolute quidditatem, sed sub ratione essendi, seu quatenus potest habere esse, & hac ratione existimat[40] dictum ab Aristotele 8. Metaphysicae, tex. 16. ens non poni in definitionibus rerum. Quam totam doctrinam videtur sumpsisse Soto ex Caietano, opusculo de ente & essentia, c. 4. proxime ante quaest. 6. ubi praeter alia dicit, Avicennam solum reprehendi, quia vocat ens praedicatum accidentale: proprie enim esse non est accidens, sed substantialis actus, non vero esse reprehensione dignum, eo quod neget, ens esse praedicatum essentiale seu quidditativum: hoc enim verum est, cum esse sit extra quidditatem, citatque Divum Thomam quodlib. 2. ar. 3. dicentem, ens de solo Deo praedicari essentialiter, quod etiam significat ⟨88b⟩ 1. part. quaest. 3. art. 4. & 5. & 1. cont. Gent. cap. 25. & 26.

40. Reading "existimat" here with C_1, C_2, G_2, M_1, M_2, M_3, P_1, P_2, S, V_1, V_2, V_3, and V_4. The following read "existimavit" instead: M_4, V_5, and Vivès.

has the act of being$_e$ or the act of existing—is used in lieu of "being," so that a being is the same as an existent. "Being" therefore formally signifies$_d$ being$_e$ or existence, which is outside the quiddity of things$_r$.

2. Touching on this opinion without mentioning Avicenna, Soto, *Antepredicaments*, ch. 4, q. 1, at the end,[154] first says that "being" is always the participle of the verb "to be," just as "existent" is the participle of the verb "to exist," and that it formally signifies being$_e$, but materially what has being$_e$. But later he explains that "being" signifies not only what actually is, as "existent" does, but what is either actually or potentially, since it is truly said of a human being who does not exist that she is a being, just as she is truly said to be an animal or a substance. And yet he nevertheless concludes that being is not said quidditatively of things$_r$, particularly created ones, since it signifies$_d$ a relation to being$_e$, and being$_e$ is outside the essence of a creature. And on this does he establish the difference between being and thing$_r$, because thing$_r$ is predicated quidditatively, since it signifies the true and fixed quiddity absolutely, and without relation to being$_e$, whereas being is not predicated quidditatively, since it does not signify the quiddity absolutely, but under the aspect$_r$ of being$_e$, or insofar as it can have being$_e$. And he believes that it is for this reason that Aristotle says in *Metaph.* VIII, text 16, that being is not put in the definitions of things$_r$.[155] Soto seems to have taken this whole doctrine from Cajetan's short work, *On Being and Essence*, ch. 4, immediately before q. 6,[156] where Cajetan says, among other things, that Avicenna is blamed only because he calls being an accidental predicate—for being$_e$ is not properly an accident, but a substantial act—and that Avicenna is not deserving of reproach for denying that being is an essential or quidditative predicate, since this

supplied. Moreover, in the same translations, the Greek "τὸ ὄν" which appears at 185b6 is rendered "id, quod est" ("that which is") or "quod est" ("what is"). See, for example, Averroes, *Aristotelis opera cum Averrois Commentariis*, vol. 4, fol. 13rD–E and 13vA, and Simplicius, *Commentarii in octo Aristotelis Physicae Auscultationis libros* (Venetiis: apud Iuntas, 1551), fol. 13ra. Cajetan and Soto both cite *Phys.* I, text 13 (185a20–27), as one in which Aristotle uses the expression "id quod est," and at 185a21 the Greek words "τὸ ὄν" do indeed appear. See Dominic Soto, *In Dialecticam Aristotelis Commentarii*, fol. 42ra, and Cajetan *In De Ente et Essentia D. Thomae Aquinatis Commentaria*, p. 88 (n. 56).

154. Dominic Soto, *In Dialecticam Aristotelis Commentarii*, fol. 42ra.

155. Aristotle, *Metaph.* VIII, ch. 6, 1045b2–3.

156. Cajetan, *In De Ente et Essentia D. Thomae Aquinatis Commentaria*, pp. 87–89 (n. 56).

Ens, & participium, & nomen.

3. Ad explicandam hanc rem, & tollendam aequivocationem utendum nobis est usitata distinctione entis, quam Caietanus & Soto supra sine causa reiiciunt, Fonseca vero merito eam amplectitur, 4. Metaphysicae cap. 2. quaest. 3. sect. 2. eamque satis insinuat Divus Thomas dict. quodlib. licet non eisdem verbis. Ens ergo, ut dictum est, interdum sumitur, ut participium verbi, *sum*, & ut sic significat actum essendi ut exercitum: estque idem quod existens actu, interdum vero sumitur ut nomen significans de formali essentiam eius rei, quae habet, vel potest habere esse, & potest dici significare ipsum esse, non ut exercitum actu, sed in potentia, vel aptitudine, sicut *vivens*, ut est participium[41] significat actualem usum vitae, ut vero est nomen, significat solum id quod habet naturam, quae potest esse vitalis operationis principium. Quod autem haec distinctio necessario a praedictis autoribus admittenda sit, patet, nam prior significatio fundata est in proprietate & rigore verbi *sum*, quod absolute dictum actuale esse seu existentiam significat unde etiam Dialectici dicunt in propositione de secundo adiacente verbum, *est*, nunquam absolvi a tempore. Et patet etiam ex communi usu, nam si quis dicat, *Adam est*, significat ipsum existere. Habet autem hoc verbum in rigore suum participium in ipso inclusum, in quod potest resolvi praedicta propositio. Rursus constat ex communi usu, *ens*, etiam sumptum pro ente reali (ut nunc loquimur) [65a] non solum tribui rebus existentibus, sed etiam naturis realibus secundum se consideratis, sive existant, sive non: quomodo Metaphysica considerat ens & hoc modo ens in decem praedicamenta dividitur. Sed *ens* in hac significatione non retinet vim participii: quia participium consignificat tempus, & ita significat actuale exercitium essendi seu existendi, & ideo haec vox, *existens*, nunquam dici potest de re quae actu non existat, quia semper retinet vim participii verbi, *existo*, ergo necesse est, *ens* in hac posteriori significatione sumi in vi nominis. Unde praedicti autores re ipsa admittunt hanc partitionem, quanvis verbis contemnant,

41. Reading "participium" here will all the older editions. Vivès has "principium" instead.

is true, for being$_e$ is outside the quiddity. And he cites St. Thomas, in *Quodlibet* II, art. 3,[157] as saying that being is predicated essentially of God alone, which he also indicates at *ST* I, q. 3, arts. 4 and 5,[158] and at *Summa Contra Gentiles* I, chs. 25 and 26.[159]

"Being" is both a participle and a noun.

3. In order to explain this matter and remove an equivocation, we must make use of the customary distinction regarding "being," which Cajetan and Soto, above, reject without reason. Fonseca rightly embraces it, *Metaph.* IV, ch. 2, q. 3, sect. 2,[160] and St. Thomas suggests it sufficiently in the mentioned *Quodlibet*, although not in the same words. "Being," then, as has been said, is sometimes taken as the participle of the verb "to be," and as such it signifies the act of being$_e$ as exercised, and it is the same as the actually existent. But sometimes it is taken as a noun formally signifying the essence of a thing$_r$ that has or can have being$_e$, and it can be said to signify being$_e$ itself, not as actually exercised, but in potency or aptitude, just as "living thing," insofar as it is a participle, signifies the actual enjoyment of life, but insofar as it is a noun signifies only that which has a nature that can be a principle of vital operations. That this distinction necessarily ought to be allowed by the mentioned authors is clear, for the first signification is founded on the proper and strict sense of the verb "to be," which, spoken absolutely, signifies actual being$_e$ or existence, for which reason also dialecticians say that in a proposition of the second adjacent[161] the verb "is" is never dissociated from time. And this is also clear from common use, for if someone says "Adam is," she signifies that Adam exists. And this verb strictly has its participle included in itself, into which the mentioned proposition can be resolved.[162] Again, it is clear from common use that being, even taken as real being (as we are now taking it), is not only attributed to existent things$_r$, but also to real natures considered in themselves, whether

157. Thomas Aquinas, *Sancti Thomae de Aquino opera omnia*, t. 25, vol. 2 (Roma & Paris: Commissio Leonina & Les Éditions du Cerf, 1996), p. 214b.

158. Thomas Aquinas, *Sancti Thomae Aquinatis opera omnia*, t. 4 (Leonina), p. 42b, pp. 43b–44a.

159. Thomas Aquinas, *Sancti Thomae Aquinatis opera omnia*, t. 13 (Leonina), p. 76b, p. 81b.

160. Pedro da Fonseca, *Commentaria in Libros Metaphysicorum Aristotelis Stagiritae*, vol. 1, cols. 739–40.

161. The verb "is" occurs as a second adjacent (*secundum adiacens*) in the proposition "a human being is."

162. I.e., "Adam is" (*Adam est*) = "Adam is a being" (*Adam est ens*).

nam perinde est dicere *ens* interdum significare rem actu existentem, interdum potentia tantum, quod dicere interdum sumi ut participium, aliquando vero ut nomen, seu, ut alii loquuntur, participialiter & nomi⟨89a⟩naliter. Quia hoc ipso, quod *ens* non significat actualem entitatem & existentiam, iam non sumitur in vi participii, sed tanquam nomen verbale. Unde Divus Thomas in dicto Quodlib. postquam tractavit de ente, prout dicitur ab actuali esse, subdit: *Sed verum est, quod hoc nomen,* ens, *secundum quod importat rem, cui competit huiusmodi esse, sic significat essentiam rei, & dividitur per decem genera.*

Quaestionis resolutio.

Ens participium quid importet.

4. Hac ergo supposita vocis significatione, facilis est quaestionis resolutio in communi sumpta. Dicendum est enim primo, sumpto ente in actu, prout est significatum illius vocis in vi participii sumptae, rationem eius consistere in hoc quod sit aliquid actu existens, seu habens realem actum essendi, seu habens realitatem actualem, quae a potentiali distinguitur, quod est actu nihil. Hoc totum, cum solum consistat in declaratione simplicissimi conceptus, non potest aliter probari, quam ex communi modo concipiendi, & ex significatione vocis a nobis explicatae. Ac denique, quia ex dictis in praecedentibus sectionibus constare potest, ens sub hac ratione posse habere unum conceptum formalem, & obiectivum communem omnibus entibus actu existentibus, cum inter se similia sint & conveniant in actuali esse & entitate, constat etiam posse conceptum illum hac voce significari: ergo entis sic sumpti, &

they exist or not: it is in this way that metaphysics considers being, and it is in this way that being is divided into the ten categories. But "being" in this signification does not retain the force of a participle, since a participle consignifies time, and so signifies the actual exercise of being$_{e}$ or existing, and therefore this word "existent" can never be said of a thing$_{r}$ that does not actually exist, since it always retains the force of the participle of the verb "to exist." Therefore, it is necessary that "being" in this second signification be taken as having the force of a noun. For this reason, the mentioned authors really allow this division, although they verbally dismiss it, for to say that "being" sometimes signifies an actually existing thing$_{r}$ and sometimes a thing that exists only potentially is the same as saying that it is sometimes taken as a participle and sometimes as a noun, or, as others say, that it is sometimes taken participially and sometimes nominally. For by the very fact that "being" does not signify actual entity and existence, it is no longer taken as having the force of a participle, but as a verbal noun. For this reason, in the mentioned *Quodlibet*, after having treated of being insofar as it is so called from actual being$_{e}$, St. Thomas adds: "But it is true that this name 'being,' insofar as it denotes a thing$_{r}$ which is capable of such being$_{e}$, in this way signifies the essence of a thing$_{r}$ and is divided into the ten genera."[163]

Resolution of the question.

What the participle "being" signifies.

4. Assuming this signification of the word, then, the question's resolution, taken in a general way, is easy. For it must be said, first, that when being is taken in act, insofar as it is the significate of that word understood as having the force of a participle, its nature$_{r}$ consists in this, that it is something actually existing, or something having a real act of being$_{e}$, or something having actual reality, which is distinguished from potential reality, which is actually nothing. All this, since it consists only in the explanation of a most simple concept, cannot be proved otherwise than from the common mode of conceiving and from the signification of the word as explained by us. And finally, because, from the things that have been said in the preceding section, it

163. Thomas Aquinas, *Sancti Thomae de Aquino opera omnia*, t. 25, vol. 2 (Leonina), p. 215a.

conceptus eius ratio, non potest in alio consistere, nec potest aliter explicari.

5. Dico secundo. Si ens sumatur prout est significatum huius vocis in vi nominis sumptae, eius ratio consistit in hoc, quod sit habens essentiam realem, id est non fictam nec chymericam, sed veram, & aptam ad realiter existendum. Probatio huius conclusionis eadem proportionaliter est, quae praecedentis, quia hic simplex conceptus non potest alio modo intelligi aut explicari.

Quid sit essentia realis.

Ens nomen quid.

6. Solum restabat exponendum, quid sit essentia realis, vel in quo ratio eius consistat: nam cum essentia sit secundum quam res dicitur, seu denominatur ens, ut Divus Thomas ait, de ente & essentia cap. 2. quod maxime verum est de ente in hac acceptione sumpto: ideo non potest satis explicari, in quo consistat ratio entis realis, nisi intelligatur, in quo consistat essentia realis. [65b] In quo duo peti possunt, quae illis duabus ⟨89b⟩ vocibus indicantur: primum, in quo consistat ratio essentiae: secundum, in quo consistat, quod realis sit. Primum non potest a nobis exponi, nisi vel in ordine ad effectus, vel passiones rei, vel in ordine ad nostrum modum concipiendi & loquendi. Primo modo dicimus, essentiam rei esse id quod est primum, & radicale, ac intimum principium omnium actionum, ac proprietatum, quae rei conveniunt, & sub hac ratione dicitur *natura uniuscuiusque rei*, ut constat ex Aristotele 5. Metaphysicae tex. 5. & notat Divus Thomas de ente & essentia cap. 1. & quodlib. 2.[42] artic. 4. & saepe alias. Secundo autem modo dicimus essentiam rei esse, quae per definitionem explicatur, ut dicit etiam Divus Thomas dicto opusculo de ente & essentia, cap. 2.

42. Reading "2" here with S, V_1, and V_2. The following read "1": C_1, C_2, G_2, M_1, M_2, M_3, M_4, P_1, P_2, V_3, V_5, and Vivès. (Scan of V_4 missing relevant portion.)

can be established that being on this conception$_r$ of it can have a single formal concept, as well as a single objective concept, common to all beings that actually exist, since they are similar to each other and agree in actual being$_e$ and entity. It is also clear that that concept can be signified by this word. Therefore, the nature$_r$ of being, thus understood, and of its concept, cannot consist in something else, nor can it be otherwise explained.

5. I say, second: if being is taken insofar as it is the significate of this word understood as having the force of a noun, then its nature$_r$ consists in this, that it is something having a real essence, that is, not a fictitious or chimerical essence, but one that is true and suited to really existing. The proof of this conclusion is proportionately the same as the proof of the preceding one, since this simple concept cannot be understood or explained in another way.

What a real essence is.

What "being" signifies when taken as a noun.

6. It remains only to explain what a real essence is, or in what its nature$_r$ consists. For since an essence is that in accordance with which a thing$_r$ is called or denominated a being, as St. Thomas says in *On Being and Essence*, ch. 2[164] (which is most especially true of being taken in this sense), one cannot sufficiently explain what the nature$_r$ of a real being consists in unless one understands what a real essence consists in. Regarding this, two things can be sought, which are indicated by those two words: first, what the nature$_r$ of an essence consists in, and second, what its being real consists in. The first cannot be explained by us except either in relation to the effects or passions of the thing$_r$, or in relation to our mode of conceiving and speaking. In the first way, we say that the essence of a thing$_r$ is that which is the first, fundamental, and innermost principle of all the actions and properties that agree with the thing$_r$, and on this conception$_r$ of it it is called the nature of each thing$_r$, as is clear from Aristotle, *Metaph.* V, text 5,[165] and as St. Thomas

164. Thomas Aquinas, *Sancti Thomae de Aquino opera omnia*, t. 43 (Leonina), p. 371a.
165. Aristotle, *Metaph.* V, ch. 4, 1014b35–1015a19.

& sic etiam dici solet, illud esse essentiam rei, quod primo concipitur de re: primo (inquam) non ordine originis: sic enim potius solemus conceptionem rei inchoare ab his, quae sunt extra essentiam rei, sed ordine nobilitatis[43] potius & primitatis obiecti: nam id est de essentia rei, quod concipimus primo illi convenire, & primo constitui intrinsece in esse rei, vel talis rei, & hoc modo etiam vocatur essentia *quidditas* in ordine ad locutiones nostras, quia est id, per quod respondemus ad quaestionem, quid sit res. Ac denique appellatur *essentia*, quia est id, quod per actum essendi primo esse intelligitur in unaquaque re. Ratio ergo essentiae his modis potest a nobis declarari.

7. Quid autem sit essentiam esse realem, possumus aut per negationem, aut per affirmationem exponere. Priori modo dicimus essentiam realem esse, quae in se se nullam involvit repugnantiam, neque est mere conficta per intellectum. Posteriori autem modo explicari potest, vel a posteriori per hoc, quod sit principium vel radix realium operationum, vel effectuum, sive sit in genere causae efficientis, sive formalis, sive materialis: sic enim nulla est essentia realis, quae non possit habere aliquem effectum vel proprietatem realem. A priori vero potest explicari per causam extrinsecam (quanvis hoc non simpliciter de essentia, sed de essentia creata verum habeat) & sic dicimus essentiam esse realem, quae a Deo realiter produci potest, & constitui in esse entis actualis. Per intrinsecam autem causam non potest proprie haec ratio essentiae explicari, quia ipsa est prima causa, vel ratio intrinseca entis, & simplicissima, ut hoc communissimo conceptu essentiae concipitur:

43. Vivès and all the earlier editions that I've consulted read "nobilitatis" here. However, the Latin text included with the Spanish translation of Rábade et. al has "notabilitatis" instead, although the translation ("en orden de excelencia y de primacía objetiva") reflects the former reading. See Francisco Suárez, *Disputaciones metafísicas*, ed. Sergio Rábade Romeo, Salvador Caballero Sánchez, and Antonio Puigcerver Zanón, vol. 1 (Madrid: Ed. Gredos, 1960), p. 419.

observes in *On Being and Essence*, ch. 1,[166] in *Quodlibet* II, art. 4,[167] and frequently elsewhere. But in the second way we say that the essence of a thing$_r$ is that which is explained by means of a definition, as St. Thomas also says in the mentioned short work, *On Being and Essence*, ch. 2,[168] and in this way it is also normally said that the essence of a thing$_r$ is that which is first conceived of the thing$_r$—first, I say, not in order of origin (for in this way we normally begin our conception of a thing$_r$ instead from those things which are outside its essence), but rather in order of excellence and the object's primacy. For belonging to the essence of a thing$_r$ is that which we conceive to agree with it primarily, and to be first constituted intrinsically in the being$_e$ of a thing$_r$, or in the being$_e$ of a thing$_r$ of a particular type, and in this way the essence is also called a quiddity in relation to our speech, since it is that by means of which we answer the question of what a thing$_r$ is.[169] And finally, it is called an *essence* because it is, in each thing$_r$, that which is understood to *be* in the first place through the act of being$_e$.[170] The nature$_r$ of an essence, then, can be explained by us in these ways.

7. We can explain what an essence's being real is either by negation or by affirmation. In the first way, we say that an essence is real when it involves no impossibility in itself and is not wholly fabricated by the intellect. In the second way, it can be explained either *a posteriori* as the principle or root of real operations or effects, whether this be in the genus of efficient cause, or in the genus of formal cause, or in the genus of material cause. For there is no real essence that cannot thus have some real effect or property. But *a priori* it can be explained through

166. Thomas Aquinas, *Sancti Thomae de Aquino opera omnia*, t. 43 (Leonina), pp. 369b–70a.

167. See Thomas Aquinas, *Sancti Thomae de Aquino opera omnia*, t. 25, vol. 2 (Leonina), pp. 215a–18b. Although in this text Aquinas identifies the nature of a thing with its essence, he does not state (as he does in the text from *On Being and Essence* just cited—see last note) that an essence is called a nature insofar as it is the first innermost principle of a thing's actions and properties.

168. Thomas Aquinas, *Sancti Thomae de Aquino opera omnia*, t. 43 (Leonina), p. 370b.

169. The Latin word for "what," in the question "what is it?" is "*quid*." A thing's quiddity is its whatness, so to speak.

170. Suárez, of course, is here assuming that his reader will recognize the connections between the abstract noun "*essentia*" ("essence"), the verb "*esse*" ("to be"), and the genitive gerund of "*esse*," "*essendi*" ("being$_e$"), which figures in the expression "*actus essendi*" ("act of being$_e$").

unde solum dicere possumus, es⟨90a⟩sentiam realem eam esse, quae ex se apta est esse, seu realiter existere. His ergo modis potest a nobis communis ratio entis declarari, magis autem exacta huius rei intelligentia pendet ex pluribus quaestionibus. Prima est, qualis sit entitas essentiae realis, quando actu non existit. Secunda, quid sit existentia actualis, & ad quid necessaria sit in rebus. Tertia, quomodo existentia distinguatur ab essentia. Sed quia hae quaestiones propriae fere sunt entis creati, & prolixam requirunt disputationem, ideo eas usque ad disputationem 7. differimus, contenti pro nunc praedicta entis & essentiae descriptione. [66a]

Ens in actu & in potentia in quo conveniant.

8. Una vero dubitatio circa duas conclusiones positas hic praetermitti non potest, quanvis attingat divisionem entis in ens in actu, & ens in potentia: scilicet an illa duplex significatio entis nominaliter, & participialiter sumpti, sit mere aequivoca, vel ita analoga, ut nullus conceptus communis utrique membro, ei respondeat: an vero habeat aliquem conceptum communem, nam si hoc posterius dicatur, nondum est a nobis communissima ratio entis satis explicata: declaravimus enim singulorum membrorum rationes, non autem rationem entis ut communis & abstrahentis ab utroque membro. Deinde difficillimus erit ad explicandum talis conceptus & ratio eius, imo & nomen, quia nec significabitur per *ens* nominaliter sumptum, nec participialiter: non potest autem fingi alius modus significandi abstrahens ab his duobus. Si vero dicatur primum, sequitur non posse dari conceptum entis communem Deo & creaturis, ut possibilibus, sed tantum ut actu existentibus, quod videtur plane falsum, & contra communem modum concip-

an extrinsic cause (although this is not true without qualification of essence, but of created essence), and in this way we say that that essence is real which can really be produced by God and constituted in the being$_{e}$ of an actual being. But this conception$_{r}$ of an essence cannot properly be explained through an intrinsic cause, since it is itself the first and simplest intrinsic cause or ground$_{r}$ of a being, insofar as it is conceived by means of this most common concept of essence. For this reason we can only say that that essence is real which is of itself suited to be or to exist really. The common nature$_{r}$ of being, therefore, can be explained by us in these ways. But a more precise understanding of this issue depends on several questions. The first is: of what sort is the entity of a real essence when it does not actually exist? Second: what is actual existence, and for what is it necessary in things$_{r}$? Third: how is existence distinguished from essence? But since these questions are for the most part proper to created being and require a lengthy discussion, we defer them to Disputation VII,[171] being satisfied for now with the preceding description of being and essence.

In what respect being in act and being in potency agree.

8. But one doubt regarding the two conclusions set forth cannot be left unmentioned here, even though it touches on the division of being into being in act and being in potency—namely, whether that twofold signification of "being" taken nominally and participially is either purely equivocal or analogical in such a way that no concept common to both members corresponds to it, or this twofold signification instead has some common concept. For if the latter is affirmed, the most common nature$_{r}$ of being has not yet been sufficiently explained by us, since we have made clear the natures$_{r}$ of the individual members, but not the nature$_{r}$ of being insofar as it is common to, and abstracts from, each member. Moreover, such a concept and its nature$_{r}$ will be most difficult to explain—and its name, too, in fact, since it will not be

171. *DM* 7 treats of the various kinds of distinction and is therefore relevant to a discussion of the questions just enumerated. But it is in *DM* 31 that Suárez explicitly addresses these questions themselves.

iendi, & contra omnia supra dicta de communissimo conceptu entis. Sequitur deinde hominem aequivoce dici de vero homine possibili, vel actu existente. Patet sequela, quia eadem est ratio de homine respectu illorum duorum membrorum, quae est de ente respectu entis in actu & in potentia, seu de ente nominaliter & participialiter sumpto: nam ut participium significat ens in actu, ita nomen ens in potentia. Consequens autem vidctur plane ſalsum: nam *homo* ex vi eiusdem impositionis significat hominem, sive actu existentem, sive possibilem: imo & simplex conceptus hominis, qui illi voci respondet, aeque repraesentat hominem existentem, vel possibilem: non est ergo ⟨90b⟩ ibi significatio aequivoca, idem ergo est proportionaliter de ente sub illa duplici ratione seu significatione sumpto, & de conceptu qui illi respondet.

Resolutio.

9. Respondetur, *ens* secundum illam duplicem acceptionem non significare duplicem rationem entis dividentem aliquam communem rationem, seu conceptum communem, sed significare conceptum entis, magis vel minus praecisum: *ens* enim in vi nominis sumptum significat id, quod habet essentiam realem, praescindendo ab actuali existentia, non quidem excludendo illam, seu negando, sed praecisive tantum abstrahendo, *ens* vero ut participium est, significat ipsum ens reale, seu habens essentiam realem cum existentia actuali, & ita significat illud magis contractum. Unde, sicut animal dictum de ipso genere praecise sumpto, & de bruto quatenus tale animal est, non dividit aliquem conceptum communem ad animal ut sic, & tale animal, sed dicit eandem rationem animalis, ut praecisam vel ut contractam, ita dicendum est de ente sub illa duplici acceptione. Magisque accommodatum exemplum est in dispositione ut significat quandam speciem qualitatis ab habitu

Exemplum accommodatum ad resolutionis intelligentiam.

signified by "being" taken nominally, nor by "being" taken participially, and another mode of signifying that abstracts from these two cannot be imagined. If, however, the former is affirmed, it follows that there cannot be a concept of being common to God and creatures insofar as creatures are possible, but only insofar as creatures are actually existent, which seems plainly false and contrary to the common mode of conceiving, and also contrary to all the things that were said above about the most common concept of being. It follows, moreover, that human being is said equivocally of a true, possible human being and an actually existing one.[172] The consequence is clear, since the argument regarding human being in relation to those two members is the same as that regarding being in relation to being in act and being in potency, or "being" taken nominally and "being" taken participially, for just as the participle signifies being in act, so does the noun signify being in potency. But the consequent seems plainly false, for "human being," by virtue of the same imposition, signifies the human being whether actually existent or possible. In fact, the simple concept of the human being which corresponds to that word equally represents an existing human being or a possible one. Therefore, the signification here is not equivocal. Therefore, the same is true proportionately both of "being" taken under that twofold conception$_r$ or signification, and of the concept that corresponds to it.

Solution.

9. I reply that, in accordance with that twofold acceptation, "being" does not signify a twofold nature$_r$ of being that divides some common nature$_r$ or common concept, but rather signifies the concept of being as prescinded more or less. For "being," understood as having the force of a noun, signifies that which has a real essence, prescinding from actual existence, not indeed excluding or denying it, but only abstracting precisively from it, whereas "being," insofar as it is a participle, signifies real being itself, or something having a real essence, together with actual existence, and thus it signifies being as more contracted. For this reason, just as "animal," as said of the genus itself taken precisely, and as said of the brute insofar as it is an animal of a particular sort, does not divide some concept common to both animal as such and a par-

172. It should be borne in mind that "human being" here and elsewhere translates a single Latin word, "*homo*."

distinctam, & genus utrique commune: non enim habet aliquam significationem communem, qua immediate significet alium conceptum communem generi, & speciei (id enim impossibile est quia generi & speciei nihil est commune praeter ipsum conceptum generis) significat ergo, vel immediate genus ipsum, vel immediate speciem quandam duplici significatione. Ita ergo *ens* non significat conceptum aliquem communem enti nominaliter, & participialiter sumpto, sed immediate habet duplicem significationem, qua significat, vel ens praescinden[66b]do ab actuali existentia, vel ens actu existens. Quocirca illa duplex significatio, vel aequivoca est, vel maxime ad aequivocationem accedit secundum quandam translationem fundatam in aliqua proportionalitate. Primo enim *ens* significasse videtur rem habentem esse reale & actuale, tanquam participium verbi essendi: inde vero translata est illa vox ad praecise significandum id quod habet essentiam realem. Cuius simile etiam est in voce illa, *dispositio*, nam ut significat genus & speciem, sine dubio habet aequivocam significationem, vel ad summum analogam secundum quandam proportionalitatem. ⟨91a⟩

10. Igitur ad exemplum de voce, *homo*, quod in contrarium afferebatur, respondetur non esse simile, nam *homo*, non habet duplicem significationem, unam qua significet hominem praecise, vel in potentia, aliam qua significet hominem existentem ut sic, sed unicam tantum, qua significat hominem praecise sive existat, sive non, quae significatio est proportionalis, vel similis illi, quam habet ens solum in vi nominis sumptum. Alia vero, quam habet in vi participii, non reperitur in hac voce, *homo*, neque est ullus terminus incomplexus & simplex, qui significet totum hoc, quod hac voce complexa significatur, *homo existens*. Quod si fingamus vocem hominis transferri ad totum hoc significandum, iam habebit duplicem significationem aequivocam, quam dicimus esse in nomine entis.

ticular type of animal, but rather signifies$_d$ the same nature$_r$ of animal as prescinded or as contracted, so must the same be said of "being" under that twofold acceptation. A more suitable example is "disposition," insofar as it signifies a certain species of quality distinct from habit and also a genus common to both.[173] For it does not have some common signification by which it immediately signifies another concept common to the genus and the species (for that is impossible, since there is nothing common to the genus and the species aside from the concept of the genus itself). Therefore, by means of a twofold signification, it either immediately signifies the genus itself, or it immediately signifies a certain species. In this way, then, "being" does not signify some concept common to "being" taken nominally and "being" taken participially, but immediately has a twofold signification by which it signifies either being, prescinding from actual existence, or actually existent being. For this reason, that twofold signification is either equivocal or very nearly approaches equivocation in accordance with a certain transference founded on some proportionality. For at first "being" seems to have signified a thing$_r$ having real and actual being$_e$, as the participle of the verb "to be." From there that word was transferred so as to signify precisely that which has a real essence. And this case is similar to that of the word "disposition," for, insofar as it signifies a genus and a species, it undoubtedly has an equivocal signification, or at most an analogical one, according to a certain proportionality.

Example suited to an understanding of the solution.

10. Therefore, as regards the example of the word "human being," which was brought forth in support of the contrary position, I reply that it is not similar. For "human being" does not have a twofold signification—one by which it signifies the human being precisely or in potency, and another by which it signifies an existing human being as such—but only one, according to which it signifies the human being precisely, whether she exists or not. And this signification is proportional or similar to that which "being" has when understood only as having the force of a noun. The other signification, which it has when understood as having the force of a participle, is not found in the case of this word, "human being," nor is there any non-complex and simple

173. See Aristotle, *Cat.* 8, 8b25–9a13.

11. Ex quo ulterius intelligitur ens sumptum in vi nominis non significare ens in potentia, quatenus privative vel negative opponitur enti in actu, sed significare solum ens ut praecise dicit essentiam realem, quod valde diversum est, sicut enim abstractio praecisiva diversa est a negativa: ita ens nominaliter sumptum, licet praecise dicat ens habens essentiam realem, non vero addit negationem, scilicet carendi existentia actuali, quam negationem seu privationem addit ens in potentia. Quod inde etiam manifeste patet, nam *ens* in vi nominis sumptum commune est Deo, & creaturis, & de Deo affirmari vere potest, ens autem in potentia nullo modo potest praedicari de Deo: imo nec de creaturis existentibus ut sic, proprie dicitur, quia iam non sunt in potentia, sed in actu: cum tamen de illis dici possit *ens*, tam ut participium, quam ut nomen, quia licet habeant actualem existentiam, vere etiam de illis dicitur, quod habent essentiam realem, praescindendo, & non negando actualem existentiam.

12. Unde tandem intelligitur, *ens* praecise sumptum, ut in vi nominis significatur, proprie dividi posse in ens in actu, & ens in potentia, & ens in actu idem esse, quod ens significatum per hanc vocem in vi participii sumptam, atque ita illa duo significare rationem entis, vel praecisam, vel determinatam ad actualem existentiam, sive haec determinatio essentialis sit, ut est in Deo, sive sit extra essentiam, ut censetur esse in creaturis, de qua re inferius disputandum est: ens autem in potentia dicit etiam reale ens, quantum ad realem essentiam, contractum & determinatum non per aliquid positivum, sed per pri⟨91b⟩vationem actualis existentiae. Ens autem sic contractum, seu prout in tali statu conceptum, non significatur per hanc vocem, *ens*, nec per aliquam aliam incomplexam, quae mihi nota sit, sed solum per hos terminos complexos, *ens possibile, ens in potentia*, & similes: quae omnia sunt diligenter advertenda: nam ex his vocum significationibus mul-

term that signifies the whole that is signified by this complex expression: "existent human being." But if we were to imagine that the word "human being" was transferred to signify this whole, then it would have the twofold equivocal signification that we say is found in the name "being."

11. From this it is further gathered that "being," understood as having the force of a noun, does not signify being in potency insofar as it is privatively or negatively opposed to being in act, but only signifies being insofar as it precisely signifies$_{d}$ a real essence, which is very different. For just as precisive abstraction is diverse from negative abstraction,[174] so also "being," taken nominally, even though it precisely signifies$_{d}$ being having a real essence, does not add a negation, namely, that of lacking actual existence, which is the negation or privation that "being in potency" adds. And this is manifestly clear from the following consideration, as well: "being," taken as having the force of a noun, is common to God and creatures, and of God it can truly be affirmed. But being in potency can in no way be predicated of God. In fact, neither is it properly said of existing creatures as such, since they are no longer in potency but in act. Nevertheless, "being"—both as a participle and as a noun—can be said of them, since, although they have actual existence, it is also truly said of them that they have a real essence, prescinding from, and not denying, actual existence.

12. From this, finally, it is understood that being, taken precisely, insofar as it is signified by the noun, can properly be divided into being in act and being in potency, and that being in act is the same as the being signified by this word when it is taken as having the force of a participle, and thus that those two signify the nature$_{r}$ of being either as prescinded from, or as determined to, actual existence, whether the latter determination is essential, as it is in the case of God, or outside the essence, as it is thought to be in the case of creatures (of which matter we shall have to treat below[175]). But "being in potency" also signifies$_{d}$ real being, as far as real essence is concerned, contracted and determined not by something positive, but by the privation of actual existence. But being, so contracted, or insofar as it is conceived in such

174. See n. 149 above.

175. See *DM* 31.6.13–14.

tum pendet vera rerum con[67a]ceptio, & ex his magna etiam ex parte obiter exposita est divisio entis in ens in actu, & ens in potentia, quam iterum postea ex professo tractabimus.

Ens an sit praedicatum essentiale.

13. Atque hinc obiter colligitur rationem entis communissimam, quae significatur per eam vocem in vi nominis sumptam, esse essentialem, & praedicari quidditative de suis inferioribus, quanvis *ens*, ut actualem dicit existentiam, & significatur per participium essendi, absolute non sit praedicatum essentiale, nisi in solo Deo. Haec posterior pars, quatenus ad Deum spectat, Theologica[44] est, & ex principiis naturalibus tractari solet infra lib. 12. & eam late disserui in tomo 1. 3. p. in disp. 11. sect. 1. & aliquid attingemus infra, disputando de Deo. Quantum vero spectat ad creaturas, pendet ex dicendis infra de distinctione existentiae ab essentia in creatura: nunc supponamus, sive distinguantur, sive non, absolute esse dicendum, existere non esse de essentia creaturae, quia potest illi dari, & ab illa auferri, & ita non habet necessariam connexionem cum essentia creaturae praecise concepta, sub qua ratione est invariabilis, & necessario dicitur de unaquaque re cuius est essentia: hac ergo ratione *ens* participialiter sumptum, dicitur non praedicari quidditative seu essentialiter de creaturis, & quoad hoc vera est opinio Avicennae supra recitata, eamque admittit D. Thom. dicto quodlib. 2. & aliis locis supra citatis, solumque potest Avicenna reprehendi vel eo quod existentiam putaverit esse verum accidens, de quo infra suo loco, vel eo quod aliam acceptionem & explicationem entis omiserit, & ideo simpliciter negandum putaverit, ens sub aliqua ratione sub qua in decem praedicamenta dividitur, esse posse essentiale omnibus illis.

44. Reading "Theologica" with none of the early editions. The following have "Theologa": M_1, P_1, P_2, S, V_1, V_2, and Vivès. The following have "Theologia": C_1, C_2, G_2, M_2, M_3, M_4, V_3, V_4, and V_5.

a state, is not signified by this word "being," nor by some other incomplex expression that is known$_n$ to me, but only by such complex terms as "possible being," "being in potency," and the like. And all these points must carefully be noted, for the true conception of things$_r$ very much depends on these significations of the words, and it is in great measure by appeal to these that we have explained, in passing, the division of being into being in act and being in potency. But we shall later treat *ex professo* of this division again.[176]

Whether being is an essential predicate.

13. And from this it is incidentally gathered that the most common nature$_r$ of being (which is signified by that word when it is understood to have the force of a noun) is essential and is predicated quidditatively of its inferiors, although being, insofar as it signifies$_d$ actual existence and is signified by the participle of the verb "to be," is absolutely not an essential predicate, except in the case of God alone. This latter point, insofar as it pertains to God, is theological, and is normally dealt with on the basis of natural principles in book XII,[177] and I have treated of it at length in volume 1 of the third part, in Disputation XI, sect. 1,[178] and we shall touch on it somewhat below, when treating of God.[179] But as regards creatures, it depends on things to be said below regarding the distinction of existence from essence in the creature.[180] For now, let us suppose that, whether they are distinguished or not, it must be affirmed absolutely that to exist does not belong to the essence of a creature, since existence can be given to it or taken from it, and so it does not have a necessary connection with the creature's essence as precisely conceived, on which conception$_r$ of it it is invariable and is necessarily said of each thing$_r$ of which it is the essence. For this reason, therefore, "being" taken participially is said not to be predicated quidditative-

176. See *DM* 31.3.

177. Sc. in connection with book XII of Aristotle's *Metaphysics*.

178. Francisco Suárez, *Commentariorum ac Disputationum in Tertiam Partem Divi Thomae Tomus Primus* (Compluti: In Collegio Societatis Iesu, ex officina Typographica Petri Madrigalis, 1590), pp. 211a–214a (p. 211 is mislabeled "209").

179. See *DM* 29 and 30.

180. See *DM* 31.6.

14. Probatur ergo altera conclusionis pars (quam immerito Soto negare videtur) quia habere essentiam realem convenit omni enti reali, estque illi maxime essentiale: ergo ens sub praedicta ratione est praedicatum essen⟨92a⟩tiale. Praeterea esse ens hoc modo convenit creaturae, etiam si non existat, quomodo haec propositio, *homo est ens*, dicitur esse aeternae veritatis: sed non convenit illi per se secundo ut proprietas aliqua, quia non supponit aliquid prius a quo dimanet tanquam passio: nam potius ille est primus conceptus cuiusvis entis realis: ergo convenit ut praedicatum essentiale, & de quidditate rei. Et hoc modo dixit D. Th. dicto quodlib. ens significare essentiam rei, & dividi per decem genera. Aristoteles autem dixit, ens non poni in definitionibus, non quia sit extra quidditatem, sed quia non dicit determinatam naturam, sed intime transcendit omnia, sicut alii dicunt de ente ut significatur hac voce *res*, de quo Soto supra concedit quidditative praedicari: quia significat absolute quidditatem realem: idem enim est significare quidditatem realem, quod significare essentiam realem, quam significat ens, ut praescindit ab actuali existentia: quia essentia, & quidditas idem omnino est, solumque etymologia nominum est diversa. Quod vero essentia aut quidditas realis sit, intelligi non potest sine ordine ad esse, & realem entitatem actualem: non enim aliter concipimus essentiam aliquam, quae actu non existit, esse realem, nisi, quia talis est, ut ei non repugnet esse entitatem actualem, quod habet per actualem existen[67b]tiam: quanvis ergo actu esse non sit de essentia creaturae, tamen ordo ad esse, vel aptitudo essendi est de intrinseco & essentiali conceptu eius: atque hoc modo ens praedicatum est essentiale.

ly or essentially of creatures, and in this respect Avicenna's opinion, rehearsed above, is true, and St. Thomas grants it in the mentioned *Quodlibet* II, and in the other places cited above. And Avicenna can only be reproached, either because he reckoned existence to be a true accident, about which we shall speak below in its place,[181] or because he neglected another acceptation and explanation of "being" and therefore thought that it was to be denied without qualification that being, on a certain conception$_{r}$ of it, according to which it is divided into the ten categories, could be essential to all of them.

14. The other part of the conclusion (which Soto seems to deny without cause) is proved, therefore, because having a real essence agrees with each real being and is most of all essential to it. Therefore, on the mentioned conception$_{r}$, being is an essential predicate. Moreover, to be a being in this way agrees with a creature even if it does not exist, just as this proposition, "a human being is a being," is said to be an eternal truth. But it does not agree with a creature *per se* in the second mode, as some property, since it does not presuppose something prior from which it emanates as a passion, for it is rather the first concept of any given real being. Therefore, it agrees as an essential predicate and belongs to the quiddity of the thing$_{r}$. And in this way, St. Thomas says in the mentioned *Quodlibet* that being signifies the essence of a thing$_{r}$ and is divided into the ten genera.[182] And Aristotle says that being is not put in definitions, not because it is outside the quiddity, but because it does not signify$_{d}$ a determinate nature, but intimately transcends all things, just as others speak about being insofar as it is signified by this word, "thing$_{r}$," which, Soto concedes in the place cited above, is predicated quidditatively, since it absolutely signifies a real quiddity.[183] For to signify a real quiddity is the same as signifying a real essence, which "being" signifies insofar as it prescinds from actual existence, since an essence and a quiddity are altogether the same and are diverse only with respect to their names' etymologies. But that an essence or quiddity is real cannot be understood without a relation

181. See *DM* 31.7.

182. Thomas Aquinas, *Sancti Thomae de Aquino opera omnia*, t. 25, vol. 2 (Leonina), p. 215a.

183. Dominic Soto, *In Dialecticam Aristotelis Commentarii*, fol. 42ra.

15. Unde obiter colligo, *ens* in vi nominis sumptum, & *rem*, idem omnino esse seu significare, solumque differre in etymologia nominum, nam *res* dicitur a quidditate, quatenus est aliquid firmum & ratum, id est, non fictum, qua ratione dicitur quidditas realis, *ens* vero in praedicta significatione dicit id, quod habet essentiam realem: eandem ergo omnino rem seu rationem realem important. Unde Avicenna *Avicen.* tract. 1. suae Metaph. cap. 6. quia non distinxit illam duplicem significationem entis, eam divisit inter ens & rem: nam ens dixit de formali significare actualem existentiam, rem vero solum quidditatem seu essentiam realem, ut notavit D. Thom. in 2. d. 37. quaest. 1. art. 1. Ergo *D. Thom.* attribuendo enti illam duplicem significationem supra explicatam, altera coincidit cum significatione nominis, *res*, scilicet illa, quae convenit enti in vi nominis sumpti. Et ita D. Thom. in dict. ⟨92b⟩ quodl. 2. dicit, nomen *ens* secundum quod importat rem cui competit esse, significare essentiam rei, & dividi per decem genera. Et per haec satisfactum est omnibus, quae circa primam opinionem adducta sunt.

to being$_e$ and to real actual entity, for we do not otherwise conceive some not-actually-existing essence to be real except because it is such that being an actual entity (which it has through actual existence) is not incompatible with it. Therefore, although to be actually does not belong to the essence of a creature, nevertheless, a relation to being$_e$, or an aptitude for being$_e$, pertains to its intrinsic and essential concept, and in this way being is an essential predicate.

15. From this I infer in passing that "being," understood as having the force of a noun, and "thing$_r$" are, or signify, altogether the same item and differ only in respect of the etymologies of the names. For "thing$_r$" is said from the quiddity, insofar as it is something stable and fixed,[184] that is, not fictional, for which reason it is called a real quiddity. But "being," in the aforementioned signification, signifies$_d$ that which has a real essence. Therefore, they convey altogether the same thing$_r$ or real nature$_r$. For this reason, since he does not distinguish that *Avicenna.* twofold signification of "being," Avicenna divides it in treatise 1 of his *Metaphysics*, ch. 6,[185] between "being" and "thing$_r$," for "being," he says, formally signifies actual existence, but "thing$_r$" only a real quiddity or essence, as St. Thomas observes, *Sent.* II, d. 37, q. 1, art. 1.[186] Therefore, *St. Thomas.* in attributing to "being" that twofold signification explained above, the one signification coincides with the signification of the name "thing$_r$," namely, that which agrees with "being" taken as having the force of a noun. And thus St. Thomas, in the mentioned *Quodlibet* II, says that the noun "being," insofar as it denotes a thing$_r$ which is capable of being$_e$, signifies the essence of a thing$_r$ and is divided into the ten genera.[187] And with this we have satisfied all of the objections that were brought forth in connection with the first opinion.

184. Scholastic philosophers commonly held that there was an etymological connection between (i) *res* ("thing"), when taken as synonymous with "real being," and (ii) "*ratus, -a, -um*" ("fixed"). See Thomas Aquinas, *Sent.* II, d. 37, q. 1, art. 1, in: *S. Thomae Aquinatis opera omnia*, vol. 1 (ed. Busa), p. 233b.

185. In a 1508 edition of Avicenna's works—*Avicenne perhypatetici philosophi*—book (or treatise) 1, ch. 6, coincides with book 1, ch. 5, of the modern edition. See *Liber de philosophia prima, sive scientia divina I–IV*, pp. 31–42.

186. Thomas Aquinas, *S. Thomae Aquinatis opera omnia*, vol. 1 (ed. Busa), p. 233.

187. Thomas Aquinas, *Sancti Thomae de Aquino opera omnia*, t. 25, vol. 2 (Leonina), p. 215a.

Sectio V.

Utrum ratio entis transcendat omnes rationes & differentias inferiorum entium, ita ut in eis intime & essentialiter includatur.

Entia completa, imo & incompleta in plures conceptus resolubilia, rationem entis participant.

1. Haec quaestio difficultatem non habet in entibus completis, vel quae per modum completorum entium ab intellectu concipiuntur, ut sunt omnia individua, species & genera, quae directe in aliquo praedicamento constituuntur usque ad summa genera: nam in haec dividitur ens, & de illis essentialiter praedicatur & consequenter de omnibus aliis inferioribus, quae sub his continentur. Deinde non solum de completis entibus, & conceptibus, sed de quibuscunque partialibus, vel incompletis entibus, quae resolubilia sunt in plures conceptus reales, est etiam indubitatum, in eis intime & essentialiter includi ens, quia, si sunt resolubilia in plures conceptus reales: ergo, ut minimum, debent resolvi in conceptum entis, qui est universalissimus omnium. Item a fortiori hoc constabit ex dicendis.

2. His suppositis est opinio Scoti in 1. d. 3. q. 3. & d. 8. q. 2. & in 2. d. 3. q. 6, ens non includi in differentiis ultimis, neque in modis intrinsecis, quibus ad prima decem genera determinatur, neque in suis propriis passionibus, quae cum ipso convertuntur, ut sunt unum, verum, bonum, de quibus alibi ipse sentit, esse positivas, & reales proprietates,

Section 5

Whether the Nature$_R$ of Being Transcends All Natures$_R$ and Differences of Inferior Beings in Such a Way That It Is Included in Them Intimately and Essentially.

Complete beings—and in fact incomplete ones as well—that are resolvable into several concepts participate in the nature$_r$ of being.

1. This question poses no difficulty in the case of complete beings, or in the case of those beings which are conceived by the intellect in the manner of complete beings, as are all individuals, species, and genera that are directly constituted in some category, all the way to the highest genera.[188] For being is divided into the latter and is predicated essentially of them, and consequently of all the other inferiors that are contained under them. Moreover, it is also certain that being is intimately and essentially included, not only in complete beings and concepts, but also in all partial or incomplete beings that are resolvable into several real concepts, since, if they are resolvable into several real concepts, they must, at least, be resolved into the concept of being, which is the most universal of all concepts. Moreover, this will be *a fortiori* clear from the things to be said.

2. With these things assumed, it is the opinion of Scotus, *Sent.* I,

188. In the first edition of the *Metaphysical Disputations*, the running header in this section reads "Whether even atomic differences include the nature of being" (*An differentiae, etiam atomae, rationem entis includant*).

ut patet in 2. d. 3. q. 2.[45] ad arg. Quid autem Scotus intelligat per differentias ultimas, obscure satis ab eo explicatur: non enim vocat ultimam differentiam illam, quae constituit ultimam speciem, nam ibi expresse dicit rationale, vel rationalitatem non esse differentiam ultimam, si anima rationalis est in re ipsa diversa a sensitiva. Igitur differentiam ultimam [68a] appellat, quae sumitur ab ultima realitate formae, differentiam autem non ultimam, quae sumitur a tota forma, ut, si est (inquit) in homine una anima, quae realiter est vegetativa, sensitiva, & rationalis, in illa distinguuntur diversi gradus seu realitates formales, & differentia, quae ab ultima rea⟨93a⟩litate sumitur, dicitur ultima, non solum quia constituit ultimam speciem, sed quia se ipsa differt ab aliis, & non est resolubilis in plures conceptus: si autem fingamus animam rationalem ut sic esse integram, & per se distinctam formam a sensitiva, & omnibus superioribus, tunc, sicut talis forma est intrinsece & quidditative ens, ita differentia ab illa sumpta, est etiam intrinsece, & quidditative ens, & ideo eius conceptus non est simpliciter simplex, sed resolvi potest in conceptum entis, & aliquem alium modum, quo determinetur conceptus entis ad esse talis differentiae, & ideo talis differentia non est ultima, quandoquidem per aliquid a se distinctum ab aliis differt.

45. Reading "q. 2" with S, V_1, and V_2. The following read "q. 1": C_1, C_2, G_2, M_1, M_2, M_3, M_4, P_1, P_2, V_3, V_4, V_5, and Vivès.

d. 3, q. 3,[189] and d. 8, q. 2,[190] and *Sent.* II, d. 3, q. 6,[191] that being is not included in ultimate differences, nor in the intrinsic modes by which it is determined to the ten primary genera, nor in its proper passions that are convertible with it, such as one, true, and good, which he himself elsewhere holds to be positive and real properties, as is clear from *Sent.* II, d. 3, q. 2, reply to the argument.[192] But what Scotus understands by an ultimate difference is explained by him in a fairly obscure way, for he does not call the difference that constitutes an ultimate species an ultimate difference, since he there expressly says that, if the rational soul is in reality diverse from the sensitive soul, rational or rationality is not an ultimate difference.[193] Therefore, he calls ultimate that difference which is taken from the ultimate reality of a form, but he calls non-ultimate that difference which is taken from a whole form. For instance, if (he says) there is one soul in the human being which is really vegetative, sensitive, and rational, then diverse formal grades or realities are distinguished in it, and the difference which is taken from the ultimate reality is called ultimate, not only because it constitutes the ultimate species, but also because it differs from other things by itself and is not resolvable into several concepts. However, if we imagine that the rational soul as such is a complete form and is *per se* distinguished from the sensitive soul and from all higher ones, then, just as such a form is intrinsically and quidditatively a being, so also is the difference taken from it intrinsically and quidditatively a being, and therefore its concept is not without qualification simple but can be resolved into the concept of being and some other mode by which the concept of being

189. John Duns Scotus, *Opera omnia*, vol. 3 (Vaticana), pp. 81–85 (ns. 131–36) and pp. 97–100 (ns. 159–61).

190. Bartolomeo Mastri (1602–73) and Raffaele Aversa (1589–1657) cite *Ord.* I, d. 8, q. 3, rather than *Ord.* I, d. 8, q. 2, in their discussions of this issue. (For Mastri, see his *Philosophiae ad mentem Scoti cursus integer tomus quartus* [Venetiis: apud Nicolaum Pezzana, 1708], p. 74b. For Aversa, see his *Philosophia Metaphysicam Physicamque complectens Quaestionibus contexta in duos Tomos distributa* [Bononiae: Ex Typographia HH. Evangelistae Ducciae, 1650], t. 1, p. 95b.) And indeed Scotus mentions the distinction between ultimate and non-ultimate differences in this question. See John Duns Scotus, *Opera omnia*, vol. 4 (Vaticana), pp. 201–202 (n. 106).

191. See John Duns Scotus, *Opera omnia*, vol. 7 (Vaticana), pp. 474–84 (ns. 168–88).

192. John Duns Scotus, *Opera omnia*, vol. 7 (Vaticana), p. 417 (n. 58).

193. John Duns Scotus, *Opera omnia*, vol. 3 (Vaticana), pp. 97–100 (ns. 159–61). See also John Duns Scotus, *Opera omnia*, vol. 7 (Vaticana), p. 479 (ns. 179–80).

Fundamentum Scoti. 3. Et hinc sumitur primum ac praecipuum fundamentum Scoti, nam una differentia non est alia, ut per se notum est: ergo vel convenit cum aliis in conceptu quidditativo entis, vel non, si non convenit: ergo non includit talem conceptum in sua quidditate & essentia, quod intendimus: si autem convenit cum aliis in illo conceptu, necesse est quod per aliquid aliud differat: ergo una differentia differet ab aliis per aliam differentiam: ergo illa differentia non erat ultima, quandoquidem in aliam ulteriorem resolvitur, & tunc ulterius eodem modo inquirendum erit de illa alia differentia, an includat conceptum quidditativum entis, in quo cum aliis conveniat, atque ita, vel procedemus in infinitum, vel sistendum erit in aliqua differentia ultima, quae ita per se differat ab omnibus aliis rebus, vel conceptibus, ut neque in conceptu entis cum illis conveniat, & consequenter, intrinsece & quidditative rationem entis non includat: nam, si includeret, conveniret in ea cum aliis, si autem conveniret, indigeret alia differentia qua differret, iuxta doctrinam *Aristoteles.* Arist. 5. Metaphys. cap. 9. & lib. 10. cap. 5. quod ea, quae inter se conveniunt, differentiis differunt. Atque haec ratio eodem modo applicari potest ad modos intrinsecos, quibus ens contrahitur ad prima decem genera: nam, cum unumquodque illorum generum concipiatur per modum entis completi, certum est, quidditative includere rationem entis, in qua omnia illa genera conveniunt: ergo oportet, ut aliquibus modis seu differentiis differant: de illis ergo modis ulterius quaeritur an includant ens: nam, si non includunt, hoc intendimus, si vero includunt, quaerendum est per quid differant ab aliis, & quomodo ad illos ⟨93b⟩ modos contrahatur ens, & ita, vel procedetur in infinitum, vel sistendum erit in aliqua differentia seu modo, qui non includat ens: ergo, cum non sit maior ratio de uno, quam de alio, sistendum erit in primo illo modo, quo contrahitur ens ad substantiam, quantitatem, &c.

is determined to the being$_e$ of such a difference, and therefore such a difference is not ultimate, inasmuch as it differs from other things through something distinct from itself.

Scotus's foundation.

3. And from this Scotus's first and chief foundation is taken. For one difference is not another, as is known$_n$ *per se*. Therefore, either it agrees with others in the quidditative concept of being, or it does not. If it does not agree, then it does not include this concept in its quiddity and essence, which is the intended conclusion. But if it agrees with others in that concept, it is necessary that it differ through something else. Therefore, one difference would differ from others through another difference. Therefore, that difference was not ultimate, since it is resolved into another, further one, and then we shall have further to inquire in the same way, regarding that other difference, whether it includes the quidditative concept of being, so that it agrees in this concept with other things, and in this way, either we shall proceed to infinity, or we shall have to stop at some ultimate difference which differs *per se* from all other things$_r$ or concepts, so that it does not agree with them in the concept of being and consequently does not intrinsically and quidditatively include the nature$_r$ of being. For if it did include it, it would agree in it with other things. But if it agreed, it would need another difference by which it might differ, according to the doctrine of Aristotle in *Metaph.* V, ch. 9, and book X, ch. 5, that those things which agree with each other differ from each other by means of differences.[194] And this argument can be applied in the same way to the intrinsic modes by which being is contracted to the ten primary genera. For, since each of those genera is conceived in the manner of a complete being, it is certain that it quidditatively includes the nature$_r$ of being, in which all those genera agree. Therefore, it must be that they differ through some modes or differences. Regarding these modes, therefore, it will further be asked whether they include being, for if they do not include it, this is the intended conclusion, but if they do include it, it must be asked, through what do they differ from other things, and how is being contracted to those modes? And so either we shall proceed to infinity, or we shall have to stop at some difference or mode that does not include

Aristotle.

194. Aristotle, *Metaph.* V, ch. 9, 1018a9–15, and *Metaph.* X, ch. 3, 1054b23–31.

Secunda ratio Scoti.

4. Atque hoc maxime confirmat secunda ratio Scoti sumpta ex proportione inter Metaphysicam & Physicam compositionem: utraque enim fit ex potentia & actu, seu (ut Scotus loquitur) ex determinabili, & determinante: sed in compositione Physica resolutio ultima fit ad ultimam potentiam determinabilem, quae in sua entitate nihil includat formae seu actus determinantis, & ad ultimam formam seu actum determinantem, quae ni[68b]hil includat potentiae determinabilis: ergo similiter in compositione Metaphysica omnium entium resolutio facienda est in ultimos conceptus determinabilem & determinantem, quorum unus alium non includat, nec e converso, sed omnis haec resolutio ex parte conceptuum determinabilium fit ultimate in conceptum entis, in quo ut sic actu non includitur aliquis modus, seu differentia determinans: ergo etiam ex parte conceptus determinantis debet correspondere aliquis modus, vel differentia, quae nullo modo includat conceptum entis determinabilem. Denique de passionibus entis plures rationes multiplicat Scotus, quas nunc omitto, quia de iis passionibus dicendum est ex professo disputatione sequente.

Opinio Scoti confutatur.

Differentiae ultimae & non ultimae explicatio Scotica impugnatur.

5. Hanc opinionem Scoti merito impugnant Thomistae, quanvis nonnulli eorum interdum illi faveant, ut infra notabo. Et primo quidem illa distinctio differentiae ultimae & non ultimae ut ab Scoto proponitur & explicatur, & supponit falsum fundamentum, & insufficiens est. Primum patet, quia re vera nulla est differentia, quae ex tota forma Physica sumatur. Primo quidem, quia iuxta veriorem sententiam in composito substantiali non est nisi una forma, & tamen omne compositum substantiale habet aliquam convenientiam cum aliis compositis, & cum omnibus substantiis creatis, & consequenter ab illius

being. Therefore, since there is no greater reason to favor one over another, we should stop with that first mode by which being is contracted to substance, quantity, etc.

Scotus's second argument.

4. And Scotus's second argument, taken from the proportion between metaphysical and physical composition, confirms this to the highest degree. For both kinds of composition are from potency and act, or (as Scotus puts it) from something determinable and something determining. But in physical composition a final resolution is made to the ultimate determinable potency, which in its entity includes nothing of form or determining act, and to the ultimate form or determining act, which includes nothing of determinable potency. Therefore, similarly, in metaphysical composition the resolution of all beings must be made to the ultimate determinable and determining concepts, the one not including the other, nor conversely. But this whole resolution, on the side of the determinable concepts, is ultimately made to the concept of being, in which, as such, some determining mode or difference is not actually included. Therefore, on the side of the determining concept as well, there must correspond some mode or difference which in no way includes the determinable concept of being. Finally, as regards the passions of being, Scotus offers a multitude of arguments, which I omit for now, since we must speak *ex professo* of those passions in the following disputation.[195]

Scotus's opinion is refuted.

The Scotist explanation of ultimate and non-ultimate differences is opposed.

5. The Thomists rightly oppose this opinion of Scotus's, although some of them occasionally favor it, as I shall note below.[196] And indeed, in the first place, that distinction between ultimate and non-ultimate differences, as set forth and explained by Scotus, both assumes a false foundation and is insufficient. The former point is clear, since really there is no difference which is taken from a whole physical form. First, indeed, because according to the truer opinion there is only one form in a substantial composite, and yet every substantial composite has some agreement with other composites and with all created sub-

195. See *DM* 3.1.
196. See *DM* 2.6.2.

forma, ut habet convenientiam cum aliis[46] sumitur aliqua differentia non ultima: ergo nulla differentia sumitur a tota forma, sed ultima sumitur ab ultimo gradu, seu rea⟨94a⟩litate eius, ut ipse Scotus loquitur. Quae ratio procedit de substantiis compositis, sed evidentior est in simplicibus, seu immaterialibus creatis, quae genere, & differentia constant, quia in eis non est nisi una simplex natura, Physice loquendo, a qua sumuntur differentiae non ultimae, & ultimae secundum diversos gradus seu conceptus eius. Et eodem modo procedit ratio in formis accidentalibus, nam ab una & eadem forma secundum rem v. g. albedine, sumitur differentia non ultima coloris, & ultima albedinis. Deinde, etiam si daremus in composito substantiali esse plures formas, nulla esset differentia sumpta a tota aliqua forma. Finge enim animam rationalem[47] in homine esse distinctam a sensitiva, &c. adhuc rationale non esset differentia sumpta a tota forma. Probatur, quia secundum illam formam homo haberet convenientiam cum angelis in intellectualitate: ergo ab illa forma sumeretur alia differentia prior: ergo differentia rationalitatis, prout est propria hominis, adhuc in eo casu non sumeretur ex tota forma, sed ex ultimo gradu eius: imo inter eam formam & alias necessario esset convenientia, vel in communi ratione formae substantialis, vel in ratione animae, & principii vitae respectu aliarum animarum realiter distinctarum: ergo secundum has omnes rationes possent ab illa sumi differentiae non ultimae: ergo nulla esset differentia, quae sumeretur a tota forma: propter similes enim rationes in formis accidentalibus nulla esse potest, a qua[48] tota aliqua differentia unica sumatur, ut Scotus fatetur.

46. Reading "aliis" here with C_1, C_2, G_2, M_1, M_2, M_3, M_4, P_1, P_2, S, V_1, V_2, V_3, and V_4. The following read "illis": V_5 and Vivès.

47. Reading "rationalem" here with C_1, C_2, G_2, M_1, P_1, P_2, S, V_1, V_2, and V_4. The following have "rationabilem": M_2, M_3, M_4, V_3, V_5, and Vivès.

48. Reading "qua" here with C_1, C_2, G_2, M_1, M_2, M_3, P_1, P_2, S, V_1, V_2, V_3, and V_4. The following have "quo": M_4, V_5, and Vivès.

stances, and consequently some non-ultimate difference is taken from its form insofar as it has an agreement with other things. Therefore, no difference is taken from a whole form. Rather, the ultimate difference is taken from its ultimate grade or reality, as Scotus himself puts it. And this argument succeeds with respect to composite substances, but it is more evident in the case of simple or immaterial created substances, which are constituted from a genus and difference, since in them there is nothing but a single simple nature, physically speaking, from which ultimate and non-ultimate differences are taken in accordance with its diverse grades or concepts. And in the same way the argument succeeds in the case of accidental forms, for from what is really one and the same form—e.g., whiteness—both the non-ultimate difference of color and the ultimate difference of whiteness are taken. Moreover, even if we granted that there are several forms in a substantial composite, there would be no difference taken from some whole form. For imagine that the rational soul in the human being is distinct from the sensitive soul, etc. Nevertheless, *rational* would not be a difference taken from a whole form. And this is proved because, in accordance with that form, the human being would have an agreement with the angels in intellectuality. Therefore, another, prior difference would be taken from that form. Therefore, the difference *rationality*, insofar as it is proper to the human being, would in that case still not be taken from a whole form, but from a form's ultimate grade. In fact, between that form and others there would necessarily be an agreement, either in the common nature$_r$ of substantial form, or, in the case of the other really distinct souls, in the nature$_r$ of soul and principle of life. Therefore, non-ultimate differences could be taken from it in accordance with all these natures$_r$. Therefore, there would be no difference that was taken from a whole form, since, for similar reasons, among accidental forms, there can be none from the whole of which some single difference is taken, as Scotus admits.

6. Unde ulterius ostendi potest insufficientem esse Scoti divisionem. Omissa enim differentia, quae sumi dicitur a tota forma, quae re vera nulla est, ut ostendi: Scotus ipse fatetur dari [69a] differentiam ultimam, quae sumitur ab ultima realitate formae: ergo necesse est, ut admittat aliud differentiarum genus, quae neque a tota forma, neque ab ultima realitate eius, sed a forma secundum aliquam communem, seu superiorem realitatem sumatur, ut erit differentia sensitivi in homine, si in eo anima sensitiva non est realiter a rationali distincta, vel sicut differentia coloris in albedine. Talis ergo differentia, neque est ultima, ut per se constat, neque est non ultima iuxta Scoti declarationem, quia non sumitur a tota forma, sed solum a quodam gradu realitatis eius: ergo insufficienter ab Scoto numerantur huiusmodi differentiae. Et quaerendum restat, an iuxta ⟨94b⟩ illius opinionem hae differentiae, quae nec sumuntur a tota forma, nec sunt ultimae, includant intrinsece & quidditative ens, necne. Nam si illae non includunt ens, sequitur, nullas omnino esse differentias reales, quae ens includant, quod & ipse negat, & per se est satis absurdum: quia, si nulla differentia est ens, nullae sunt in rebus differentiae reales, & consequenter nec per eas constituuntur essentiae reales, neque essentialiter distinguuntur. Si autem illae differentiae includunt ens: ergo idem dicendum est de ultimis differentiis, etiam si non sumantur a tota forma, sed ab ultimo gradu eius. Probatur haec consequentia, primo, quia hae differentiae subalternae, v. g. sensibile, non sumuntur a tota forma, sed a quodam gradu reali eius, & hoc satis est, ut includant ens: ergo multo magis id sufficiet, ut ultimae differentiae includant ens. Patet consequentia, quia talis differentia sumitur a perfectiori gradu illius formae, ut v. g. sensibile, & rationale, supposita vera sententia de unitate animae in homine, sunt differentiae, quarum neutra sumitur a tota forma, & sensibile sumitur ab illa secundum gradum superiorem minusque perfectum, tamen, quia forma etiam secundum illum praecisum gradum considerata, realis est, verumque ens, ideo differentia illa ens intrinsece & essentialiter includit: rationale autem sumitur ab eadem forma secundum inferiorem gradum realem, magisque perfectum, & forma a qua sumitur, etiam secundum illam considerationem est realis verumque ens: ergo multo maiori ratione talis[49] differentia

Differentiae etiam infimae.

49. Reading "talis" with C_1, C_2, G_2, M_1, M_2, M_3, M_4, P_1, P_2, S, V_1, V_2, V_3, and V_4. The following read "realis": V_5 and Vivès.

6. From this it can further be shown that Scotus's division is insufficient. For, setting aside the difference that is said to be taken from a whole form (which is really nothing, as I have shown), Scotus himself grants that there is an ultimate difference which is taken from the ultimate reality of a form. Therefore, it is necessary that he admit another genus of difference, a difference that is taken, neither from a whole form, nor from its ultimate reality, but from the form in accordance with some common or higher reality, as the difference *sensitive* in the case of the human being will be if the sensitive soul in her is not really distinct from the rational soul, or as color's difference is in the case of whiteness. Therefore, such a difference is neither ultimate, as is clear *per se*, nor is it not ultimate, according to the explanation of Scotus, since it is not taken from a whole form, but only from a certain grade of its reality. Therefore, such differences are insufficiently enumerated by Scotus. And it remains to be asked whether, in his opinion, these differences, which are neither ultimate nor taken from a whole form, intrinsically and quidditatively include being, or not. For if they do not include being, it follows that there are no real differences whatsoever that include being, which even he denies, and as is *per se* absurd enough. For if no difference is a being, there are no real differences in things[r], and consequently real essences are not constituted or essentially distinguished by them. If, however, these differences include being, the same must be said of ultimate differences, even if they are not taken from a whole form, but from its ultimate degree. This consequence is proved, first, because these subaltern differences—e.g., *sensitive*—are not taken from a whole form, but from a certain real grade of a form, and this is enough for them to include being. Therefore, for all the more reason, this will be enough for ultimate differences to include being. The consequence is clear, since such a difference is taken from a more perfect degree of that form. For instance, *sensitive* and *rational* (assuming the true opinion regarding the unity of the soul in the human being) are differences neither of which is taken from a whole form, and *sensitive* is taken from that form according to a grade that is higher and less perfect. Nevertheless, since the form, even considered according to that prescinded grade, is real and a true being, that difference intrinsically and essentially includes being. But *rational* is taken

Lowest differences as well.

includet[50] intime & essentialiter ens. Praeterea nulla est maior ratio de una, quam de alia, nam tam simplex est conceptus differentiae sensibilis, sicut conceptus differentiae rationalis, neuter enim alterum includit formaliter, neque e contrario. Quod sic declaro, nam ut ipse Scotus indicat, haec differentia *rationale* proprie non differt ab aliis per aliam differentiam, sed per se ipsam, quia, dum ipsa est quo aliud differt, simul etiam est se ipsa differens, ne in infinitum procedamus, ipsamque differentiam speciem faciamus, utpote ex genere & alia differentia constantem: sed totum hoc eodem modo procedit in differentia superiori, scilicet *sensibile*, quia etiam illa non constat alia differentia, neque est species, sed se ipsa differt ab alia sibi opposita, quatenus dividit, & contrahit superius genus, & constituit suam propriam subalternam speciem: est ergo eadem ⟨95a⟩ ratio utriusque differentiae, & idem est de omnibus superioribus. Quod si dicas huiusmodi differentias subalternas esse determinabiles per differentias ultimas, hoc in primis nil refert, ut illae potius, quam hae ens includant, imo iuxta discursum Scoti supra factum potius sequitur has differentias prout determinabiles sunt [69b] per inferiores, non includere illas, & quatenus determinant superiores, etiam non posse ipsas superiores includere, & consequenter esse tam simplices, quantum esse possunt differentiae ultimae. Et praeterea etiam differentiae ultimae, maxime secundum opinionem Scoti, sunt determinabiles per differentias individuales: ergo etiam in hoc est eadem ratio de illis.

Item differentiae individuales.

7. Unde videtur tandem sequi, consequenter loquendo iuxta opinionem Scoti, solas differentias individuales debere dici ultimas, nam illae solae sumuntur ex ultima realitate formae, & per alias nullo modo differunt, neque ut per differentias constituentes (quod commune est

50. Reading "includet" with C_1, C_2, G_2, M_1, M_2, M_3, P_1, P_2, S, V_1, V_2, V_3, and V_4. The following read "includit": M_4, V_5, and Vivès.

from the same form according to a real grade that is lower and more perfect, and the form from which it is taken, according to that consideration as well, is real and a true being. Therefore, with much greater reason will such a difference intimately and essentially include being. In addition, there is no weightier reason in the one case than there is in the other, for the concept of the difference *sensitive* is as simple as the concept of the difference *rational*, since the one does not formally include the other, or vice versa. And this I make clear in the following way, for as Scotus himself points out, this difference, *rational*, properly does not differ from other things through another difference, but *per se*, since, while it is itself that through which another thing differs, it is at the same time also different by itself, lest we proceed to infinity and make the difference itself a species, as consisting in a genus and another difference. But all this holds true in the same way in the case of the higher difference, namely, *sensitive*, since it too is not constituted from another difference, nor is it a species, but it differs by itself from the other difference opposed to it, insofar as it divides and contracts a superior genus and constitutes its own proper subaltern species. Both differences, therefore, have the same character$_r$, and the same is true of all higher differences. But if you say that such subaltern differences are determinable by ultimate differences, in the first place, this is not relevant to the question of whether the former, rather than the latter, include being. In fact, according to the argument of Scotus outlined above, it follows, rather, that the former differences, insofar as they are determinable by inferior ones, do not include the latter, and insofar as they determine superior ones, they also cannot include these superior ones, and consequently, they are as simple as ultimate differences can be. And moreover, ultimate differences also, especially according to the opinion of Scotus, are determinable by individual differences. Therefore, in this respect also there is the same account$_r$ regarding them.

Individual differences too.

7. From this, finally, it seems to follow, speaking consistently in accordance with the opinion of Scotus, that only individual differences should be called ultimate, for they alone are taken from the ultimate reality of a form, and they differ in no way through other differences—neither through constituting differences (which is common to all differences, as has been said), nor through differences which contract

omnibus differentiis, ut dictum est) neque ut per differentias contrahentes ad inferiora, quia illas non habent, quod est proprium harum differentiarum individualium. Sed neque Scotus in hoc sensu est locutus de differentiis ultimis, ut patet ex locis citatis, & ex his, quae adduximus, neque de illis dici potest, quod ens non includant, propter alias rationes supra tactas, scilicet, quia etiam hae sumuntur a materia vel forma secundum veram realitatem earum. Item, quia conceptus differentiae individualis in se non est simplicior, quam conceptus differentiae specificae, vel genericae, etiam si non sit ita communis, vel contrahibilis: hoc enim nihil refert ad simplicitatem conceptus: nam potius superiora, & universaliora solent esse simpliciora. Et praeterea rationes, quas de modis intrinsecis faciemus, de his etiam differentiis individualibus probabunt, nam, ut ostendam, eadem est seu proportionalis earum ratio.

Modi intrinseci entis rationem entis imbibunt.

8. Iam igitur de modis intrinsecis falsa etiam ostenditur opinio Scoti primo, quia, vel illi modi sunt positivi & reales, vel non. Hoc secundum, neque ab Scoto dicitur, neque est verum, ut contra aliquos ostendam sectione sequenti: quomodo enim possent constituere varias rerum essentias, & essentiale discrimen inter illas, si non essent reales modi, & positivi? Si autem huiusmodi sunt, quomodo mente concipi potest, eos non in⟨95b⟩cludere intrinsece & essentialiter ens? Nam ut praecedente sect. ostendimus, ens intrinsece est, quod habet veram & realem essentiam, aut ergo hi modi habent aliquam realem essentiam, & ita intrinsece & essentialiter sunt ens: vel nullam habent, & sic nec possunt essentiam realem constituere, neque aliquid reale addere ad contrahendum superiorem conceptum, & constituendam determinatam essentiam, & distinguendam illam ab aliis. Et confirmatur, nam si hi modi non sunt ens: ergo nihil sunt: ergo nihil conferre possunt ad essentias reales constituendas. Respondent aliqui, hos modos non esse ens ut quod, tamen esse ens ut quo, seu aliquid entis, & ideo[51] neque esse simpliciter, & univoce ens, ut Scotus loquitur, neque omnino nihil. Sed haec responsio solum videtur in verbis consistere, quoniam esse ens ut quo nihil aliud est, quam esse formam seu actum realem in Metaphysica constitutione seu compositione: nulla autem potest

51. Reading "ideo" with S, V_1, and V_2. The following read "inde": C_1, C_2, G_2, M_1, M_2, M_3, M_4, P_1, P_2, V_3, V_4, V_5, and Vivès.

to inferiors, since they do not have such differences (which is something proper to these individual differences). But Scotus did not speak in this sense of ultimate differences, as is clear from the passages cited and from the things that we have adduced, nor can it be said of them that they do not include being, because of the other arguments touched on above—namely, because these too are taken from the matter or form according to their true reality. And also, because the concept of an individual difference in itself is not simpler than the concept of a specific or generic difference, even if it is not so common or contractible, for this is not relevant to the simplicity of a concept, since it is rather higher and more universal things that are wont to be simpler. And in addition, the arguments that we shall make regarding intrinsic modes have probative value as regards these individual differences as well, for, as I will show, their character$_r$ is the same or proportional.

Intrinsic modes of being include the nature$_r$ of being.

8. Scotus's opinion regarding intrinsic modes, then, is now shown to be false as well. First, because either those modes are positive and real, or they are not. The latter is not said by Scotus, nor is it true, as I will show against some people in the following section.[197] For how could they constitute the various essences of things$_r$, and the essential distinction between them, if they were not real and positive modes? But if they are such, how can it be conceived by the mind that they do not intrinsically and essentially include being? For as we showed in the preceding section, intrinsically a being is what has a true and real essence. Therefore, either these modes have some real essence, and thus intrinsically and essentially are beings, or they have none, and thus cannot constitute a real essence or add something real in order to contract a higher concept, constitute a determinate essence, and distinguish that essence from others. And this is confirmed, for if these modes are not beings, they are nothing. Therefore, they can help not at all in constituting real essences. Some reply that such a mode is not a being in the sense of "that which," but a being in the sense of "that by which," or something belonging to a being, and that it is therefore not a being without qualification and univocally, as Scotus puts it, nor altogether nothing. But this reply seems to consist merely in words,

197. See *DM* 2.6.2.

esse forma, vel actus realis alicuius, nisi in se sit aliquid reale, quod est esse in se ens reale: ergo repugnat dicere aliquid esse reale quo, & non ens ut quod, nam illud quo in huiusmodi quod necessario fundari debet. Quod in omni compositione Physica inductione ostendi potest: est autem eadem ratio in Metaphysica compositione: quia etiam in illa [70a] potentia & actus concipiuntur ut constituentia integram realitatem, seu essentiam: unde in se etiam considerata necessario concipi debent ut habentia aliquid realitatis seu essentiae saltem partialis: alias non possent concipi ut apta ad constituendum & complendum essentiam realem: & haec ratio applicari potest ad omnes differentias tam ultimas, quam non ultimas, genericas, specificas, & individuales.

9. Secundo possunt e contrario hic applicari rationes factae de differentiis, praesertim illa, quod differentia non ultima, id est subalterna, ideo includit ens, quia sumitur a forma secundum aliquem gradum realitatis eius, sed etiam hi modi intrinseci sumuntur a forma, vel natura secundum aliquem gradum realitatis eius: ergo etiam includunt ens. Minor declaratur, nam in substantia modus per se sumitur ex realitate cuiuscunque naturae substantialis, quatenus cum aliis convenit in aptitudine subsistendi, & ita in substantiis immaterialibus ille modus sumitur ex tota forma simplici secundum eam praecisam rationem, in materialibus vero ex tota forma Metaphysica, seu natura integra, & con⟨96a⟩sequenter ex materia, quatenus ex parte sua confert ad subsistendum: & ex forma, quatenus absolute constituit substantialem naturam. Tenet ergo prima consequentia a paritate rationis, & quia sicut hic modus intrinsecus immediate determinans ens concipitur ut quid simplex, se ipso & non per alium modum differens ab aliis, ita etiam differentia tam subalterna quam ultima, ut declaratum est.

since to be a being in the sense of "that by which" is nothing other than to be a form or real act in a metaphysical constitution or composition. But nothing can be the form or real act of something unless it is in itself something real, which is to be in itself a real being. Therefore, it is contradictory to say that something is a real "that by which" and not a being in the sense of "that which," for that "by which" must necessarily be founded on such a "that which." And this can be shown by induction in every physical composition, and the same consideration$_r$ applies to metaphysical composition, since in the latter, too, potency and act are conceived as constituting a whole reality or essence. For this reason, even considered in themselves, they must necessarily be conceived as having some—at least partial—reality or essence. Otherwise, they could not be conceived as suited to constituting and completing a real essence. And this argument can be applied to all differences, ultimate ones no less than non-ultimate ones, generic, specific, and individual.

9. Second, the arguments made regarding differences can, in their turn, be applied here—especially this one: a non-ultimate, i.e., subaltern, difference includes being because it is taken from a form according to some grade of its reality. But these intrinsic modes are also taken from a form or nature according to some grade of its reality. Therefore, they too include being. The minor is made clear, for in a substance the mode of [existing$_e$] *per se* is taken from the reality of any substantial nature insofar as it agrees with others in the aptitude for subsisting. And thus in immaterial substances that mode is taken from the whole simple form according to that prescinded nature$_r$, while in material substances it is taken from the whole metaphysical form[198] or complete nature, and consequently from both matter (insofar as matter contributes, on its side, to subsistence) and form (insofar as form absolutely constitutes the substantial nature). The first consequence, therefore, holds by parity of reasoning, and because, just as this intrinsic mode immediately determining being is conceived as something simple that differs from other things by itself and not through another mode, so likewise is a difference, whether subaltern or ultimate, as has been made clear.

198. On metaphysical form, see *DM* 15.11.

Ens esse genus, & modum entis veram differentiam infertur ex Scoti opinione.

10. Tertio, quia, si conceptus substantiae resolvitur in conceptum entis, & conceptum modi omnino condistincti ab ente, & contrahentem, & non includentem ipsum, nihil deesse potest huic modo quominus vera differentia sit, neque enti quominus genus sit, praesertim, cum Scotus supponat, ens esse univocum. Sequela quoad priorem partem probatur, quia de ratione differentiae nihil aliud est, nisi quod essentialiter contrahat superius praedicatum univocum, & quidditativum, non includendo ipsum, & cum illo constituendo gradum essentialem aliquem per modum formae eius, ex quo habet, quod praedicetur (ut aiunt) in quale quid, & consequenter quod faciat differre ab aliis: haec autem omnia conveniunt modis contrahentibus ens iuxta doctrinam Scoti. Quoad alteram vero partem probatur sequela, quia de ratione generis solum est, quod sit praedicatum univocum, & quidditativum, seu in quid non exprimens totam quidditatem usque ad ultimum gradum (propter quod dici solet praedicari in quid incomplete) & quod sit aptum contrahi & determinari per differentias essentialiter distinctas, ex quo habet, quod de pluribus essentialiter differentibus praedicetur, sed hoc totum convenit enti iuxta principia Scoti. Unde e contrario Arist. 3. Metaphys. tex. 10. inde probat, ens non posse esse genus, quia in omnibus differentiis, & modis, quibus contrahitur, essentialiter includitur, quod repugnat generi, ut idem Arist. probat 6. Topic. c. 3.

Responsio Scoti ad illatum inconveniens refutatur.

Respondet Scotus, ens non esse genus, quia licet non in omnibus, saltem in aliquibus differentiis includitur, scilicet in differentiis non ultimis, quae sumuntur a tota forma. Sed hoc in primis ostensum est supponere falsum, quia nullae sunt differentiae, quae sumantur a tota forma in sensu ab Scoto intento, id est, quae sumantur a tota forma totaliter (ut sic dicam) & non secundum aliquem praecisum ⟨96b⟩ gradum, [70b] seu conceptum. Et deinde non satisfacit, nam quid refert, quod ens includatur in quibusdam [non][52] ultimis & remotis differentiis, ut non sit genus respectu substantiae, & accidentis, in quae proxime & univoce dividitur per differentias proprias, & extra sui rationem? Imo e contrario iuxta Scoti sententiam inferendum esset illas differentias non ultimas prout ab ipso finguntur, non esse proprias differentias,

52. Reading "non" here in accordance with a suggestion by Charles Berton in the Vivès edition. See Francisco Suárez, *Opera Omnia*, vol. 27, p. 368b. None of the earlier editions that I've consulted reads "non" here.

From Scotus's opinion it follows that being is a genus & that a mode of being is a true difference.

10. Third, because if the concept of substance is resolved into the concept of being and the concept of a mode altogether condistinguished from being, which both contracts being and does not include it, then this mode can lack nothing that is required to be a true difference, and being can lack nothing that is required to be a genus, particularly since Scotus supposes that being is univocal. The consequence is proved with respect to its first part because nothing pertains to the nature$_r$ of a difference except that it essentially contract a superior, univocal, and quidditative predicate which it does not include, and that it constitute with this superior predicate, in the manner of a form of it, some essential grade, with the result that it is predicated (as they say) *in quale quid* and consequently makes something differ from other things. But all this is true of the modes that contract being, according to the doctrine of Scotus. The consequence is proved with respect to its other part because it pertains to the nature$_r$ of a genus merely that it be a univocal and quidditative, or *in quid*, predicate, not expressing the entire quiddity as far as the ultimate grade (for which reason it is normally said to be predicated *in quid* incompletely), and also that it admit of being contracted and determined by essentially distinct differences, so that it is predicated of several essentially different things. But all this is true of being, according to Scotus's principles. For this reason, in *Metaph.* III, text 10, Aristotle proves, to the contrary, that being cannot be a genus, since it is essentially included in all the differences and modes by which it is contracted, which is incompatible with being a genus,[199] as the same Aristotle proves in *Topics* VI, ch. 3.[200] Scotus replies that being is not a genus because, although it is not included in all differences, it is at least included in some, namely, in non-ultimate differences, which are taken from a whole form.[201] But this, in the first place, has been shown to suppose something false, since there are no differences that are taken from a whole form in the sense intended by Scotus—that is: taken from a whole form wholly (so to speak), and not according to some prescinded grade or concept. And second, this is insufficient, for how does being's inclusion in certain [non-]ultimate and

Scotus's reply to the problem is refuted.

199. Aristotle, *Metaph.* III, ch. 3, 998b22–27.
200. Aristotle, *Top.* VI, ch. 6, 144a31–b3.
201. John Duns Scotus, *Opera omnia*, vol. 3 (Vaticana), pp. 98–99 (n. 160).

sed quasdam species entis: nam resolubiles sunt in conceptum entis quidditativum, & univocum ipsis, & in aliquam differentiam ultimam, quae non includat ens: nihil ergo ibi deerit ad constitutionem & compositionem speciei.

11. Quarto hi modi intrinseci sunt inaequales in perfectione entitativa: ergo sunt entia. Antecedens patet, quia substantia est perfectior accidente, & non ratione eius, in quo conveniunt, ergo ratione eius in quo differunt: ergo ratione sui proprii modi intrinseci. Quod etiam per se notum est, ideo enim substantia perfectior est, quia est per se, accidens vero in alio: ergo ipse modus per se essendi perfectior est modo existendi in alio, ergo uterque habet aliquam perfectionem: ergo entitatem, nam perfectio sine entitate reali concipi non potest: aut enim sunt idem, aut perfectio supponit entitatem, & est proprietas eius. Unde novum argumentum, vel confirmatio confici potest: nam in his modis (& idem est de omnibus differentiis) reperiuntur passiones entis, sunt enim aliquid: nec enim sunt nihil: & unum, nam unusquisque modus est in se indivisus,[53] & distinctus a quolibet alio: & bonum, quia habent suam definitam perfectionem, & appetibilitatem, & verum, quia non sunt conficti, & per se intelligibiles sunt. Tandem modus quo constituitur substantia, aliquo modo substantia esse debet: nam ut dixit Arist. 1. Phys. c. 6. substantia non constituitur ex non substantiis, & idem proportionaliter est de modo accidentis, sed quod est substantia, est etiam ens: ergo.

Aristoteles.

Sententiae Scoti, quae fingi posset, explicatio.

12. Hinc vero sumere potest aliquis occasionem ad explicandam sententiam Scoti, vel certe novam aliam introducendam. Differentia

53. Reading "indivisus" here with C_1, C_2, G_2, M_1, M_2, M_3, P_1, P_2, S, V_1, V_2, V_3, and V_4. The following read "divisus": M_4, V_5, and Vivès.

remote differences keep it from being a genus in relation to substance and accident, into which it is immediately and univocally divided by proper differences outside its nature$_r$? In fact, to the contrary, according to the opinion of Scotus, it would have to be inferred that those non-ultimate differences, as they are imagined by him, are not proper differences, but certain species of being. For they are resolvable into a concept of being which is quidditative and univocal with respect to them and into some ultimate difference which does not include being. Therefore, there will be nothing lacking here for the constitution and composition of a species.

11. Fourth, these intrinsic modes are unequal in entitative perfection. They are, therefore, beings. The antecedent is clear, since substance is more perfect than accident, and not by virtue of that in which they agree. Therefore, by virtue of that in respect of which they differ. Therefore, by virtue of its proper intrinsic mode. And this is also known$_n$ *per se*, for substance is more perfect because it exists$_e$ *per se*, whereas an accident exists$_e$ in another. Therefore, the very mode of existing$_e$ *per se* is more perfect than the mode of existing in another. Therefore, both have some perfection, and therefore entity, for perfection without real entity cannot be conceived, since either these are the same, or perfection presupposes entity and is a property of it. Hence a new argument or confirmation can be devised. For the passions of being are found in these modes (and the same goes for all differences): for they are *something*, since they are not nothing, and *one*, since each mode is undivided in itself and distinct from any other thing, and *good*, since they have their own determinate perfection and desirability, and *true*, since they are not fabricated and are *per se* intelligible. Finally, the mode by which a substance is constituted must in some way be a substance, since, as Aristotle says in *Physics* I, ch. 6, a substance is not constituted from non-substances,[202] and the same is proportionately true of the mode of accident. But that which is a substance is also a being. Therefore.

Aristotle.

Explanation of a view that might be imagined to be Scotus's.

12. Someone might take the opportunity here to explain Scotus's view, or, at any rate, to introduce another, new view. For the difference

202. Aristotle, *Phys.* I, ch. 6, 189a33.

enim seu modus constituens substantiam, non est substantia completa, sed incompleta: hac enim ratione substantia, quae est generalissimum praedicamenti substantiae, habere potest differentias, in quibus non includatur, quia genus illud tantum est substantia ⟨97a⟩ completa, differentia autem est solum incompleta substantia: ad hunc ergo modum dici potest ens, quod determinatur ad esse substantiae, quantitatis, & aliorum, quae in rectis lineis praedicamentorum ponuntur, solum esse ens completum, & ideo non includi in modis intrinsecis quibus determinatur, imo neque in differentiis, quae etiam sunt incompleta entia, & in hoc sensu omnes rationes factae non procedunt contra hanc sententiam, quia non negatur, differentias & modos esse aliquo modo entia, sed solum esse entia completa, quod nullam habet absurditatem.

Aliena ab Scoti mente & falsa ostenditur.

13. Sed haec expositio, neque est ad mentem Scoti, neque in se vera est. Primum patet, quia Scotus specialiter negat, ens includi in differentiis ultimis, in non ultimis autem concedit includi: non loquitur ergo de ente completo, quia hoc modo nulla differentia est completum ens. Deinde Scotus loquitur de universalissimo conceptu entis realis, quem mens nostra potest abstrahere, ut manifeste constat ex citatis locis: ens autem completum praedicto modo explicatum non est universalissimus conceptus entis, nam, cum entia [71a] incompleta aliquid entitatis habeant, convenientiam aliquam realem habent cum entibus completis: ergo concipi potest ratio entis universalior, quae secundum rationem ab his praescindat. Quod autem illa sententia in se falsa sit, tribus rationibus ostenditur. Prima est tantum ad hominem, supposita sententia Scoti, quod ens sit univocum: tunc enim evidentius sequitur iuxta praedictam interpretationem, ens completum esse unum genus commune ad decem praedicamenta, quia habet differentias reales extra sui rationem, & omnia alia requisita ad rationem generis, ut patet applicando rationem supra factam.

14. Secunda ratio est, quia ens communissime sumptum, ut est transcendens, & obiectum Metaphysicae, vel intellectus, abstrahit a completo & incompleto: nam haec omnia, ut ex modo significandi patet, se habent per additionem ad ens inquantum ens, in ordine ad praecisionem vel expressionem nostrorum conceptuum. Et saltem du-

or mode that constitutes substance is not a complete substance, but an incomplete one. For this reason, substance, which is the most general item in the category of substance, can have differences in which it is not included, since that genus is only complete substance, whereas a difference is only an incomplete substance. In the same way, therefore, it might be said that being, which is determined to the being$_e$ of substance, quantity, and the other items placed in the direct lines of the categories, is only complete being, and therefore is not included in the intrinsic modes by which it is determined, nor, in fact, in differences, which are also incomplete beings. And in this sense all the arguments made do not succeed against this view, since it is not denied that differences and modes are in some way beings, but only that they are complete beings, which involves no absurdity.

The view is shown to be foreign to the thought of Scotus and false.

13. But this explanation is neither in accord with the thought of Scotus nor true in itself. The first point is clear, since Scotus specifically denies that being is included in ultimate differences, but he concedes that it is included in non-ultimate ones. He is not, therefore, speaking of complete being, since in this way no difference is a complete being. Moreover, Scotus speaks of the most universal concept of real being that our mind can abstract, as is manifestly clear from the cited passages. But complete being, explained in the mentioned way, is not the most universal concept of being, for, since incomplete beings have some entity, they have some real agreement with complete beings. Therefore, a more universal nature$_r$ of being can be conceived, one which rationally prescinds from these. And that this opinion is false in itself is shown by means of three arguments. The first is only *ad hominem*, assuming Scotus's view that being is univocal. For then it more evidently follows on the mentioned interpretation that complete being is a single genus common to the ten categories, since it has real differences outside its nature$_r$, as well as all the other things required for the nature$_r$ of a genus, as is made clear by applying the argument made above.

14. The second argument is: because being taken in the most common way, insofar as it is transcendental and the object of metaphysics or the intellect, abstracts from complete and incomplete being. For these, as is clear from their mode of signifying, are related to being as being through addition, in relation to the precision or expression of

bium non est, quin possit ens in hac generalitate significari & concipi, ut paulo antea dicebam: sic autem nunc nos loquimur de ente, quia ut sic est obiectum Metaphysicae: ergo huiusmodi ens intrinsece includitur in differentiis & modis intrinsecis. Quod si fortasse autores praedictae ⟨97b⟩ sententiae dicant, se non loqui de huiusmodi ente, sed de ente completo, in primis non loquuntur ad rem, de qua nunc agimus. Deinde non effugiunt difficultatem, quae in tota hac sententia praecipue declarari intenditur, scilicet, quomodo ens ad inferiora descendat: nam, licet dicant, ens completum contrahi ad substantiam per quendam modum, qui nec est ens completum nec omnino nihil, sed incompletum ens, restat illis explicandum, quomodo & per quid ens communissimum determinetur ad esse entis completi vel incompleti. Nam de eo, quod addit ens completum supra ens, inquiram, an includat ens communissime sumptum: nam, si non includit, erit nihil, & procedent omnia argumenta facta, si autem includit: ergo differentia seu modus contrahens vel dividens, includit ipsummet divisum. Unde de illo modo restabit inquirendum, per quid distinguatur ab ipso ente in communi quod in se includit, & per quid differat ab aliis entibus, & ita incidet haec explicatio in difficultates, quas Scotus vitare intendit.

15. Tertia ratio & maxime propria est, quia ille conceptus entis completi communis decem praedicamentis, prout in rectis lineis constituuntur, & non aliis rebus, est impossibilis, quia perfectiora entia sunt incompletae substantiae, quae non ponuntur directe in praedicamento substantiae, quam accidentia, quae ponuntur directe in praedicamento accidentis. Quod patet, sive consideremus physice substantias incompletas, sive Metaphysice, nam materia prima perfectior est, magisque habet de entitate, quam quantitas, & forma substantialis, magis quam qualitas. Similiter rationalitas, prout est differentia substantialis, perfectius quid est, quam quodlibet accidens: ergo ens prout est commune ad substantiam, & accidentia, multo magis commune est ad substantias incompletas, & consequenter ad omne id, quod quacunque ratione entitatem includit: nam haec sola convenientia considerari potest

our concepts. And there is, at least, no doubt that being can be signified and conceived in this generality, as I was saying a little earlier. But we are now speaking of being in this way, since as such it is the object of metaphysics. Therefore, being of this sort is intrinsically included in differences and intrinsic modes. But if, by chance, the authors of the mentioned opinion say that they are not speaking of this sort of being, but of complete being, in the first place, they are not speaking to the issue that we are now dealing with. Second, they do not escape the difficulty that we especially aim to highlight in this whole opinion, namely, that of how being descends to its inferiors. For, although they say that complete being is contracted to substance by a certain mode which is neither a complete being nor altogether nothing, but rather an incomplete being, nevertheless, it remains for them to explain how, and by what, being, taken in the most common way, is determined to the being$_{e}$ of complete or incomplete being. For regarding that which complete being adds to being, I will inquire whether it includes being taken in the most common way. For if it does not include it, it will be nothing, and all of the arguments that have been made will apply. But if it does include it, then a dividing or contracting difference or mode includes the very thing that is divided. For this reason, regarding that mode, it will remain to inquire what distinguishes it from that very being in general which it includes within itself, and what makes it differ from other beings, and so this explanation will fall into the difficulties that Scotus aimed to avoid.

15. The third and most appropriate argument is: because that concept of complete being which is common to the ten categories insofar as they are constituted in direct lines, and not to other things$_{r}$, is impossible, since incomplete substances, which are not placed directly in the category of substance, are beings that are more perfect than accidents which are placed directly in an accidental category. And this is clear, whether we consider incomplete substances physically or metaphysically, for prime matter is more perfect and has more entity than quantity, and substantial form is more perfect and has more entity than quality. Similarly, rationality, insofar as it is a substantial difference, is something more perfect than any accident. Therefore, being, insofar as it is common to substance and accidents, is *a fortiori* common to incomplete substances as well, and consequently to everything that,

inter substantiam & accidens. Unde conceptus ille entis completi, si sit conceptus entis, quod sit per se unum, tantum esse potest conceptus substantiae. [71b]

Quaestionis resolutio.

16. Dicendum est ergo, ens, in quantum ens, intrinsece includi in omni ente, & in omni conceptu positivae differentiae, aut modi entis realis. Ita docet D. Thom. 1. cont. Gen. cap. 25. & quaest. 21.[54] de verit. artic. 1. & indi⟨98a⟩cat quodlib. 2. art. 3. & 1. part. quaest. 3. art. 4. quaest. 4. ar. 3. ad 1. quaest. 5. ar. 1. & docent Thomistae, Caiet. de ente & essentia cap. 1. Soncin. 5. Metaphys. quaest. 14. Soto in Antepraed. cap. 4. Idem tenet Fonseca 4. Metaphy. q. 4. c. 2. q. 3. & sumitur ex Arist. 3. Metaph. tex. 10. quem supra citavi. Et suppositis iis, quae contra Scotum dicta sunt, sufficienter probatur inductione, quia, si loquamur Physice de rebus, ratio entis includitur in omnibus substantiis, & in[55] omnibus partibus earum, & in omnibus accidentibus, & in omnibus modis positivis realibus: nam omnia haec habent aliquo modo essentiam veram, id est, non fictam, nec imaginariam, sed realem, aptam ad existendum extra nihil. Si autem Metaphysice res considerentur, ens includitur in omnibus generibus, & speciebus, & individuis absque controversia, & ostensum a nobis est includi etiam in differentiis, & in modis positivis intrinsecis, sed praeter haec nihil est in rebus.

D. Thom. *Caietan.* *Soncin.* *Soto.* *Fonseca.* *Aristot.*

54. Reading "21" with S, V_1, and V_2. The following read "31": C_1, C_2, G_2, M_1, M_2, M_3, M_4, P_1, P_2, V_3, V_4, V_5, and Vivès.

55. Reading "in" here with all the older editions. Vivès omits this word.

for whatever reason, includes entity, for only this agreement can be observed between substance and accident. For this reason, that concept of complete being, if it is the concept of a being that is *per se* one, can only be the concept of substance.

Resolution of the question.

16. It must, therefore, be said that being as being is intrinsically included in every being and in every concept of a positive difference or mode of real being. St. Thomas teaches this in *Summa Contra Gentiles* I, ch. 25,[203] and in *On Truth*, q. 21, art. 1,[204] and he indicates it in *Quodl.* II, art. 3,[205] and *ST* I, q. 3, art. 4, q. 4, art. 3, ad 1, and q. 5, art. 1.[206] And the Thomists teach it: Cajetan, *On Being and Essence*, ch. 1,[207] Soncinas, *Metaph.* V, q. 14,[208] and Soto, *Antepredicaments*, ch. 4.[209] Fonseca holds the same view, *Metaph.* IV, q. 4, ch. 2, q. 3,[210] and it is taken from Aristotle, *Metaph.* III, text 10, which I cited above.[211] And, assuming the things that were said against Scotus, it is sufficiently proved by induction, since, if we speak physically of things$_r$, the nature$_r$ of being is included in all substances and in all of their parts, and in all accidents and in all positive real modes. For all of these in some way have a true essence, that is, not a fictitious or imaginary essence, but rather a real one, suited to existing outside of nothingness. And if things$_r$ are considered metaphysically, being is incontrovertibly included in all genera and species and individuals, and it has been shown by us that it is included also in differences and in positive intrinsic modes. But aside from these there is nothing in things$_r$.

St. Thomas.

Cajetan. Soncinas. Soto. Fonseca. Aristotle.

203. Thomas Aquinas, *Sancti Thomae Aquinatis opera omnia*, t. 13 (Leonina), pp. 76b–77a.

204. Thomas Aquinas, *Sancti Thomae de Aquino opera omnia*, t. 22, vol. 3, fasc. 1 (Leonina), pp. 592b–93a.

205. Thomas Aquinas, *Sancti Thomae de Aquino opera omnia*, t. 25, vol. 2 (Leonina), pp. 214a–15b.

206. Thomas Aquinas, *Sancti Thomae Aquinatis opera omnia*, t. 4 (Leonina), pp. 42a–b, 54a–b, 56a–b.

207. Cajetan, *In De Ente et Essentia D. Thomae Aquinatis Commentaria*, p. 27 (n. 14).

208. Paul Soncinas, *Quaestiones Metaphysicales acutissimae*, p. 62b.

209. Domingo de Soto, *In Dialecticam Aristotelis Commentarii*, fol. 41va–vb.

210. Pedro da Fonseca, *Commentaria in Libros Metaphysicorum Aristotelis Stagiritae*, vol. 1, cols. 739–44.

211. Aristotle, *Metaph.* III, ch. 3, 998b22–27. For the earlier citation, see *DM* 2.5.10 above.

Obiectioni respondetur.

17. Dices, passiones entis esse praeter haec omnia, de quibus nihil dictum est. Respondetur. De his passionibus in controversia positum est, an formaliter dicant aliquid positivum ex natura rei distinctum ab ente, vel solum negativum, aut ens rationis. Si hoc ergo posterius verum est, consequenter dicendum est, passiones illas formaliter non includere ens, neque hoc esse contra conclusionem, quia illae passiones formaliter non dicunt differentias, aut modos realiter determinantes, aut afficientes ens. Si autem prior sententia vera est, consequenter asserendum est, has passiones in formali conceptu suo includere ens propter easdem rationes supra adductas, & contineri has passiones sub enumeratione facta, quia dicunt modos reales entis illi adaequatos, seu convertibiles cum ipso: quae autem harum opinionum verior sit, sequente disputatione tractabitur. Ratio autem a priori[56] conclusionis iam etiam tacta est, & sumitur ex ratione entis supra explicata, quae est habere essentiam realem, in quo non includitur, quod illa essentia sit perfecta, vel imperfecta, integra, vel partialis, sed solum quod realis sit: hoc autem necesse est includi in omnibus rebus, & modis, seu differentiis realibus. A posteriori autem generalis etiam ratio est, quia in his omnibus reperitur semper aliquis effectus, seu quasi effectus realis, quod non potest intelligi sine inclusione alicuius entitatis: nam constituunt, complent, aut integrant, ac distinguunt ⟨98b⟩ ens reale, adeo ut etiam ille modus, quo nostro more intelligendi determinatur ens in communi ad Deum seu ens increatum, concipiatur tanquam constituens tale ens: unde non potest concipi nisi sub ratione alicuius entitatis. Item huiusmodi differentiae, vel modi solent esse radices proprietatum, vel actionum realium: ergo.

18. Ad primum Scoti fundamentum respondetur, unam differentiam quantumvis ultimam posse esse diversam ab alia, etiam si cum illa in communi entis ratione conveniat, sicut de primis generibus [72a] generalissimis omnes docent, quae propterea non proprie differre, sed primo diversa esse dicuntur, quia alias non essent suprema genera,

56. Reading "a priori" here with S, V_1, and V_2. The following read "aptior": C_1, C_2, G_2, M_1, M_2, M_3, M_4, P_1, P_2, V_3, V_4, V_5, and Vivès.

An objection is answered.

17. You will say that the passions of being are other than all these things, and that nothing has been said about them. I reply: regarding these passions, it is matter of dispute whether they formally signify$_{d}$ something positive that is *ex natura rei* distinct from being, or only something negative, or a being of reason. If the latter is true, it must consequently be said that those passions do not formally include being, and that this is not contrary to the conclusion, since those passions do not formally signify$_{d}$ differences or modes that really determine or affect being. But if the former opinion is true, then it must consequently be asserted that these passions include being in their formal concept, for the reasons adduced above, and that these passions are contained under the enumeration that was made, since they signify$_{d}$ real modes of being adequate to it or convertible with it. However, which of these opinions is truer will be dealt with in the following disputation.[212] But an *a priori* argument for the conclusion has already been touched on and is taken from the nature$_{r}$ of being explained above—which is to have a real essence—and this does not require that that essence be perfect, or imperfect, whole or partial, but only that it be real. This, however, is necessarily required in the case of all things$_{r}$ and all real modes or differences. There is also an *a posteriori* and general argument: because in all of these some real effect or quasi-effect is always found, which fact cannot be understood without the involvement of some entity. For they so far constitute, complete or make entire, and distinguish, real being, that, in our manner of understanding, even the mode by which being in general is determined to God or uncreated being is conceived as something which constitutes a particular being. For this reason, it cannot be conceived except under the notion$_{r}$ of some entity. Moreover, such differences or modes are normally the sources of real properties or actions; therefore.

18. To Scotus's first foundation, I reply that one difference, however ultimate, can be diverse from another even if it agrees with that other one in the common nature$_{r}$ of being, just as all teach regarding the first most general genera, which, for this reason, do not properly differ, but are said to be primarily diverse, since otherwise they would not

212. See *DM* 3.1. Cf. *DM* 4.2.

sed sub alio superiori contenta, praesertim posita univocatione entis, quam Scotus ponit: quo modo autem hoc intelligendum sit, in sequente sectione declarabitur. Ad secundum respondetur in primis non esse necessariam illam proportionem inter compositionem physicam, & Metaphysicam, alioqui, sicut de omni forma verum est nihil includere materiae, & de materia, nullam includere formam, ita de omni genere seu conceptu determinabili verificandum esset, quod nullam includat differentiam, & e contrario de omni differentia, quod non includat ens quod est primum determinabile. Secundo dicitur, illam proportionem servari posse inter compositionem Metaphysicam, & Physicam, quamdiu in eis sistitur, & tenet in hoc, quod nec genus differentiam, nec differentia genus includit, sicut nec materia formam, nec forma materiam: si autem resolvendo Metaphysicam compositionem pervenitur ad simplices conceptus non compositos ex genere & differentia, iam in illis respectu praedicatorum superiorum transcendentium non oportet servari praedictam proportionem, quia in eis iam non reperitur ille determinationis modus, sed alius iam explicandus.

be supreme genera, but would rather be contained under some other superior genus, especially granted the univocation of being that Scotus posits. But how this is to be understood will be made clear in the next section. To the second foundation, I reply, first of all, that that proportion between physical and metaphysical composition is not necessary. Otherwise, just as it is true of every form that it includes no matter, and of matter that it includes no form, so also would it have to be verified of every genus or determinable concept that it includes no difference, and conversely, of every difference it would have to be verified that it does not include being, which is the first determinable. Second, I say that that proportion between metaphysical and physical composition can be defended as long as it is limited and understood as follows: that the genus does not include the difference nor the difference the genus, just as matter does not include form, nor form matter. But if in resolving a metaphysical composition one arrives at simple concepts that are not composed from a genus and difference, in their case the mentioned proportion must not be maintained in relation to higher transcendental predicates, since that mode of determination is not found in them, but another one, which must now be explained.

Sectio VI.

Quomodo ens in quantum ens ad inferiora contrahatur seu determinetur.

Difficultas quaestionis.

1. Haec est potissima difficultas, ob quam Scotus, Caietanus & alii in sententias extreme oppositas declinarunt. Alii negando conceptum entis praecisum, & abstractum, ut nulla sit necessaria eius contractio, vel determinatio, quia haec nullo convenienti modo intelligi potest: quia nec fieri potest per non ens ut ostensum est ⟨99a⟩ section. praeced. neque etiam per aliquod ens, alioqui in illo ente supponetur iam facta determinatio, & procedetur in infinitum. Sed haec sententia, si intelligatur de abstractione secundum rem seu fundata in distinctione aliqua ex natura rei, vera est, & quoad hoc satisfacit, si vero intelligatur de abstractione secundum rationem tantum, non est vera ut ostendimus, & ideo etiam secundum rationem explicare oportet, quomodo haec contractio seu determinatio fiat. Alii ergo ita praescindunt, & abstrahunt conceptum entis, ut contrahi & determinari existiment per aliquid quod intrinsece non sit ens, quomodo philosophatur Scotus, qui non solum secundum rationem, sed etiam ex natura rei huiusmodi praecisionem excogitavit, tamen in duobus deceptus est, ut probavi: primo ponendo talem modum abstractionis, & praecisionis realis, secundo supposita illa fingendo modos, seu differentias positivas reales, quae entia non sint.

Section 6

How Being as Being Is Contracted or Determined to Its Inferiors.

Difficulty of the question.

1. This is the greatest difficulty, on account of which Scotus, Cajetan, and others have turned to altogether opposed views. Some reject a prescinded and abstracted concept of being, so that no contraction or determination of it is necessary, on the grounds that this determination can be understood in no suitable way. For it cannot occur through a non-being, as was shown in the preceding section, nor also through some being, otherwise in this being an already-made determination would be presupposed, and there would be an infinite regress. However, this opinion, if it is understood to concern an abstraction that is real or founded on some distinction *ex natura rei*, is true and to this extent satisfactory, but if it is understood to concern only an abstraction according to reason, it is not true, as we have shown, and therefore it must be explained how this contraction or determination occurs even according to reason. Others, therefore, prescind and abstract the concept of being in such a way that they think it is contracted or determined by something that is not intrinsically a being, as Scotus philosophizes, and he devises such a precision not only according to reason, but also *ex natura rei*. However, he erred in two respects, as I have shown: first, by positing such a mode of real abstraction and precision, and second, having supposed this, by fashioning real, positive modes or differences that are not beings.

2. Aliter vero favet huic parti Soncin. 4. Metaph. quaest. 1. ad 2. & quaest. 19. ad 7. & lib. 5. quaest. 14. dum ait modum constituentem substantiam, & consequenter determinantem ens ad illam esse tantum negationem, vel ens rationis. Unde (inquit) licet ens includatur quidditative in substantia, non tamen in eo per quod contrahitur ad conceptum substantiae, quia id solum est quaedam negatio, quam circunscribimus hac voce *per se*. Sed non vi[72b]deo quid Soncinatem in eam sententiam induxerit, cum ipse non ponat conceptum obiectivum entis praecisum ab hoc disiuncto, *substantia vel accidens*, quia, si ab his non abstrahit, nullo modo contrahente indiget, sed sola ablatione alterius membri alterum determinatum relinquitur, id autem quod relinquitur, non potest intrinsece constitui per solam ablationem alterius membri, sed per id quod intrinsece est. Qua enim ratione intelligi potest substantia constitui in ratione substantiae, quae perfectissima est per solam negationem, aut per ens rationis? Unde omnia fere argumenta, quibus contra Scotum probavimus, modum entis includere ens, procedunt contra hanc sententiam, scilicet, quia substantia non nisi ex substantiis coalescere, vel constitui potest. Item quia alias, etiam modus quo determinatur ens ad ens increatum, esset negatio. Praeterea conceptus substantiae de formali esset privativus, ⟨99b⟩ aut per rationem confictus, & non realis: quia id, per quod formaliter constituitur, dicitur esse negativum seu ens rationis. Denique alias etiam accidens per negationem a fortiori constitueretur, cum sit minus perfectum, quam substantia, erit ergo quidam circulus, quia substantia constituetur per negationem inhaerentiae, accidens vero per negationem perseitatis, quod vix est intelligibile. Quocirca, quanvis haec simplicia interdum a nobis per negationes explicentur, tamen mens recte[57] concipit res ipsas reales non constitui negationibus: sic differentiam bruti per irrationale explicamus, quod non propterea concipimus negatione constitui: similiter infinitatem Dei, negatione declaramus, quam in summa quadam, & positiva perfectione consistere recte concipimus: sic ergo, quanvis substantiam per se esse interdum explicemus per negationem inhaerendi in alio, tamen mente concipimus non per eam negationem formaliter constitui, sed per positivam perfectionem, qua intelligitur

Non admisso conceptu praeciso entis, nulla contractio ipsius necessaria.

57. Reading "recte" here with C_1, C_2, G_2, M_1, M_2, M_3, M_4, P_1, P_2, S, V_1, V_2, V_3, and V_4. The following read "recta": V_5 and Vivès.

2. Soncinas, *Metaph.* IV, q. 1, ad 2, and q. 19, ad 7, and book V, q. 14,[213] inclines to this view in another way when he says that the mode which constitutes substance, and consequently determines being to substance, is only a negation or being of reason. Thus (he says) although being is quidditatively included in substance, still, it is not included in that by which it is contracted to the concept of substance, since this is only a certain negation which we designate by the expression "*per se*." But I do not see what led Soncinas to this opinion, since he himself does not posit an objective concept of being prescinded from this disjunctive [concept], *substance or accident*, for if it does not abstract from these, it in no way requires something that contracts it, but by the mere removal of one of the two members the other is left determined, and that which is left cannot be constituted intrinsically by the mere removal of the other member, but [only] by that which it intrinsically is. Nonetheless, how can a substance be understood to be constituted in the nature$_r$ of substance (which is the most perfect nature$_r$) by a mere negation or by a being of reason? Accordingly, almost all the arguments by means of which we have proved against Scotus that a mode of being includes being succeed against this opinion, namely: because a substance can only take root in, or be constituted from, substances. Further, because otherwise the mode by which being is determined to uncreated being would also be a negation. Also, because the concept of substance would formally be privative, or made up by reason, and not real, since that by which it is formally constituted is said to be negative or a being of reason. Finally, because otherwise an accident too would *a fortiori* be constituted by a negation, since it is less perfect than a substance. There will, therefore, be a kind of circle, since a substance will be constituted by the negation of inherence while an accident is constituted by the negation of perseity, which is hardly intelligible. Therefore, although these simple things are sometimes explained by us by means of negations, nevertheless, the mind rightly conceives that real things$_r$ themselves are not constituted by negations. Thus we explain the difference of the brute by *irrational*, but we do not for this reason conceive the brute to be constituted by a negation. Similarly, we explain God's infinity by means of a negation, but we rightly conceive it to consist in a certain

If a prescinded concept of being is not granted, no contraction of it is necessary.

213. Paul Soncinas, *Quaestiones Metaphysicales acutissimae*, p. 3a, p. 30b, pp. 62a–63a.

formalem vim habere ut sit per se absque subiecto, cui inhaereat: sicut e contrario in accidente intelligimus esse talem positivam naturam, quae postulat adhaesionem ad aliud ut esse possit.

Substantia & accidens per positivas perfectiones constituuntur.

3. Tertia ergo sententia admittit contractionem seu determinationem entis ad inferiora per modos positivos, & reales: haec autem determinatio dupliciter explicari potest. Primo, ut sit per modum compositionis ex ente & modo aliquo, ex quibus tanquam ex partibus Metaphysicis conceptus substantiae, v. g. componitur, & in eosdem est resolubilis: quae compositio non est ex genere & differentia, solum quia ens includitur in ipso modo: in his enim compositionibus quae tantum sunt per rationem non reputatur inconveniens, quod determinabile, quando transcendens est, includatur in conceptu determinantis. Et hac ratione aiunt conceptum[58] substantiae & aliorum supremorum generum, vel differentiarum vocari simpliciter simplices, non quia non sunt resolubiles in duos conceptus: hoc enim est proprium solius entis, sed quia non sunt resolubiles in duos conceptus mutuo praescindentes, quia unus necessario debet in alio includi, scilicet ens in modo, quanvis e converso modus in ente actualiter non includatur.

Aliqui qualiter ens determinari existiment.

4. Quod si obiicias, quia repugnat fieri talem resolutionem in duos conceptus, & al⟨100a⟩terum in altero includi, nam si in conceptu modi *per se* includitur ens, & ipsum *per se*: ergo in eo includitur totum id, quod in conceptu substantiae: ergo nulla facta est resolutio: Responderi potest includi quidem ens in modo [73a] per se, aliter vero quam in substantia, nam in substantia includitur ut in completo & perfecto ente: in modo vero solum ut in incompleto. Item substantia includit modum *per se* ut partem metaphysicam formaliter constituentem ipsam, atque illa est totum constitutum ex ente & modo: modus autem *per se* includit

58. Reading "conceptum" here with M_1, M_2, M_3, M_4, P_1, S, V_1, V_2, V_3, and V_4. The following read "conceptus" instead: C_1, C_2, G_2, P_2, V_5, and Vivès.

supreme and positive perfection. In the same way, then, although we sometimes explain a substance's existing$_e$ *per se* by the negation of inherence in another thing, nevertheless, we do not conceive in our minds that it is formally constituted by that negation, but by a positive perfection, by means of which it is understood to have the formal power to exist$_e$ *per se* without a subject in which to inhere—just as, conversely, we understand that in an accident there is a positive nature of a sort that requires adhesion to another thing in order for it to be able to exist$_e$.

Substance & accident are constituted by positive perfections.

3. The third opinion, then, grants the contraction or determination of being to inferiors by positive and real modes, but this determination can be explained in two ways. First, as occurring by way of a composition from being and some mode, from which, as from metaphysical parts, the concept of substance (for example) is composed, and into which it is resolvable. And this composition is not from a genus and difference merely because being is included in the same mode. For in these compositions which are only through reason it is not reckoned problematic that the determinable, when it is transcendental, should be included in the concept of the determining. And for this reason they say that the concepts of substance and the other highest genera, or the concepts of differences, are called simple without qualification, not because they are not resolvable into two concepts (for this is proper to being alone), but because they are not resolvable into two concepts that are mutually prescinding, since one must necessarily be included in the other, namely, being in the mode, although the mode is not, conversely, included actually in being.

How some think that being is determined.

4. But if you object because it is impossible for such a resolution to be made into two concepts and for the one to be included in the other—since, if both being and [the mode of existing$_e$] *per se* are included in the concept of the mode of [existing$_e$] *per se*, then everything that is included in the concept of substance is included in this concept, and so no resolution has been made—to this it can be replied that being is indeed included in the mode of [existing$_e$] *per se*, but in a way different from the way it is included in substance, for it is included in substance as in a complete and perfect being, but in the mode only as in an incomplete being. Moreover, substance includes the mode of [existing$_e$] *per se* as a metaphysical part that formally constitutes it, and it is a whole

seipsum, seu potius est ipsemet, non ut pars sui, sed ut id quo constituitur substantia, & hac ratione vera fit resolutio substantiae in ens, & per se: neque idem omnino includitur in modo, quod concipiebatur in substantia.

5. Quod si ulterius urgeatur difficultas supra tacta, de contractione seu determinatione entis ad ipsum modum *per se* per quid fiat, aut quomodo non procedatur in infinitum. Duplex est modus respondendi. Prior est determinari ens ad *per se* per alium modum, ita ut modus ipse[59] per se[60] resolubilis sit in duos conceptus, scilicet in conceptum entis, & alterius modi innominati, ratione tamen distincti ab ipso per se[61] minusque perfecti: nam eadem ratio, quae probat substantiam ipsam esse sic resolubilem, probare etiam videtur de modo per se[62]: nam in eo est ratio entis modificata, & aliter, quam in substantia, & aliter etiam quam in modo accidentis: ergo potest ibi ratione distingui ratio entis, quae modificatur, & ratio illam modificans ratione distincta ab illa, qua modificatur ad substantiam, ut modificatio ipsa diversae rationis sit. Iuxta hanc vero sententiam consequenter dicendum est, illum etiam alium modum esse resolubilem in alios similes duos conceptus, & consequenter ita posse in infinitum procedi, quia non est maior ratio sistendi in uno, quam in alio. Hoc autem esset magnum inconveniens, si ponerentur isti conceptus ex natura rei distincti, quia oporteret fingere in substantia infinitos modos ex natura rei distinctos, & in perfectione inaequales, habentes terminum ex parte modi perfectissimi & proxime constitutivi ipsius substantiae, non vero ex alio extremo: ita ut omnes illi modi simul ibi sint: & tamen in eis nullum sit assignare infimum[63] in perfectione: haec enim & similia re vera sunt absurda. At vero si asseratur solum esse inter haec distinctionem rationis, & omnem hanc resolutionem & compositionem esse ⟨100b⟩ per praecisionem, & denominationem intellectus, non videtur mag-

59. Reading "ipse" here with S, V_1, and V_2. The following omit "ipse": C_1, C_2, G_2, M_1, M_2, M_3, M_4, P_1, P_2, V_3, V_4, V_5, and Vivès.

60. Vivès italicizes "per se" here. The older editions do not.

61. Vivès italicizes "per se" here. The older editions do not.

62. Vivès italicizes "per se" here. The older editions do not.

63. Reading "infimum" here with S, V_1, and V_2. The following read "infinitum": C_1, C_2, G_2, M_1, M_2, M_3, M_4, P_1, P_2, V_3, V_4, V_5, and Vivès.

constituted from being and that mode, but the mode of [existing$_e$] *per se* includes itself, or rather is its very self, not as a part of itself, but as that by which substance is constituted, and for this reason a true resolution of substance into being and [existing$_e$] *per se* is made. Nor is altogether the same thing that was conceived in substance included in the mode.

5. But if one insists on the difficulty touched on above regarding the contraction or determination of being to the mode of [existing$_e$] *per se* itself—i.e., through what is it done? or how does one not proceed to infinity?—there are two ways of replying. The first is that being is determined to [the mode of existing$_e$] *per se* by another mode in such a way that the mode of [existing$_e$] *per se* is itself resolvable into two concepts, namely, the concept of being and the concept of another unnamed mode, which is nevertheless rationally distinct from, and less perfect than, [the mode of existing$_e$] *per se*. For the same argument which proves that substance itself is thus resolvable seems also to prove this regarding the mode of [existing$_e$] *per se*, since in this mode the nature$_r$ of being is modified, and modified otherwise than it is in substance, and also otherwise than it is in the mode of accident. Therefore, one can there rationally distinguish the nature$_r$ of being that is modified and the nature$_r$ modifying it, which is rationally distinct from that by which [the nature$_r$ of being] is modified to substance, so that the modification itself is of a different kind$_r$. But according to this opinion it must consequently be said that that other mode, too, is resolvable into two other similar concepts, and that consequently one can in this way proceed to infinity, since there is no greater reason to make a stop at the one than at the other. And this would be a great problem if these concepts were supposed distinct *ex natura rei*, since it would be necessary to imagine in a substance infinite modes distinct *ex natura rei* and unequal in perfection, having a terminus on the side of the most perfect mode that is immediately constitutive of the substance itself, but not on the side of the other extreme, and this in such a way that all those modes are simultaneously there, while yet none among them can be designated lowest in perfection. For these and similar things are really absurd. But if it is asserted that between these there is only a distinction of reason, and that this whole resolution and composition is through a precision and denomination of the intellect, it does not seem to be a great problem to

num inconveniens totum hoc admittere: nam intellectus potest infinitis modis res inter se conferre aut praescindere, & abstrahere: sicut potest etiam inter duas species infinita genera,[64] vel in infinitum praescindere & abstrahere, quatenus inter duas species possunt aliae intermediae in infinitum multiplicari. Sed nihilominus haec responsio non est probanda, etiam in hac sententia: quia mens statim abhorret processum in infinitum, quia alias nullus esset modus aut terminus resolutionis ad rem distincte concipiendam, nec posset mens inchoare, vel efficere huiusmodi abstractionem, & determinationem, nisi sistendo semper in conceptu ulterius resolubili in duos alios conceptus, & incipiendo ab alio simili. Unde autores omnes conati sunt hunc processum vitare; *Aristot.* & videtur sane repugnare Aristot. 2. Metaph. cap. 2. text. 10. & 11. ubi negat posse procedi in infinitum in praedicatis quidditativis: oppositum enim aperte sequitur ex praedicto processu: & statim addemus alias rationes, quae com[73b]munes sunt, etiam contra hanc responsionem.

6. Secunda ergo responsio esse potest, modum *per se* non esse ulterius resolubilem in duos conceptus, sed seipso distingui a quolibet alio completo, vel incompleto ente: nam cum procedimus resolvendo quod constituitur, in id quo constituitur, sistendum est in eo quo, ne procedamus in infinitum. Nam quod est ratio constituendi, seu distinguendi aliud, hoc ipso est per se distinctum a quolibet alio: sic enim in rebus physicis forma est quae distinguit unum compositum ab alio, ipsa vero per se est distincta: & in universum actus est qui distinguit, ipse vero actus per se est distinctus. Sic ergo modus *per se* (& idem est de caeteris) contrahit ens ad substantiam, quam constituit, & distinguit ab aliis, simulque se ipsum ab aliis etiam separat, & per se se determinat ens ad se ipsum: & sic cessat processus in infinitum. Haec responsio est probabilis, tamen non est satis consequenter dicta, nec rem satis declarat, ut ex dicendis in sequente[65] sententia patebit.

64. Reading "infinita genera," with S, V_1, and V_2. The following have "in infinita genera,": C_1, C_2, G_2, M_1, M_2, M_3, M_4, P_1, P_2, V_3, V_4, V_5, and Vivès. (But see Charles Berton's note on this, at Francisco Suárez, *Opera Omnia*, vol. 27, p. 368b.)

65. Reading "sequente" with S, V_1, V_2, V_3, and V_4. The following have "consequente": C_1, C_2, G_2, M_1, M_2, M_3, M_4, P_1, P_2, V_5, and Vivès.

grant all this. For the intellect can compare things$_{r}$ to each other or prescind and abstract them in infinite ways, just as it can also, between two species, prescind and abstract infinite genera, i.e., prescind and abstract genera to infinity, inasmuch as, between two species, other intermediate ones can be multiplied to infinity. But nevertheless, this reply is not to be approved even as regards this opinion, for the mind immediately shrinks from a progression to infinity, since otherwise there would be no mode or terminus of the resolution so as to conceive the thing$_{r}$ distinctly, nor could the mind begin or complete such an abstraction or determination except by always stopping at a concept further resolvable into two other concepts and by beginning from another similar one. For this reason, all authors have endeavored to avoid this progression, and it certainly seems to be incompatible with what Aristotle says in *Metaph.* *Aristotle.* II, ch. 2, texts 10 and 11, where he denies that one can proceed to infinity in quidditative predicates,[214] for the opposite clearly follows from the mentioned progression. And against this reply we shall also presently add other arguments which are general.

6. The second reply, then, can be that the mode of [existing$_{e}$] *per se* is not further resolvable into two concepts, but is distinguished from any other complete or incomplete being by itself. For when we proceed by resolving what is constituted into that from which it is constituted, a stop must be made at this "by which," so as not to proceed to infinity. For that which is a nature$_{r}$ constituting or distinguishing something else is for this very reason distinguished *per se* from any other thing. For in this way, in the case of physical things$_{r}$, it is the form that distinguishes one composite from another, but the form itself is distinguished *per se*. And in general the act is what distinguishes, but the act itself is distinguished *per se*. It is in this way, therefore, that the mode of [existing$_{e}$] *per se* (and similarly for the others) contracts being to substance, which it constitutes and distinguishes from other things, and at the same time it also distinguishes itself from other things and *per se* determines being to itself. And in this way a progression to infinity is avoided. This reply is plausible, but it is not advanced with sufficient consistency and does not sufficiently clarify the issue, as will become clear from the things to be said in connection with the following opinion.

214. Aristotle, *Metaph.* II, ch. 2, 994b16–25.

Explicatur vera sententia.

7. Quarta igitur opinio, & quae mihi probatur, est, hanc contractionem seu determinationem conceptus obiectivi entis ad inferiora non esse intelligendam per modum ⟨101a⟩ compositionis, sed solum per modum expressioris conceptionis alicuius entis contenti sub ente: ita ut uterque conceptus, tam entis, quam substantiae, v. g. simplex sit, & irresolubilis in duos conceptus, solumque differant, quia unus est magis determinatus, quam alius. Quod in ordine ad conceptus formales recte explicatur: differunt enim solum quia per unum expressius concipitur res prout est in se, quam per alium, quo solum confuse concipitur, & praecise secundum aliquam convenientiam cum aliis rebus: hoc autem totum fieri potest sine propria compositione per solam cognitionem confusam, vel distinctam, praecisam, vel determinatam. Sic igitur his conceptibus formalibus intelliguntur correspondere duo obiectivi simplices, & irresolubiles in plures conceptus; quorum unus dicitur superior, vel abstractior alio, solum quia respondet confusiori conceptui formali, per quem non concipitur res secundum determinatum modum quo est in se: sed confuse, & praecise. Potest etiam intelligi ille conceptus superior includi in inferiori sine propria compositione inferioris: quia totum id, quod confuse concipitur in illo conceptu praeciso, reperitur in alio obiecto expressius concepto, & in toto illo, quacunque ratione consideretur. Ac denique intelligitur determinatio superioris ad inferius, & additio inferioris ad superius non quasi per additionem partis ad partem, sed per solam maiorem determinationem, vel expressionem, aut confusionem eiusdem rei in ordine ad diversos conceptus mentis.

8. Talem modum explicandi hanc rem indicavit D. Thom. quaest. 1. de verit. art. 1. dicens; *Quod primo intellectus concipit, quasi notissimum, & in quo omnes conceptiones resolvit, est ens: unde oportet quod omnes aliae conceptiones intellectus accipiantur ex additione ad ens: sed enti nihil potest addi quasi extranea natura per modum quo differentia additur generi, quia quaelibet natura essentialiter est ens: sed secundum*

The true opinion is explained.

7. The fourth opinion, then, and the one I approve, is that this contraction or determination of the objective concept of being to inferiors is not to be understood by way of composition, but only by means of a more express conception of some being contained under being, and this in such a way that both concepts—for example, the concepts of being and substance—are simple and irresolvable into two concepts and differ only because one is more determinate than the other. And this is rightly explained in relation to the formal concepts, for these differ only because the thing$_r$ as it is in itself is conceived more expressly by the one concept than it is by the other, the thing$_r$ being conceived by the latter only confusedly and precisely according to some agreement with other things$_r$. But all this can occur without a proper composition, merely by means of cognition that is confused or distinct, prescinded or determined. In this way, therefore, it is understood that to these formal concepts there correspond two objective concepts that are simple and irresolvable into several concepts, one of which is said to be superior to, or more abstract than, the other solely because it corresponds to a more confused formal concept, by means of which the thing$_r$ is not conceived in accordance with the determinate mode in which it exists$_e$ in itself, but confusedly and precisely. That superior concept can also be understood to be included in the inferior one without a proper composition in the inferior concept, since everything that is confusedly conceived in that prescinded concept is found conceived more expressly in the other object, and in all of it, in whatever way it is considered. And finally, the determination of the superior to the inferior, as well as the addition of the inferior to the superior, is understood, not by an addition of part to part, as it were, but only by a greater determination, i.e., expression, or confusion of the same thing$_r$ in relation to diverse concepts of the mind.

8. St. Thomas, in *On Truth*, q. 1, art. 1, signals such a way of explaining this matter, saying: "What the intellect first conceives as most known$_n$, and into which it resolves all conceptions, is being, for which reason it is necessary that all other conceptions of the intellect be obtained by means of an addition to being. But to being nothing can be added as an extraneous nature in the way a difference is added to a

hoc aliqua [74a] *dicuntur addere supra ens, inquantum exprimunt ipsius modum, qui nomine ipsius entis non exprimitur*: & infra, *Substantia non addit supra ens aliquam differentiam, sed nomine substantiae exprimitur specialis modus essendi*. Idem significat quaest. 21. de verit. art. 1. Eundem item dicendi modum significavit Scot. 1. dist. 8. quaest. 3. differt tamen in ratione explicandi: ut ex dictis facile constat. ⟨101b⟩

Scotus.

Modus contrahendi ens assignatus possibilis esse probatur.

9. Praeterea, hunc modum abstractionis & determinationis intellectualis esse possibilem probatur exemplis: nam cum dividimus quantitatem in bicubitam, tricubitam, &c. non potest intelligi, quod conceptus bicubitae quantitatis resolvatur in conceptum quantitatis & bicubiti, quia impossibile est concipere bicubitum non concepta quantitate, signum ergo est, illos duos conceptus solum distingui sicut expressum & confusum. Idem fere est in conceptu caloris & caloris ut octo: cuius signum etiam est, quod conceptus communis caloris non solum includitur in toto calore ut octo, sed etiam in singulis gradibus eius: cum ergo dicitur calor ut octo, non additur modus distinctus faciens compositionem cum calore ut sic, sed exprimitur & concipitur calor, prout est in re. In praesente etiam hoc est manifestum in determinatione entis ad ens infinitum, neque enim concipi potest infinitas, tanquam aliquis modus additus enti, vel tanquam aliquid minus ipso ente infinito: solum ergo est ibi expressior, magisque determinatus conceptus cuiusdam simplicissimi entis: & hac ratione ens ipsum non est simplicius Deo, quanvis in modo quo concipitur, sit abstractius. Ita ergo recte intelligi potest in conceptu substantiae & accidentis.

Ad omnes difficultates enodandas talis modus aptissimus.

10. Si autem hic modus possibilis est, quod in praesente sufficiat, & ita fieri censendum sit, facile suaderi potest. Primo, quia hoc modo expeditur facile difficultas saepe inculcata in superioribus: & explicatur, quomodo ens possit dicere conceptum praecisum secundum rationem, & nihilominus determinari ad inferiora, & intime includi in omnibus illis absque processu in infinitum, & absque propria compositione. Secundo, quia hoc modo salvatur optime, quomodo suprema

genus, since any nature is essentially a being. But conformably with this, some things are said to add to being insofar as they express a mode of it which is not expressed by the name 'being' itself." And farther on: "Substance does not add some difference to being, but a special mode of existing$_e$ is expressed by the name 'substance.'"[215] And he signifies the same thing in *On Truth*, q. 21, art. 1.[216] Moreover, Scotus refers to the same manner of speaking in *Sent.* I, d. 8, q. 3,[217] although he differs in his way of explaining it, as can easily be established from the things that have been said.

Scotus.

9. Moreover, that this mode of intellectual abstraction and determination is possible is proved by means of examples. For when we divide quantity into two-cubit, three-cubit, etc., it cannot be understood that the concept of a two-cubit quantity is resolved into the concept of quantity and the concept of two-cubit, since it is impossible to conceive two-cubit without conceiving quantity. This, therefore, is a sign that these two concepts are distinguished only as express and confused. Almost the same goes for the concept of heat and the concept of eight degrees of heat. Also a sign of this is the fact that the common concept of heat is not only included in the whole eight degrees of heat, but also in its individual degrees. When, therefore, we speak of eight degrees of heat, a distinct mode that enters into composition with heat as such is not added; rather, a heat is expressed and conceived as it is in reality. In the present case, this is also clear from the determination of being to infinite being, for infinity cannot be conceived as some mode added to being, or as something less than infinite being itself. Therefore, in this case there is only a more express and determinate concept of some most simple being. And for this reason being itself is not simpler than God, even if it is more abstract in its manner of being conceived. The concepts of substance and accident can therefore be correctly understood in this way.

It is proved that the mentioned mode of contracting being is possible.

10. But if this mode [of contraction] is possible, it can easily be shown that it suffices in the present case and that [the contraction of being] should be judged to occur in this way. First, because in this way

Such a mode [of contraction] is the best suited to resolving all the difficulties.

215. Thomas Aquinas, *Sancti Thomae de Aquino opera omnia*, t. 22, vol. 1, fasc. 2 (Leonina), p. 5a.

216. Thomas Aquinas, *Sancti Thomae de Aquino opera omnia*, t. 22, vol. 3, fasc. 1 (Leonina), pp. 592b–93a.

217. See John Duns Scotus, *Opera omnia*, vol. 4 (Vaticana), pp. 221–27 (ns. 136–50).

genera dicant conceptus simpliciter simplices: & nihilominus possit ab eis abstrahi conceptus entis per solam praecisionem intellectus, quae non consistat quasi in separatione unius ab alio, scilicet, formalis a materiali, vel materialis a formali, ut fit in abstractione generis a differentiis: sed quae consistat in cognitione aliquo modo confusa, qua consideratur obiectum, non distincte & determinate prout est in re, sed secundum aliquam similitudinem, vel convenientiam, quam cum aliis habet; quae convenientia in ordine ad conceptum entis est in rebus secundum totas ⟨102a⟩ entitates, & modos[66] reales earum: & ideo confusio, seu praecisio talis conceptus non est per separationem praecisivam unius gradus ab alio, sed solum per cognitionem praecisivam conceptus confusi a distincto & determinato. Unde potest tertio hoc ostensive probari, quia conceptus entis non est praecisus secundum rem, sed secundum rationem, ut probatum est: praecisio autem secundum rationem potest contingere illis duobus modis; ut ostensum est, & non facile poterit alius fingi, vel excogitari. Rursus praecisio quasi formalis per exclusionem unius [74b] gradus ab alio non habet locum in ente propter illimitationem suam, & transcendentiam: & quia convenientia[67] in qua fundatur eius conceptus, aeque est in tota entitate secundum se totam: ergo solum potest in ente habere locum altera praecisio per confusionem conceptus: ergo etiam e contrario modificatio, seu determinatio ad inferiora genera solum esse potest per simplicem conceptum magis expressum, & determinatum, quia contractio debet proportionate respondere abstractioni, & expressio seu determinatio praecisioni.

66. Reading "modos" here with C_1, C_2, G_2, M_1, M_2, M_3, M_4, P_1, P_2, S, V_1, V_2, V_3, and V_4. The following have "modus": Vivès and V_5.

67. Reading "convenientia" here with S, V_1, and V_2. The following read "continentia" instead: C_1, C_2, G_2, M_1, M_2, M_3, M_4, P_1, P_2, V_3, V_4, V_5, and Vivès.

the difficulty often pressed above is easily resolved, and it is explained how being can signify$_{d}$ a rationally prescinded concept and nevertheless be determined to inferiors and be intimately included in all of them without a progression to infinity and without a proper composition. Second, because in this way one best explains how the highest genera signify$_{d}$ concepts that are without qualification simple, while yet allowing that the concept of being can be abstracted from them by a mere precision of the intellect that does not consist, as it were, in the separation of one thing from another (namely, in the separation of the formal from the material, or of the material from the formal, as happens in the abstraction of a genus from differences), but consists, rather, in a cognition that is in some way confused, by means of which the object is considered, not distinctly and determinately as it is in reality, but according to some similarity or agreement that it has with other things—which agreement, in relation to the concept of being, is in things$_{r}$ with respect to their whole entities and real modes. And therefore the confusion or precision of such a concept is not by means of a separation precisive of one grade from another, but only by means of a cognition precisive of a confused concept from a distinct and determinate one. For this reason, in the third place, it can be proved ostensively as follows. For the concept of being is not prescinded in reality, but rationally, as has been proved. But a rational precision can happen in those two ways, as has been shown, and another way cannot easily be imagined or devised. And again, a precision that is, as it were, formal, through the exclusion of one grade from another, has no place in the case of being, on account of its limitlessness and transcendence, and because the agreement on which its concept is founded is equally in the whole entity in its entirety. Therefore, in the case of being, only the other precision, through the confusion of a concept, can take place. Therefore also, conversely, a modification or determination to inferior genera can only occur by means of a simple concept that is more express and determinate, since a contraction must correspond proportionately to an abstraction, and an expression or determination to a precision.

11. Tandem contra hanc sententiam sic explicatam non occurrit difficultas alicuius momenti: nihil enim se offert quo ostendi possit hunc modum abstractionis & contractionis secundum rationem repugnare, aut non sufficere ad omnia, quae de ente & eius inferioribus dici solent, aut concipi, & ad omnem experientiam, quae ex modo concipiendi nostro sumatur, vel percipi possit. Solum video posse obiici Philosophi testimonium, lib. 3. Metaph. tex. 3. dicentis, non posse commune praedicatum contrahi per differentiam quae per se includat ipsum commune praedicatum. Sed ut omittam testimonia, quae ex illo libro sumuntur non esse firmae autoritatis, quia Arist. nihil in illo libro docet asserendo, sed argumentando, & dubitando: tamen falso citatur, quia non loquitur de quolibet communi praedicato, sed de genere, de quo est alia ratio, ens autem non est genus, imo hoc ipsum vult ibi Aristoteles concludere. Unde quod aliqui id extendunt ad omne praedicatum commune, vel univocum, gratis dictum est, & praeter mentem Philosophi. De qua re iterum infra redibit sermo, tractando de universalibus, & de analogia, vel communitate entis, & accidentis.

12. Hinc sequitur conceptum substantiae, & conceptum perseitatis, seu ⟨102b⟩ modi *per se* obiective non distingui, sed tantum ex modo concipiendi, ut quod, vel ut quo: sicut Deus, & Deitas; quia in re proprie non est quo, & quod, sed tantum quod: mens autem, quia non potest explicare simplicia, nisi ad modum compositorum, utitur illis concipiendi modis. Et ideo supra dicebam, recte quidem dici unum ex his modis distingui ab alio se ipso, tamen, consequenter loquendo, idem esse dicendum de ipsis generibus, quae apprehenduntur ut constituta per tales modos: quia re vera ibi nulla est constitutio per modum compositionis, sed per simplicem, & adaequatam identitatem (sicut dicunt Theologi de relatione & persona divina) quia quidquid unum includit, includit aliud. Neque est ulla ratio ob quam modus *per se*, magis se ipso distinguatur ab alio modo, quam substantia; cum proxime etiam sit sub ente, & intime ac totaliter includat illud. Atque hac ratione optime dicuntur suprema genera primo diversa, non quia in nullo communi conceptu confuso conveniant, sed quia non habent

Qua ratione suprema genera dicantur primo diversa.

11. Finally, against this opinion, thus explained, no significant difficulty presents itself, for there is nothing by which it can be shown that this mode of abstraction and contraction according to reason is impossible, or that it is insufficient for all the things that are normally said or thought about being and its inferiors, or for every experience that is based on our mode of conceiving or admits of being perceived by us. The only objection I see is one based on a testimony of the Philosopher, *Metaph.* III, text 3, where he says that a common predicate cannot be contracted by a difference which *per se* includes that common predicate itself.[218] But, setting aside the fact that the testimonies which are taken from that book are not of great authority, since Aristotle teaches nothing in that book by asserting, but only by arguing and doubting, still, the passage is erroneously appealed to, since he is not speaking there of any common predicate, but of a genus, of which there is a different account$_r$, and being is not a genus. In fact, this is the very thing that Aristotle wishes to conclude there. For this reason, it is pointless and at odds with the thought of the Philosopher to say that some people extend this conclusion to every common or univocal predicate. We shall return to a discussion of this matter below, when we deal with universals and with the analogy or community of being and accident.[219]

12. Hence it follows that the concept of substance and the concept of perseity (or the concept of the mode of [existing$_e$] *per se*) are not distinguished objectively, but only according to our way of conceiving, as "that which" and "that by which," in the way God and Divinity are. For properly in reality there is not "that by which" and "that which," but only "that which." However, the mind, since it cannot explain simple things except in the manner of composite things, uses these ways of conceiving. And therefore, above, I said that it is indeed correctly affirmed that one of these modes is distinguished from another by itself. But speaking consistently, the same must be said of the genera themselves that are apprehended as constituted by such modes, since in their case there really is no constitution by way of composition, but

218. *Metaph.* III, text 3, is 996a18–b26. In this text, Aristotle does not make the observation that Suárez here attributes to him. Suárez likely has in mind *Metaph.* III, ch. 3, 998b22–27.

219. See *DM* 6.8, *DM* 28.3, *DM* 32.2, *DM* 39.3.

determinatas differentias, quae sint extra rationem illius communis seu entis, sed se ipsis habent diversitatem in propriis ac determinatis naturis, quanvis etiam habeant imperfectam similitudinem in ratione entis: haec enim duo non repugnant, ut in superioribus declaratum est.

by simple and adequate identity (as theologians say regarding the divine relation and person), since whatever the one includes the other includes also. Nor is there any reason why the mode of [existing$_e$] *per se* should be more distinguished by itself from another mode than substance is, since it too is immediately under being and intimately and totally includes it. And for this reason the highest genera are rightly said to be primarily diverse, not because they agree in no confused common concept, but because they do not have determinate differences which are outside the nature$_r$ of that common concept, i.e., outside the nature$_r$ of being. Rather, they have a diversity by themselves in respect of their proper and determinate natures, even though they also have an imperfect similarity in the nature$_r$ of being. For these two things are not incompatible, as we made clear above.

Why the highest genera are said to be primarily diverse.

BIBLIOGRAPHY

Editions of Suárez's *Disputationes Metaphysicae* cited in the notes on the Latin text

C_1 = Francisco Suárez, *R. Patris Francisci Suarez e Societate Iesu Metaphysicarum Disputationum Tomus Prior.* Coloniae: Excudebat Franciscus Helvidius, 1608.

C_2 = Francisco Suárez, *R. Patris Francisci Suarez e Societate Iesu Metaphysicarum Disputationum … Tomi Duo.* Coloniae: Excudebat Franciscus Helvidius, 1614.

G_2 = Francisco Suárez, *R. Patris Francisci Suarez e Societate Iesu Metaphysicarum Disputationum … Tomi Duo.* Coloniae Allobrogum [i.e., Genevae]: apud Philippum Gamonet, 1636.

M_1 = Francisco Suárez, *R. Patris Francisci Suarez e Societate Iesu Metaphysicarum Disputationum … Tomi Duo.* Moguntiae: Excudebat Balthasarus Lippius, Sumptibus Arnoldi Mylii, 1600.

M_2 = Francisco Suárez, *R. Patris Francisci Suarez e Societate Iesu Metaphysicarum Disputationum … Tomi Duo.* Moguntiae: Excudebat Balthasarus Lippius, Sumptibus Arnoldi Mylii, 1605.

M_3 = Francisco Suárez, *R. Patris Francisci Suarez e Societate Iesu Metaphysicarum Disputationum … Tomi Duo.* Moguntiae: Sumptibus Hermanni Mylii Birckmanni, Excudebat Hermannus Meresius, 1614.

M_4 = Francisco Suárez, *R. Patris Francisci Suarez e Societate Iesu Metaphysicarum Disputationum … Tomi Duo.* Moguntiae: Sumptibus Hermanni Mylii Birckmanni, Excudebat Hermannus Meresius, 1630.

P_1 = Francisco Suárez, *R. Patris Francisci Suarez e Societate Iesu Metaphysicarum Disputationum … Tomi Duo.* Parisiis: apud Michaelem Sonnium, via Iacobaea, sub scuto Basiliensi, 1605.

P_2 = Francisco Suárez, *R. Patris Francisci Suarez e Societate Iesu Metaphysicarum Disputationum … Tomi Duo.* Parisiis: apud Petrum Ménier, ad portam sancti Victoris, 1619.

S = Francisco Suárez, *Metaphysicarum Disputationum … Tomus Prior.* Salmanticae: apud Ioannem & Andream Renaut Fratres, 1597.

V_1 = Francisco Suárez, *Metaphysicarum Disputationum … Tomus Prior.* Venetiis: apud Baretium Baretium, & Socios, 1599.

V_2 = Francisco Suárez, *Metaphysicarum Disputationum … Tomus Prior.* Venetiis: apud Io. Baptistam Colosinum, 1605.

V_3 = Francisco Suárez, *Francisci Suarez e Societate Iesu, Metaphysicarum Dispu-*

tationum ... Tomi Duo. Venetiis: apud Haeredes Melchioris Sessae, 1610.

V_4 = Francisco Suárez, *Francisci Suarez e Societate Iesu, Metaphysicarum Disputationum ... Tomi Duo.* Venetiis: apud Petrum Mariam Bertanum, 1619.

V_5 = Francisco Suárez, *R. P. Francisci Suarez Granatensis e Societate Jesu, Doctoris Eximii, Metaphysicarum Disputationum ... Pars Prima.* Venetiis: apud Sebastianum Coleti, 1751.

Vivès = Francisco Suárez, *Opera Omnia.* Vol. 25. Parisiis: apud Ludovicum Vivès, 1861.

Other Primary Sources

Alexander of Aphrodisias. *Super Priora resolutoria Aristotelis subtilissima Explanatio.* Venetiis: apud Hieronymum Scotum, 1560.

[Ps.-]Alexander of Hales [Alexander Bonini]. *In Duodecim Aristotelis Metaphysicae Libros Dilucidissima Expositio.* Venetiis: apud Simonem Galignanum de Karera, 1572.

Al-Ghazali. *Algazel's Metaphysics: A Mediaeval Translation.* Edited by J. T. Muckle. Toronto: Institute of Mediaeval Studies, 1933.

Antonius Andreas. *Questiones Antonii Andree super xii libros metaphysice novissime diligenti examine recognite: ac novis additionibus textuum: aliisque quampluribus postillis in margine decorate.* Venetiis: Heredes Octaviani Scoti, 1523.

Aristotle. *Aristoteles Latinus I.1–5, Categoriae vel Praedicamenta.* Edited by L. Minio-Paluello. Bruges & Paris: Desclée de Brouwer, 1961.

Averroes. *Aristotelis De Anima Libri Tres cum Averrois Commentariis.* Venetiis: apud Junctas, 1562.

———. *Aristotelis opera cum Averrois Commentariis.* 10 vols. in 12. Venetiis: apud Junctas, 1562.

Aversa, Raffaele. *Philosophia Metaphysicam Physicamque complectens Quaestionibus contexta in duos Tomos distributa. Auctore P. Raphaele Aversa a Sanseverino Clericorum Regularium Minorum Sac. Theologiae Professore et Praeposito Generalo. Nunc denuo in lucem edita ab eodem Auctore recognita. Tomus Primus, In quo de Ente in communi & primis eius generibus accurate disseritur: Et omnia quae spectant ad Aristotelis libros Metaphysicae & Physicae Auscultationis continentur.* Bononiae: Ex Typographia HH. Evangelistae Ducciae, 1650.

Avicenna. *Avicenne perhypatetici philosophi: ac medicorum facile primi opera in lucem redacta: ac nuper quantum ars niti potuit per canonicos emendata.* Venetiis: Heredes Octaviani Scoti, 1508.

———. *Liber de philosophia prima, sive scientia divina I–IV.* Edited by S. Van Riet. Louvain & Leiden: Peeters & Brill, 1977.

Boethius. *In Categorias Aristotelis libri quatuor.* Patrologiae Cursus Completus: Series Latina 64. Edited by J.-P. Migne. Paris: apud Garnier Fratres, 1891.

Busse, Adolfus, ed. *Commentaria in Aristotelem graeca.* Vol. 4, part 1. Berolini: Typis et Impensis Georgii Reimer, 1887.

Cajetan, Cardinal. See Vio, Tommaso de.

Collegium Complutense Sancti Cyrilli [Antonio de la Madre de Dios, aka Antonio de Olivera]. *Artium Cursus sive Disputationes in Aristotelis Dialecticam, et Philosophiam naturalem.* Compluti: apud Ioannem de Orduña, 1624.

Deza, Diego. *Didaci deza archiepiscopi hispalensis novarum deffensionum doctrine angelici doctoris beati Thome de aquino super primo libro sententiarum questiones profundissime ac utilissime.* Hispali: Arte et ingenio Iacobi Kronberger Alemani, 1517.

Dominic of Flanders. *In Duodecim Libros Metaphysicae Aristotelis.* Coloniae Agrippinae: Typis Arnoldi Kempensis, 1621.

Eustachius a Sancto Paulo. *Quarta pars Summae Philosophicae, Quae est Metaphysica.* Parisiis: apud Carolum Chastellain, 1609.

Fonseca, Pedro da. *Commentariorum Petri Fonsecae D. Theologi Societatis Iesu In Libros Metaphysicorum Aristotelis Stagiritae Tomus primus.* Romae: apud Franciscum Zanettum & Bartholomeum Tosium socios, 1577.

———. *Commentariorum Petri Fonsecae Lusitani, Doctoris Theologi Societatis Iesu, In Libros Metaphysicorum Aristotelis Stagiritae Tomi Quatuor. Continet hic Tomus Primus quatuor priorum librorum explicationem.* Coloniae: Sumptibus Lazari Zetzneri Bibliopolae, 1615.

Gregory of Rimini. *Lectura super Primum et Secundum Sententiarum.* T. 2. Edited by A. D. Trapp, V. Marcolino, and M. Santos-Noya. Berlin & New York: Walter de Gruyter, 1982.

Hervaeus Natalis. *Quolibeta.* Venetiis: Heredes Octaviani Scoti, 1513. [Reprint: Ridgewood, N.J.: Gregg Press Inc., 1966.]

Javelli, Crisostomo Giovanni. *Chrysostomi Iavelli Canapicii, ordinis Praedicatorum, Philosophi & Theologi nostrae aetatis eruditissimi omnia, quotquot inveniri potuerunt, Opera, quibus quicquid ad Rationalem, Naturalem, Moralem ac Divinam Philosophiam pertinet* [...], *tomus primus.* Lugduni: apud Antonium de Harsy, 1580.

John Capreolus. *Defensiones Theologiae Divi Thomae Aquinatis.* Edited by Ceslaus Paban and Thomas Pègues. Vol. 1 and vol. 2. Turonibus: Sumptibus Alfred Cattier, Bibliopolae Editoris, 1900.

John Duns Scotus. *Opera omnia.* Vol. 6. Parisiis: apud Ludovicum Vivès, 1892.

———. *Opera omnia.* Vol. 3. Civitas Vaticana: Typis Polyglottis Vaticanis, 1954.

———. *Opera omnia.* Vol. 4. Civitas Vaticana: Typis Polyglottis Vaticanis, 1956.

———. *Opera omnia.* Vol. 7. Civitas Vaticana: Typis Polyglottis Vaticanis, 1973.

Mastri de Meldula, Bartolomeo. *Philosophiae ad mentem Scoti cursus integer tomus quartus: Metaphysicorum pars prior.* Venetiis: apud Nicolaum Pezzana, 1708.

Micraelius, Johannes. *Lexicon Philosophicum Terminorum Philosophis Usitatorum.* Jenae: impensis Jeremiae Mamphrasii, 1653.

Pereira, Benedict. *Benedicti Pererii Societatis Iesu, De Communibus omnium rerum naturalium Principiis & Affectionibus, Libri Quindecim.* Parisiis: apud Micaëlem Sonnium, 1579.

Philoponus. *In libros Priorum resolutivorum Aristotelis.* Venetiis: apud Hieronymum Scotum, 1555.

Rubio, Antonio. *Logica Mexicana.* Lugduni: Sumptibus Antonii Pillehotte, 1620.
Simplicius. *Commentarii in octo Aristotelis Physicae Auscultationis libros.* Venetiis: apud Iuntas, 1551.
Soncinas, Paul [Paulo Barbo]. *Quaestiones Metaphysicales acutissimae.* Lugduni: apud Carolum Presnot, 1579.
Soto, Domingo de. *In Dialecticam Aristotelis Commentarii.* Salmanticae: Excudebat Andreas à Portonariis. S. C. M. Typographus, 1564.
———. *Super octo libros Physicorum Aristotelis Commentaria.* Salmanticae: ex Officina Ildefonsi à Terranova & Neyla, 1582.
Suárez, Francisco. *Commentariorum ac Disputationum in Tertiam Partem Divi Thomae Tomus Primus.* Compluti: In Collegio Societatis Iesu, ex officina Typographica Petri Madrigalis, 1590.
———. *R. P. Francisci Suarez, E Societate Jesu, Opera Omnia.* Vol. 3. Parisiis: apud Ludovicum Vivès, 1856.
———. *R. P. Francisci Suarez, E Societate Jesu, Opera Omnia.* Vol. 25. Parisiis: apud Ludovicum Vivès, 1861.
———. *R. P. Francisci Suarez, E Societate Jesu, Opera Omnia.* Vol. 26. Parisiis: apud Ludovicum Vivès, 1861.
———. *R. P. Francisci Suarez, E Societate Jesu, Opera Omnia.* Vol. 27. Parisiis: apud Ludovicum Vivès, 1878.
———. *Disputaciones metafísicas.* Edited and translated by Sergio Rábade Romeo, Salvador Caballero Sánchez, and Antonio Puigcerver Zanón. 7 vols. Madrid: Ed. Gredos, 1960–66.
———. *A Commentary on Aristotle's* Metaphysics, *or "A Most Ample Index to the* Metaphysics *of Aristotle."* Translated by John P. Doyle. Milwaukee: Marquette University Press, 2004.
———. *Metaphysical Disputation I: On the Nature of First Philosophy or Metaphysics.* Translated by Shane Duarte. Washington, D.C.: The Catholic University of America Press, 2021.
Thomas Aquinas. *Sancti Thomae Aquinatis opera omnia.* T. 1. Romae: Ex Typographia Polyglotta, Sacra Congregatio de Propaganda Fide, 1882.
———. *Sancti Thomae Aquinatis opera omnia.* T. 4. Romae: Ex Typographia Polyglotta, Sacra Congregatio de Propaganda Fide, 1888.
———. *Sancti Thomae Aquinatis opera omnia.* T. 5. Romae: Ex Typographia Polyglotta, Sacra Congregatio de Propaganda Fide, 1889.
———. *Sancti Thomae Aquinatis opera omnia.* T. 6. Romae: Ex Typographia Polyglotta, Sacra Congregatio de Propaganda Fide, 1891.
———. *Sancti Thomae Aquinatis opera omnia.* T. 13. Romae: Typis Riccardi Garroni, 1918.
———. *In duodecim libros metaphysicorum Aristotelis expositio.* Taurini & Romae: Marietti, 1950.
———. *Quaestiones Disputatae.* 9th ed. Vol. 2. Taurini & Romae: Marietti, 1953.
———. *Sancti Thomae de Aquino opera omnia.* T. 22, vol. 1, fasc. 2. Romae: ad Sanctae Sabinae, 1970.
———. *Sancti Thomae de Aquino opera omnia.* T. 22, vol. 3, fasc. 1. Romae: ad Sanctae Sabinae, 1973.

———. *Sancti Thomae de Aquino opera omnia.* T. 43. Romae: Editori di San Tommaso, 1976.
———. *S. Thomae Aquinatis opera omnia.* Ed. Roberto Busa. Vol. 1. Stuttgart-Bad Cannstatt: Frommann-Holzboog, 1980.
———. *Sancti Thomae de Aquino opera omnia.* T. 25, vol. 2. Roma & Paris: Commissio Leonina & Les Éditions du Cerf, 1996.
Toledo, Francisco de. *Commentaria una cum quaestionibus in universam Aristotelis logicam.* Venetiis: apud Juntas, 1580.
Trombetta, Antonio. *Antonii trombette Patavini minoriste theologi Opus in Metaphysicam Arist. Padue in thomistas discussum: Cum questionibus perutilissimis antiquioribus adiectis in optimam seriem redactis: et formalitates eiusdem cum additionibus et dilucidatione diligenti exculte.* Venetiis, 1504.
Vio, Tommaso de. *In De Ente et Essentia D. Thomae Aquinatis Commentaria.* Cura et studio P. M.-H. Laurent. Taurini: Marietti, 1934.
———. *Scripta Philosophica: De Nominum Analogia, De Conceptu Entis.* Edited by N. Zammit, reviewed again by H. Hering. Romae: apud Institutum «Angelicum», 1952.

Other Resource

Oxford Latin Dictionary. Edited by P. G. W. Glare. Oxford: Clarendon Press, 1996.

Secondary Sources

Alcorta, José Ignacio. *La teoría de los modos en Suárez.* Madrid: Consejo Superior de Investigaciones Científicas, 1949.
Anfray, Jean-Pascal. "A Jesuit Debate about the Modes of Union: Francisco Suárez vs. Pedro Hurtado De Mendoza." *American Catholic Philosophical Quarterly* 93, no. 2 (2019): 309–34.
Ashworth, E. J. "Signification and Modes of Signifying in Thirteenth-Century Logic: A Preface to Aquinas on Analogy." *Medieval Philosophy and Theology* 1 (1991): 39–67.
———. "Analogical Concepts: The Fourteenth-Century Background to Cajetan." *Dialogue* 31, no. 3 (1992): 399–413.
———. "Analogy and Equivocation in Thirteenth-Century Logic: Aquinas in Context." *Mediaeval Studies* 54 (1992): 94–135.
———. "Suárez on the Analogy of Being: Some Historical Background." *Vivarium* 33, no. 1 (1995): 50–75.
Aubenque, Pierre. "Sur la naissance de la doctrine pseudo-Aristotélicienne de l'analogie de l'être." *Les Études philosophiques* 3/4 (1989): 291–304.
———. "Suárez et l'avènement du concept d'être." In *Francisco Suárez (1548–1617): Tradição e modernidade.* Edited by Adelino Cardoso, António Manuel Martins, and Leonel Ribeiro dos Santos, 11–20. Lisbon: Colibri, 1999.
Bastit, Michel. "Interprétation analogique de la loi et analogie de l'être chez Suárez: De la similitude à l'identité." *Les Études philosophiques* 3/4 (1989): 429–43.

Brown, Stephen. "Gerard of Bologna's *Quodlibet I, Quaestio 1:* On the Analogy of Being." *Carmelus* 31 (1984): 143–70.

Courtine, Jean-François. "Le projet suarézien de la métaphysique." *Archives de Philosophie* 42, no. 2 (1979): 235–74.

———. "Le statut ontologique du possible selon Suárez." *Cuadernos salmantinos de filosofía* 7, no. 1 (1980): 247–67.

———. "Ontologie ou métaphysique?" *Giornale di metafisica* 7, no. 1 (1985): 3–24.

———. "Différence ontologique et analogie de l'être: Le tournant suarézien." *Bulletin de la Société française de Philosophie* 83, no. 2 (1989): 41–76.

———. *Suárez et le système de la métaphysique.* Paris: PUF, 1990.

———. *Inventio Analogiae: Métaphysique et ontothéologie.* Paris: Librairie Philosophique J. Vrin, 2005.

Cronin, Timothy J. *Objective Being in Descartes and in Suárez.* Rome: Gregorian University Press, 1966.

D'Ettore, Domenic. "The Fifteenth-Century Thomist Dispute over Participation in an Analogous Concept: John Capreolus, Dominic of Flanders, and Paul Soncinas." *Mediaeval Studies* 76 (2014): 241–73.

———. *Analogy after Aquinas: Logical Problems, Thomistic Answers.* Washington, D.C.: The Catholic University of America Press, 2019.

Darge, Rolf. "«Ens in quantum ens»: Die Erklärung des Subjekts der Metaphysik bei F. Suarez." *Recherches de théologie et de philosophie médiévales* 66, no. 2 (1999): 335–61.

———. "Grundthese und ontologische Bedeutung der Lehre von der Analogie des Seienden nach F. Suárez." *Philosophisches Jahrbuch* 106, no. 2 (1999): 312–33.

———. *Suárez' transzendentale Seinsauslegung und die Metaphysiktradition.* Leiden & Boston: Brill, 2004.

———. "Die Transformation der aristotelischen Analogielehre bei Cajetan und Suárez." In *Der Aristotelismus an den europäischen Universitäten der frühen Neuzeit.* Edited by Rolf Darge, Emmanuel J. Bauer, and Günter Frank, 57–81. Stuttgart: W. Kohlhammer, 2010.

———. "Suárez on the Subject of Metaphysics." In *A Companion to Francisco Suárez.* Edited by Victor M. Salas and Robert L. Fastiggi, 91–123. Leiden & Boston: Brill, 2015.

Doig, James C. "Suárez, Descartes, and the Objective Reality of Ideas." *The New Scholasticism* 51, no. 3 (1977): 350–71.

Doyle, John P. "Suárez on the Reality of the Possibles." *The Modern Schoolman* 45, no. 1 (1967): 29–48.

———. "Suárez on the Analogy of Being." *The Modern Schoolman* 46, no. 3 (1969): 219–49.

———. "Suárez on the Analogy of Being." *The Modern Schoolman* 46, no. 4 (1969): 323–41.

———. "Heidegger and Scholastic Metaphysics." *The Modern Schoolman* 49, no. 3 (1972): 201–220.

Elorduy, Eleuterio. "El concepto objetivo en Suárez." *Pensamiento* 4 (1948): 335–423.

Forlivesi, Marco. "La distinction entre concept formel et concept objectif: Suárez, Pasqualigo, Mastri." *Les Études philosophiques* 1 (2002): 3–30.
Gentile, Luigi. "Valenza logico-metafisica dell'«*analogia entis*» in F. Suárez." In *Christoph Clavius e l'attività scientifica dei gesuiti nell'età di Galileo. Atti del Convegno Internazionale (Chieti 28–30 aprile 1993)*. Edited by Ugo Baldini, 209–22. Roma: Bulzoni, 1995.
Gilson, Étienne. *L'Être et l'Essence*. 2nd ed. Paris: J. Vrin, 1962.
Gracia, Jorge J. E. "Suárez's Conception of Metaphysics: A Step in the Direction of Mentalism?" *American Catholic Philosophical Quarterly* 65, no. 3 (1991): 287–309.
———. "Suárez and Metaphysical Mentalism: The Last Visit." *American Catholic Philosophical Quarterly* 67, no. 3 (1993): 349–54.
Guy, Alain. "L'Analogie de l'être selon Suárez." *Archives de Philosophie* 42, no. 2 (1979): 275–94.
Heider, Daniel. "Is Suárez's Concept of Being Analogical or Univocal?" *American Catholic Philosophical Quarterly* 81, no. 1 (2007): 21–41.
———. "El concepto de ser in Suárez: ¿unívoco o análogo?" In *Suárez en perspectiva, 1617–2017*. Edited by Julio Söchting Herrera, 99–120. Special issue of *Studium: Filosofía y Teología* 40 (2017).
Hellín, José. *La analogía del ser y el conocimiento de Dios en Suárez*. Madrid: Gráficas Uguina, 1947.
———. "La teoría de los modos en Suárez." *Pensamiento* 6 (1950): 216–26.
———. "Existencialismo escolástico suareciano: La existencia, constitutivo del ente." *Pensamiento* 12 (1956): 157–58.
———. "Existencialismo escolástico suareciano: La existencia es lo principal en el ente." *Pensamiento* 13 (1957): 21–38.
Hochschild, Joshua P. *The Semantics of Analogy: Rereading Cajetan's* De Nominum Analogia. Notre Dame, Ind.: University of Notre Dame Press, 2010.
Hoeres, Walter. "Francis Suárez and the Teaching of John Duns Scotus on *Univocatio Entis*." In *Studies in Philosophy and the History of Philosophy*. Vol. 3: *John Duns Scotus, 1265–1965*. Edited by John K. Ryan and Bernardine M. Bonansea, 263–90. Washington, D.C.: The Catholic University of America Press, 1965.
Honnefelder, Ludger. *Scientia transcendens: Die formale Bestimmung der Seiendheit und Realität in der Metaphysik des Mittelalters und der Neuzeit*. Hamburg: F. Meiner, 1990.
Hurtado, Guillermo. "Entes e modos en las *Disputationes Metafísicas*." In *Francisco Suárez (1548–1617): Tradição e modernidade*, 99–117.
Ippolito, Benedetto. *Analogia dell'Essere: La metafisica di Suàrez tra onto-teologia medievale e filosofia moderna*. Milano: Franco Angeli, 2005.
Marion, Jean-Luc. *Sur la théologie blanche de Descartes*. Paris: PUF, 1981.
Menn, Stephen. "Suárez, Nominalism and Modes." In *Hispanic Philosophy in the Age of Discovery*. Edited by Kevin White, 226–56. Washington, D.C.: The Catholic University of America Press, 1997.
Panaccio, Claude. "From Mental Word to Mental Language." *Philosophical Topics* 20, no. 2 (1992): 125–47.

———. *Mental Language: From Plato to William of Ockham.* Translated by Joshua Hochschild and Meredith Ziebart. New York: Fordham University Press, 2017.

Pasnau, Robert. "Form and Matter." In *The Cambridge History of Medieval Philosophy.* Edited by Robert Pasnau and Christina van Dyke, 635–46. Cambridge: Cambridge University Press, 2010.

Pereira, José. *Suárez: Between Scholasticism and Modernity.* Milwaukee: Marquette University Press, 2007.

Renemann, Michael. "Suárez's Doctrine of Concepts: How Divine and Human Intellection Are Intertwined." In *A Companion to Francisco Suárez,* 313–35.

Riva, Franco. "La dottrina suareziana del concetto e le sue fonti storiche." *Rivista di Filosofia Neo-Scolastica* 71, no. 4 (1979): 686–99.

Roig Gironella, Juan. "La analogía del ser en Suárez." *Espíritu* 36 (1987): 5–48.

Salas, Victor. "Francisco Suárez: End of the Scholastic ἐπιστήμη?" In *Francisco Suárez and His Legacy: The Impact of Suárezian Metaphysics and Epistemology on Modern Philosophy.* Edited by Marco Sgarbi, 9–28. Milano: Vita e Pensiero, 2010.

———. "Francisco Suárez, the Analogy of Being, and Its Tensions." In *Suárez's Metaphysics in Its Historical and Systematic Context.* Edited by Lukáš Novák, 87–104. Berlin: De Gruyter, 2014.

———. "Between Thomism and Scotism: Francisco Suárez on the Analogy of Being." In *A Companion to Francisco Suárez,* 336–62.

Schneider, Marius. "Der angebliche philosophische Essentialismus des Suárez." *Wissenschaft und Weisheit* 24 (1961): 40–68.

Thompson, Augustine. "Francisco Suárez's Theory of Analogy and the Metaphysics of St. Thomas Aquinas." *Angelicum* 72, no. 3 (1995): 353–62.

Wells, Norman J. "*Esse Cognitum* and Suárez Revisited." *American Catholic Philosophical Quarterly* 67, no. 3 (1993): 339–48.

Yela Utrilla, Juan Francisco. "Modo y límite en Suárez." In *Actas del Congreso Internacional de Filosofía, Barcelona, 4–10 octubre 1948, con motivo del Centenario de los filósofos Francisco Suárez y Jaime Balmes.* Vol. 3, pp. 533–46. Madrid: Instituto "Luis Vives" de Filosofía, 1949.

Zavalloni, Roberto. *Richard de Mediavilla et la controverse sur la pluralité des formes: Textes inédits et étude critique.* Louvain: Éditions de l'Institut Supérieur de Philosophie, 1951.

INDEX

Metaphysical Disputation II: On the Essential Concept or Concept of Being was designed in Minion with Hypatia Sans display type and composed by Kachergis Book Design of Pittsboro, North Carolina. It was printed on 60-pound Maple Eggshell Cream B18 and bound by Maple Press of York, Pennsylvania.